Memory Work

School for Advanced Research
Advanced Seminar Series

James F. Brooks
General Editor

Memory Work

Contributors

Susan D. Gillespie
Department of Anthropology, University of Florida

Rosemary A. Joyce
Department of Anthropology, University of California, Berkeley

Lisa J. Lucero
Department of Anthropology, University of Illinois, Urbana-Champaign

Lynn Meskell
Department of Cultural and Social Anthropology, Stanford University

Barbara J. Mills
Department of Anthropology, University of Arizona

Axel E. Nielsen
Consejo Nacional de Investigaciones Científicas y Técnicas and the Universidad Nacional de Córdoba, Argentina

Timothy R. Pauketat
Department of Anthropology, University of Illinois at Urbana-Champaign

Joshua Pollard
Department of Archaeology and Anthropology, University of Bristol

Ann B. Stahl
Department of Anthropology, University of Victoria

William H. Walker
Department of Sociology and Anthropology, New Mexico State University

Memory Work

Archaeologies of Material Practices

Edited by Barbara J. Mills and William H. Walker

School for Advanced Research Press

Santa Fe

School for Advanced Research Press

Post Office Box 2188
Santa Fe, New Mexico 87504-2188
www.sarpress.sarweb.org

Co-Director and Editor: Catherine Cocks
Manuscript Editor: Tom Ireland
Designer and Production Manager: Cynthia Dyer
Proofreader: Sarah Soliz
Indexer: Catherine Fox
Printer: Thomson Shore, Inc.

Library of Congress Cataloging-in-Publication Data:

Memory work : archaeologies of material practices / edited by Barbara J. Mills and
William H. Walker. – 1st ed.
    p. cm.
  Includes bibliographical references and index.
  ISBN 978-1-930618-88-6 (pa : alk. paper)
  1. Social archaeology. 2. Archaeology and history. 3. Memory—Social aspects—History. 4. Material
culture—History. 5. Landscape—Social aspects—History. 6. Historic buildings. 7. Historic sites.
8. Excavations (Archaeology) 9. Civilization, Ancient. I. Mills, Barbara J., 1955–
II. Walker, William H., 1964–

CC72.4.M46 2008
930.1–dc22

                        2007050197

Cover illustration: Buried mosaic "mask" at La Venta, Mexico. Box 23 (Slides, 1943–1971), Slide #232,
the Robert Fleming Heizer Papers, National Anthropological Archives. © Smithsonian Institution.

Contents

Figures

Tables

Acknowledgments

The idea for this seminar began during a lunchtime discussion in Tucson in which we lamented the fact that archaeologists working on the topics of ritual, memory, and depositional practice seemed to have increasingly small citation circles. We also saw a gap between those working on either side of the Atlantic. We approached Richard Leventhal, then president of the School of American Research, who encouraged us to submit a proposal for a short seminar. Scheduling the seminar was delayed, and only after George Gumerman came on board as interim president were we able to put the pieces into place. SAR did a stellar job in helping us carry out the seminar, which was held in February of 2005. We especially thank George Gumerman for his continued support and encouragement, Nancy Owen Lewis for her help with logistics, Doug Dearden for IT support, and Leslie Shipman and her staff for making us feel at home (and of course, well fed).

We thank our wonderful seminar participants for preparing stimulating papers in advance of our session at SAR. Although we did not know each other well before the seminar, we found that we shared many of the same theoretical interests and had used many of the same interpretive methods. Rosemary Joyce served as our seminar discussant, later preparing her own paper, which is included in this volume. We then "road tested" our seminar at the 2005 American Anthropological Association annual meeting, and we thank the Archeology Division for its support. At the AAA, Lynn Meskell served as our discussant, and her comments round out our volume as the final chapter. Several of us also presented in a session together at the Theoretical Archaeology Group in Exeter, England, in 2006. Joshua Pollard is to be thanked for helping to arrange that session—and his memorable tours of Stonehenge and Avebury.

We would also like to thank our two peer reviewers, Robert Preucel and Julia Hendon, for their insightful comments on our manuscript. They provided many new ideas that we incorporated into our discussions and that were especially helpful in preparing our introduction.

Finally, we thank Catherine Cocks of SAR Press for her guidance in bringing our project to its printed form and James F. Brooks, president of SAR, for his continued commitment to the project. James saw the potential of our seminar and encouraged us to submit the manuscript for publication in the advanced seminar series while director of SAR Press. His support has been important to our project, and we are happy to have this volume appear in the series.

Memory Work

1

Introduction

Memory, Materiality, and Depositional Practice

Barbara J. Mills and William H. Walker

This volume focuses on ways in which material culture engages in the transmission of memory and how archaeologists use knowledge of these interactions to interpret identity, ritual practice, political action, and other facets of past societies. There has been a resurgence of interest in material culture studies in recent years, and many of these studies address how people and objects intersect in the construction and transmission of social memory. The basis of much of this new research on material culture is a focus on the interaction of humans and materials within different social contexts or sets of interrelationships, or what is now being called the *materiality* of social life (Meskell 2004:6; see also Buchli 2004; DeMarrais et al. 2004; Graves-Brown 2000; Meskell 2005; Miller 2005; Preucel and Meskell 2004). This research is opening up many new ways of thinking about the manner in which people and objects shape each other, including the meaning objects have for those who use them.

In tandem with the renewal of interest in material culture, memory studies have become a growing topic of interdisciplinary study (Climo and Cattell 2002; Olick and Robbins 1998). We also view our work as contributing to memory studies, a field that has seen remarkable growth but with highly disparate methods, theories, and interpretations. Memory studies have great potential for archaeology because of their diachronic focus on the transmission and transformation of social practices. Although many of these studies of social memory use objects or other forms of material culture as illustrative, fewer explicitly concentrate on how memory and material practices are interdependent features of social life. Important exceptions include the work of a number of material culture theorists specifically focusing on memory (for example, Küchler 1987, 1993, 1997, 2002; Küchler and Melion 1991), the contributors to an edited volume entitled *Archaeologies of Memory* (Van Dyke and Alcock 2003), studies of mortuary ritual and memory (for example, Chesson 2001; Hallam and Hockey 2001; Tarlow 1999; Williams 2004), and pieces directly addressing how materiality and memory intersect (for example, Hendon 2000; Joyce 2000a; Meskell 2004). Our work builds on this previous research and seeks to understand how memory work is related to the objects, features, and deposits that are the basis for archaeological interpretations. In this volume, we look at material practices through a number of archaeological projects to understand how people constructed social life through their memory work.

Our use of the term "memory work" in this book has two meanings. First, it refers to the many social practices that create memories, including recalling, reshaping, forgetting, inventing, coordinating, and transmitting. As several anthropologists and sociologists have observed in their use of the concept of memory work, memories are made, not just experienced (Jansen 2007; Krause 2005; Litzinger 1998; Stoler and Strassler 2000). It is in this active construction that material traces are left behind and that the contributors of this book, as archaeologists, are especially adept at uncovering. Memory work is not just about the material traces left behind, however; it also is about understanding the materiality of those practices or the interaction of humans and materials within a set of social relationships (Meskell 2004:6). Once understood within their cultural contexts, all material traces are the residues of memory-making relationships, albeit in different social, spatial, and temporal settings. In this book we focus on a set of case studies that illustrate how social memories were made through repeated, patterned, and engaged social and material practices. These practices themselves were quite varied from case to case, but the essays are linked by the evidence they bring to bear on the materiality of memory making.

Second, "memory work" also refers to the interpretive activities we scholars follow when studying social memory. Collectively the contributors to this book form a group of archaeologists who have made it our project to understand the ways in which social memory can be looked at in past and present societies. We came together initially as part of a seminar at the School of American Research (now the School for Advanced Research), reworked our papers for a session at the American Anthropological Association meetings, and then reworked them again for this book. Although this volume contains contributions that focus on contexts from around the world, we share a consistent perspective on the need to inform memory studies through a theoretical approach that incorporates practice, agency, and materiality.

We also share a common goal to map out the different ways in which social memories in past societies can be programmatically and tangibly studied. Our goal is to use our memory work to construct new interpretations about these societies that otherwise might not be possible. Such an approach requires that we confront the intersections of a number of fundamental theoretical issues such as those between memory and materiality, knowledge and practice, subjects and objects, and the past and the present. We do not construe these intersections dichotomously, but instead emphasize the layers of complexity within or between these categories—an approach that is more consistent with the many ways that people made the past into the present through their interactions with material things.

In this chapter we provide brief overviews of contemporary memory and material culture/materiality studies. Our goal is to bring out how anthropologists, including archaeologists, have been looking at the intersection of these two subjects. Lastly, we place the case studies in this volume within the context of this literature, emphasizing key themes that have emerged from our work.

FROM COLLECTIVE MEMORY TO MEMORY WORK

The study of memory is a truly interdisciplinary project with prominent research in literature, philosophy, psychology, history, sociology, and anthropology. Archaeological research on memory is relatively recent, and as the volume edited by Ruth Van Dyke and Susan Alcock (2003) demonstrates, archaeologists draw somewhat eclectically from these sources, especially from history, sociology, and anthropology. The literature in anthropology and its allied fields is vast, but there are several important changes in the literature that have emerged (see especially the reviews of Climo and Cattell 2002; Jansen 2007:958; Olick and Robbins 1998). These include (1) a fundamental theoretical shift from the study of social structures to that of "practice theory" (for example, Bourdieu 1977, 1990) and agency, which has led to the rejection of the broader term of "collective memory" in favor of "social memory"; (2) greater attention to how memory is an important part of everyday life (de Certeau 1984)—not just of large-scale commemorative events; (3) how memory work is replete with "semiotic textures" (Jansen 2007:958) showing how memory and meaning are inextricably related; and (4) that memory work subsumes a range of practices, including remembering and forgetting (Litzinger 1998:226). The above trends crosscut several disciplines, making scholarship on memory studies highly interdisciplinary. In addition, as Jansen (2007) points out, current trends in memory research are highly dependent on the empirical topics of interest. Today, memory studies variably emphasize different social scales of analysis (the individual, group, or nation), the context (sites) of memory-making events and places, the selective and exclusive nature of memory work, and/or the symbolic tools of memory work and their manipulation.

Although agency theory does not preclude the agency of groups, one of the most important historical shifts in memory studies has been in directing attention away from the Durkheimian idea of a "collective memory" that is somehow separate from the memories of individuals. This term, originally coined by Émile Durkheim and elaborated upon by his student Maurice Halbwachs (1925, 1992), is still used in the literature, although there has been a preference by many authors to replace it with "social memory" to highlight the many social contexts in which memories are made and the role of individuals in the process of remembering (Climo and Cattell 2002; Fentress and Wickham 1992; Wertsch 2002). Memory does not reside in, and is not transmitted by, cultures but in people as members of social groups. Fentress and Wickham (1992), for example, entitled their book *Social Memory* to emphasize that it is the interaction of individuals as members of different collectives who engage in memory making that is important. The vast literature on oral history is one venue in which anthropologists, public historians, and others have studied how individuals engage in the process of remembering because this is one area where there is reliance on individuals' memory rather than on texts (Fentress and Wickham 1992:2). The authors of the chapters in our volume also use the term "social memory" instead of "collective memory" to mark the importance of different social scales and the various roles of individuals and agency in memory work. As we discuss below, however, our emphasis is on material culture, although oral histories may be important sources for understanding the persistence of some material practices through time (for example, Mills, Pauketat, and Walker, this volume).

Paul Connerton's (1989) book, *How Societies Remember,* also emphasizes the idea that it is membership in a social group—rather than the collective or culture as a whole—that defines the degree of similarity in remembering. His research is transitional in the anthropological literature because he recognized that memory was a part of the construction of individual personhood and therefore an important part of social identity. The literature on identity and memory is now quite vast, but importantly, Connerton presented two ways in which the performative, habitual aspects of commemorative practices produce social memory: through bodily or incorporating practices and through inscribing practices, including writing. Drawing on a number of sources, especially Pierre Bourdieu (1977, 1990), Connerton's terminology and approach have had an impact on the ways in which archaeologists have applied memory studies in their work. But rather than seeing social memories as adhering rather mechanically to either incorporating or inscribing practices, these practices should be viewed as working together to illustrate how memory is transmitted and embodied through practice. In this way, social memory becomes more active and is better described through acts of remembering, rather than as an objectified albeit intangible thing or something that is discoverable existing outside of people's lived experience.

Thus, in contrast to Connerton's explicit emphasis on commemorative ceremonies, another shift in the literature is the recognition that memory construction is part of everyday life. It contains strategies and tactics that are the result of "models of interaction" (de Certeau 1984). The strategies and tactics of memory construction may include the more visible and more easily studied commemorative acts, but materially marked moments of memory work are everywhere. As we discuss below, the prevalence of these materially marked moments allows memory work to be studied in many different contexts and through a range of material practices. In some research (for example, Stahl's and Nielsen's chapters in this volume), it allows a blurring of the distinction between the everyday and the ritual for situating memory work (see also Bradley 2003, 2005; Brück 1999). Nonetheless, because rituals can produce highly visible material records that are well preserved archaeologically, and because rituals are highly charged moments of memory work, other contributors to our volume focus on the ways in which memory work was expressed through small- and large-scale events that were part of ritual practice (in the sense of Bell 1992, 1997).

Whether dealing with daily or more periodically marked events, the shift in attention to the range of contexts in which memory work takes place underscores the importance of seeing the process as constitutive of social life (Giddens 1984), rather than simply a tool used by particular social actors. Thus, there has been an explicit shift in language from "memory" to "remembering" (for example, Wertsch 2002:17). Memory is not something out there to be discovered but a process that is continually changed through the active engagement of people in remembering (and other forms of memory work). An overobjectification of social memory diminishes the value of memory studies for understanding how the process of remembering can be transformative. This emphasis parallels the theoretical shift from instrumentalist to constructivist positions in the social sciences. Nonetheless, the distinction can be overemphasized: memory making is a process that constructs social life, but it also may be used as a means to an end, particularly in political actions. For example, the selective remembering that can occur when events are intentionally erased from national histories is instrumental at the same time as it reconstructs the social life of those who lived that history and the lives of their descendants. Similarly, the past may be used to legitimize the present—even if that past never happened in what Hobsbawm (1983) calls "the invention of tradition."

A final trend in memory studies is greater attention to the ways in which meaning is ascribed during memory work. Representation has always been important in the process of historical recollection. The topic of representation has been of increasing importance in the anthropological literature on memory and material culture (for example, Küchler and Melion 1991) and museum studies. Each cultural relationship ascribes a different form of meaning to objects within social interactions. For those who use them, the value of objects may be derived from their intrinsic qualities, such as their color or brilliance (Hosler 1994; Jones and MacGregor 2002; Saunders 1999, 2001), their place of origin (Bradley 2000; Helms 1993), and/or the networks that they have passed through.

Museums are an example of sites of memory (Nora 1989) in that they provide a space for housing and displaying the material objects that are used in commemorative practices, whether they are images, three-dimensional objects, or texts. Sites of memory are not restricted to museums and may also include parks and other places and landscapes. In some of them, historically documented events occurred; in others, the past is interpreted for the public (for example, Shackel 2000). Others may be places that are known from traditional histories and become important loci for memory work through their incorporation into contemporary ethnohistorical documentation (for example, Ferguson and Colwell-Chanthaphonh 2006).

The spatial dimension of memory work is one with which archaeologists have a particular affinity. Research on representation therefore intersects with sites of memory in the archaeological literature on landscapes and memory (for example, Alcock 2002; Ashmore and Knapp 1999; Bender, ed. 1993; Bradley 1998; Edmonds 1999; Hirsch and O'Hanlon

1995; Thomas 1999b; Tilley 1994; Van Dyke 2003). Many of these studies have taken an explicitly phenomenological approach inspired by Christopher Tilley. Although some of the contributors to these volumes tack back and forth between places and the objects deposited in these places, the vast majority of these studies foreground the ways in which monuments were transformed and then themselves became transformative of social practices. In short, landscapes *of* memory became an important bridge to the discussion of landscapes *in* memory (Bender 1993:11), as in Parmentier's (1985) distinction between signs in history and signs of history (see also Ferguson and Preucel 2005; Preucel 2006:85–86). The idea of landscapes in memory is exemplified in the chapter in this volume by Susan Gillespie, who discusses how architecture and features, once created, control future practices by channeling or concretizing subsequent depositional practices in places or sites of memory. Gillespie reexamines the stratigraphic evidence at the Olmec site of La Venta (900–500 BCE) to define relationships between collective memories and building activities. She focuses on how practice creates sacred places and how those places in turn recreate people and their memories. She traces the biography or life history of the complex's platforms, altars, and spectacular deposits of serpentine to construct a new interpretation of the history of La Venta.

That memory work includes a number of different practices, including both remembering and forgetting, has been a theme in many anthropological studies. Through her work on the destruction of monuments (Küchler 1999), and especially the New Guinea *malanggan* (Küchler 1987, 1993, 2002), Susanne Küchler has been at the forefront of bringing the memory practice of forgetting into the anthropological study of social memory (see also Forty and Küchler 1999; Küchler and Melion 1991). Much of the work in this area analyzes the ways in which memory work can be influenced by political action, but it also addresses a key area in interdisciplinary studies: how are memories selectively constructed, by whom, and for what purpose? Remembering and forgetting are important parts of memorials to the deceased, and thus this theme has become an integral part of mortuary studies in anthropology (for example, Chesson 2001; Hallam and Hockey 2001). The often paradoxical relationship between remembering and forgetting is discussed in our volume by Mills. She emphasizes that there are many ways in which this intersection is realized, including secreting or hiding (Hendon 2000), intentional destruction, and the retirement of rooms, objects, and settlements when residents migrate to new places.

As our brief discussion indicates, anthropologists' and especially archaeologists' research on memory has often involved the intersection of memory work with material things. Whether concerned with monuments or modifications of the landscape, mnemonics for tracing back lineages, memorials to important historical figures, or images that capture events or people, the literature on memory is replete with material culture. Archae-ologists have found the anthropological works that discuss the intersection of memory with the material world the most rewarding. But at the same time that memory studies have been transformed by wider trends in the discipline, so, too, have material culture studies.

FROM MATERIAL CULTURE TO MATERIALITY

As Bjørnar Olsen (2003) recently pointed out, material culture has tended to be marginalized in the contemporary social science research despite the fact that things are a fundamental part of social life. Yet there has been a resurgence of interest in material culture on the part of ethnographers and archaeologists, who have made important contributions to building theories of material life (for example, Appadurai 1986; Buchli 2002; Knappett 2005; Meskell 2004; Miller 2005; Myers 2001; Schiffer and Miller 1999). Many of these scholars are archaeologists who have turned to modern material culture studies in order to look at consumption and commodification as part of globalization processes and/or to show how theories of material culture bridge relations between people and things in multiple cultural contexts.

A pivotal volume in the burgeoning new material culture studies was *The Social Life of Things: Commodities in Cultural Perspective* (Appadurai 1986). Although most of the contributors are not archaeologists, several of the themes in this volume have been extensively drawn upon by archaeologists (including innumerable versions of the title). Two of the most important themes in this volume are that things have different values and meanings depending on their cultural contexts, and that the same object can endure through changes in valuation and meaning depending on its biography. For example, things that were originally produced as goods for exchange have one set of meanings, but when they later circulate as commodities in the global market, they have another. That objects may have transient values depending on the point in their life history was especially brought out in the chapter by Igor Kopytoff (1986) on the cultural biographies of things. The biographical approach can be used to show how the process of taking objects from one context and placing them in another transforms their value and meaning.

The topic of object or artifact biographies is now encountered in a number of works by archaeologists (Gosden and Marshall 1999; Meskell

2004) and historians of technology (for example, Hoskins 1998). The concept is a broad one, however, encompassing a number of theoretical and methodological approaches. Current studies of material culture in archaeology are spread across a number of different archaeologies, including behavioral/processual, cognitive/processual, and postprocessual approaches. Various terms are used, including "life histories," "structured deposition," and "object biographies." All of these are genealogical approaches to some extent, but with different assumptions and outcomes. The term "materiality" is being incorporated more and more, but often there is little specificity in its definition. Nonetheless, there is a common theme that objects have histories—that is, they have genealogies.

One of the earliest genealogical approaches in archaeology was developed in the behavioral archaeology of Michael Schiffer and his colleagues, which explicitly focuses on the life history of artifacts (for example, LaMotta and Schiffer 1999; Schiffer 1975, 1976; Schiffer and Skibo 1997; Walker 1995; Walker et al. 2000). Life histories of artifacts are based on the concept of behavioral chains, which link different activities to all stages of artifact production, distribution, and consumption. The life history approach is more encompassing than the similar-sounding *chaîne opératoire* approach begun by André Leroi-Gourhan (1964) and developed by French archaeologists to study artifact manufacture (especially chipped stone artifacts; see Bleed 2001). In contrast to the chaîne opératoire approach, the life history approach also considers what happens to objects after they are manufactured. Thus, methodologically, it is closer to the object biographies discussed by Kopytoff (1986), although there has not been the same attention to the value and meaning of objects in different social settings. Earlier work of the behavioral/processual school focused on using life histories to understand the technological choices that were made in production, largely relating production to use (for example, Schiffer and Skibo 1997). More recent contributions within this approach to life histories have focused on the consumption and discard portions of the behavioral chain, such as Schiffer's engagement with modern material culture (for example, Schiffer 1991, 1994), LaMotta and Schiffer's (1999) discussion of cultural and noncultural formation processes that structure the deposition and depletion of objects in houses, and Walker's (1995, 1999; Walker et al. 2000; Walker and Lucero 2000; Walker and Schiffer 2006) observations on how ritual objects are differentially deposited based on their histories as singularities. Walker's more recent work, especially with Lucero, explicitly incorporates agency theory to look at how artifact life histories, ritual, and politics intersect.

Paralleling the study of life histories by the behavioral/processualists in the United States was the use of the term "structured deposition" in the United Kingdom. Originally coined by Richards and Thomas (1984), it referred to Neolithic deposits that were distinct in some way from everyday domestic trash and instead were the result of ritual activity (see Pollard, this volume). They interpreted structured deposits as purposefully created and symbolically motivated. Richards and Thomas's interpretations were part of a break from processual archaeology, incorporating many of the ideas of symbolic and structural archaeology that were just beginning to be introduced into the literature (for example, Hodder 1982). As Pollard's chapter in this volume discusses, the concept of structured deposition presented several problems, largely because all deposition is structured in some way and because these deposits were seen as somehow distinct from everyday life. Nonetheless, we think that the concept of structured deposition is quite important in the development of a set of interpretive methods that uses depositional practice to look at memory and materiality.

Gosden (2005) has recently suggested that there are two basic ways to look at object biographies: their genealogy and source. His separation of these two parts of the interartifactual domain reflects increasing interest on the part of archaeologists with the idea that where something originally came from (including where the raw materials were procured) is something that adds significance to the object. This concept is similar to that of Bradley's (2000) "pieces of places," in which objects have meaning because of the association of those places with important events, people, and so on. The genealogy of objects is also important, and we can view these along a continuum of objects that are expediently collected, used, and discarded on one end (and therefore having little genealogy), and highly valued heirlooms that are often inalienable goods on the other (Weiner 1992; see also Lillios 2003; Mills 2004).

Although many archaeologists focus exclusively on genealogies of particular objects (the biographical approach), we think that a more productive approach is to focus on genealogies of practices. Pauketat and Alt (2005) emphasize the latter in their discussion of "agency in a postmold." Importantly, these are practices that have great time depth and are revealing in the degree of similarity of practice—including memory practices—that characterize Mississippian societies over long periods of time. Like Joyce and Lopiparo (2005), Pauketat and Alt view agency as something that is archaeologically accessible. In Joyce and Lopiparo's case, they advocate the idea that archaeology's unique contribution to studies of agency (and materiality) is by viewing the past practices of past peoples through sequences of actions, chains, networks, and citations. These sequences are, however, not simply about the traditional idea of behavioral chains, or châines opératoires, but rather about viewing them as embedded within the materiality of past practices. Thus, there is a difference between object biographies and genealogies of practice: the latter is more inclusive than the former.

This embedding of object biographies within a broader field of material practices is one of the reasons that there has been a rejection of the term "structured deposits" (for example, Richards and Thomas 1984) to refer to intentional acts of object burial. As Pollard discusses in his chapter in this volume, the fallacy of the idea that deposits can be unstructured undermines the use of structured deposits as a separate entity. All deposits are structured in some way, and it is in how those deposits are structured that engages us in memory studies. Pollard addresses the evolving theoretical consideration of the concept of structured deposition, arguing that some of the most fruitful approaches entail recognizing that objects are also subjects in many cultures and that deposits provide "a context in which the status and roles" of human and other material participants (artifacts, architecture) "are highlighted and brought to the fore." Like Stahl (this volume), he recognizes that the variable nature or character of the agency of people and objects will vary cross-culturally and that the organization of deposits provides archaeologists with a window into these past object worlds (in the sense of Meskell 2004). He illustrates his argument in a case study of Etton Closure, a fourth century BCE British ditch monument. Like the people, animals and things (cattle, axes, and fossils) were "gathered/herded, controlled, killed, and combined to forge new relationships between agent laden people and things." In part the attempt to "control, channel and pay respect to these various agencies" led to the depositional patterns at this site, and these practices are examples of genealogies of practice.

Despite the fact that contemporary material culture studies may emphasize concepts of interest to archaeologists, most do not build the necessary linkages that are required for interpreting memory from the archaeological record. These linkages must be built by tacking back and forth between social interpretations and archaeological deposits. Key to this interpretive process is that there must be some grounding in the material practices that render social memory visible in the archaeological record. These practices are not unique, disconnected events but part of a string of repeated actions that are learned, transmitted, and transformed. People construct social memories through their engagement with other people (living as well as ancestral) and through their interaction with varieties of material culture. The latter may include different kinds of substances, sediments, buildings, artifacts, unmodified objects, and even animals that are used and deposited in archaeological sites.

Thus, within the literature on "things" (to use the broadest term), there has been an important change from the use of the term "material culture" to that of "materiality" that is important for linking memory to things. This shift in meaning is similar to the change from "memory" to "remembering" in that it emphasizes the shift from objects to the ways in which objects (and monuments, features, and so on) are actively used in social practices. Many of the contributors to this volume also explicitly link their research on memory work to studies of materiality, practice, and agency (DeMarrais et al. 2004; Gosden 1994; Graves-Brown 2000; Joyce 2000a; Meskell 2003, 2004, 2005; Miller 1987; Miller, ed. 2005; Mills 2004; Owoc 2005; Pauketat 2003b; Pauketat and Alt 2004; Preucel and Meskell 2004; Thomas 1997, 1999b, 2000). Unlike studies of material culture, the concept of materiality expresses a fundamental assumption about the physicality of practice and the ways that objects and people interact.

Central to understanding materiality is its relationship to agency. Much of the intersectional work on materiality and agency builds on the ideas of Bruno Latour (1993, 1999, 2005) and Alfred Gell (1993, 1996, 1998). Latour and Gell each have questioned the anthropocentric assumption that only people possess agency. In so doing they have challenged the boundary between people as subjects and artifacts as objects. Latour argues that artifacts cause actions and that their effects have consequences. Some of those materials or simply "nonhumans" (Latour 1999) are perceived as animate and possessing agency, and some are not. But in all cases they impact action and exist in a symmetrical relationship to human social actors (Latour 1999:182). Therefore he prefers to describe them as social actors as important as any human and applies the linguistic term "actants" to them to emphasize the symmetrical or equal nature of people and things. Within Latour's actor network theory, all actants have agency. This leads him to deny many of the fundamental assumptions of the modern/postmodern debate, preferring to go beyond a social theory based on humans as the ultimate source of agency. In many ways this is a return to pre-Durkheimian notions of the social because it does not place objects in opposition to people (Pinney 2005:258). Thus, like several other anthropologists (for example, Strathern 1990; Weiner 1992), Latour shows stronger connections to the approaches of Marcel Mauss when addressing material things. In this volume, Rosemary Joyce makes the use of the term "actant" more explicit for archaeologists by framing Latour's ideas within an approach that sees all actants (humans and nonhumans) as part of a network "whose changing articulations become our focus."

Although Gell was less willing to make a total commitment to nonhumans as actants, he sought to understand how people's agency is conditioned by their reactions to objects and even their attribution of agency to objects. He coined the term "secondary agency" to describe the effects of human agency as realized through objects and thereby stopped short of according them the full-blown analytical equality sought by Latour. Miller (2005:13) summarizes their different approaches: "While Latour is looking for the nonhumans below the level of human agency, Gell is looking through the objects to embedded human agency we infer they contain." He notes a tension between the abstraction of theoretical solutions to the subject/object dilemma, which he refers to as a philosophical argument, and the grounded albeit "messy terrain of ethnography," which he believes provides a healthy check on such abstractions. Because ours is an archaeological volume, it incorporates this tension between social theory and ethnography over the materiality of subjects and objects and complicates it by applying another layer of tension—that between the abstraction of theory-laden inferences and the terrain of archaeological deposits. Shanks and Tilley (1987) once called this the double hermeneutic of archaeology.

Inspired by Gell's notion of agency as the abduction or inference of agency by people to things (see also Gosden 2005; Olsen 2003) and Latour's desire to seek a nonanthropocentric solution to the subject/object problem, Walker (this volume) considers the role of materiality in the study of prehistoric religion. He argues that archaeologists can identify the life histories of spirits by examining the reactions of people to things they may have inhabited. He finds that anthropocentric thinking hampers an archaeological study of religion and draws on Pueblo people's memory work or oral traditions that link the underworld of the dead with the world of the living to explain the deposition of dogs and human remains in ceremonial buildings. He argues that a nonanthropocentric understanding of society encourages archaeologists to interpret specific kinds of deposits as the results of interactions between human and nonhuman agents, including animals and spiritual forces. He finds that when we recognize that dogs, witches, and buildings are potential members of societies, then the material patterns of the archaeological record become more comprehensible.

Similarly, Lucero explores the processes of ensoulment and then de-animation among Classic Maya commoners at the site of Saturday Creek, Belize. She argues that strata associated with household funerary practices involved the simultaneous making of sacred places and the memories about those places. Mortuary customs required the creation of new houses, which involved dedication ceremonies, the de-animation of older houses, and the particular inclusion of grave goods. The logic of such practices is similar across wealthier and poorer households, albeit the elite nature of the objects involved differed between the two contexts. Perhaps one might argue that the houses, like the people, were also themselves poorer or richer rather than simply the products of the poor and rich. As a result status was created and maintained through the very interaction involved in the ensoulment and de-animation of houses. Therefore, as she notes, "The depositional sequence of a structure thus embodies histories of the people who lived and died within its walls just as much as it chronicles building, razing, and re-building."

Thus, whether or not we take a Latourian approach, in which these objects, materials, or simply "nonhumans" are viewed as social actors in their own right, we recognize that many materials were perceived as animate and possessing agency by those who made, used, and deposited them. It is in what Gell (1998) calls this "interartifactual domain" that "connectivities," "attachments," and "resemblances" are created—a domain in which "subjects and objects do not stand in opposition from each other" (Küchler 2005:210) but are complementary. Memory work is therefore understood as an active process in which "making and doing constitutes both persons and things" (Myers 2005:74).

RELATING MEMORY TO MATERIAL PRACTICES

Archaeological deposits are contexts in which memory practices are materialized. As we stated in the beginning of this introduction, we ascribe to the view that all memory practices have material consequences—that they are materialized through practice. Thus, a practice approach is at the heart of how, archaeologically, we can begin to differentiate different forms of memory work in the past. Understanding the spatial and temporal distribution of practices that produced archaeological deposits is a fundamental part of connecting memory and materiality. It requires the same skills that archaeologists use in any research program, but with the added layer of attention to the relationality of materials (including people). This is an important tenet of actor network theory, but it should be familiar to all archaeologists. Context is everything, and in order to understand materiality, it is important that archaeologists differentiate depositional processes produced as part of human practice from those produced through natural forces, and that the content, form, frequency, and distribution of materials be assessed.

Because interpretations of memory and materiality focus on practice, there has been a recursive relationship of techniques of archaeological fieldwork and the scale and precision with which interpretations of practice have been attempted. For example, it would be difficult to talk about the daily practices without being able to differentiate deposits that were made at this level of temporality from those that were produced during more occasional calendrical events, such as annual large-scale feasting. Both can be the subject of studies of the reproduction of memory and its intersection with practice, but the interpretations of daily practices rest on finer-grained (literally) studies of how sediments accumulate within deposits using techniques such as micromorphology and the differentiation of layers of plaster (for example, Hodder and Cessford 2004), while large-scale feasting might better be understood in terms of deviations from these smaller-scale accumulations.

The issue of intentionality is implied in many of the previous studies of depositional practice and materiality. We do not agree that it is necessary to assign intentionality to the archaeological materials that we study. Many practices are small in scale, and the results of these activities in the archaeological record are not necessarily the result of intentional acts of discard. In fact, it is this blurring of the distinction between acts of deposition and habitual practices that results in the accumulation of deposits over long periods of time, and that is underscored by several of the authors in this volume (see especially the chapters by Joyce, Pauketat, and Stahl). Whether intentional or not, archaeological deposits are created through different practices, and it is in the differentiation of those social practices and their relationships to memory production that we find our toehold on interpretation, not in whether those practices were intentional or not.

In this volume, Joyce tackles the deeper issues of intentionality entailed in the study of materiality and depositional practices. She illustrates her ideas using examples from Early and Middle Formative (1100–700 BCE) sites in Honduras. She applies Latour's (2005) insight that analyses of networks of human and nonhuman things should ask how nonhuman participants (artifacts, strata, buildings) cause other participants to act. She recognizes that while objects do not have intentions, they can cause practices to happen. Small platforms such as the one found in the early sequence of Los Naranjos, for example, did not intend to grow into large pyramids, yet the presence of the platform encouraged or facilitated the possibility of new practices, including placement of human burials and other activities that changed consciousness about history and would eventually collectively contribute to the making of the later pyramid (compare

Gillespie, this volume). She concludes that the structured deposits "to which we can draw attention are the likeliest remaining pieces of past networks of knowledge and memory, intentionality and action, personhood and embodied dispositions."

The chapters in this volume clearly draw on several different theories of connectivity or relationality to understand memory practices. These include concepts such as enchainment, gathering, and citation. For example, the concept of enchainment is one that has been discussed by John Chapman (2000a) within his theory of fragmentation. Although Chapman's discussion of fragmentation as a way of looking at chains of people places undue emphasis on object breakage and material pieces, the practical aspects of building relationships between people through time, whether with whole or fragmentary objects, are most salient. The concept of gathering together, discussed in many chapters in this volume (for example, Gillespie, Pollard, and Mills) owes its intellectual roots to archaeologists working with small, yet highly diverse Neolithic assemblages (for example, Barrett 1999; Bradley 1990, 2000; Hill 1995; Jones 2002; Pollard 2001; Pollard and Ruggles 2001; Thomas 1999b). In these cases, fragments of objects with diverse origins were deposited together, linking places and people. Citation, or the reference back to something else during an activity, is another concept of connectivity that comes from Jacques Derrida (1982) through Judith Butler (1993, 1997; see also Jones 2001, 2005; Joyce 2003a). Butler's ideas on embodiment, in particular, provide an important way to think about how personhood and identity are expressed within memory practices. Citations to the past are ways in which genealogies of practices are built, forming bridges between people across large expanses of time and space, and these can be expressed at different social scales ranging from the individual to larger social fields or collectives.

As an example of the use of citation and enchainment, Pauketat (this volume) looks at the continuity and change associated with the spread of a founder's cult from Cahokia into Wisconsin in the eleventh century. Like Joyce he questions the role of intentionality in discussions of agency, noting that agency is not something exclusive to individuals but is instead dispersed across fields of relationships between people and things. Radical changes in history reflect significant reorderings of fields of power, but not necessarily intentionality. To explore how disjunctions in history occur, such as the creation of a founders' cult during the emergence and promotion of an ancient ruler, Pauketat focuses on how practice, defined as the tangible aspects of culture, highlights particular images, people, and things in a citational process (in the sense of Butler 1993). Highlighted or cited relations grow and change through an enchainment of people and things. He argues that the end of effigy mound construction in Wisconsin after 1050 CE was a consequence of the decoupling of the region's old practices from their referents (out-of-date citations) and their enchainment to the new referents from Cahokia, those of a foreign founders' cult centered at a distant place (Cahokia) where the powers of *wa-kaⁿ-da* were being gathered.

Mills's chapter combines the concepts of gathering and citation to look at memory practices in Chaco Canyon at different social scales. She points out that Chacoan depositional practices brought together objects with diverse origins and histories. Dedicatory caches for round rooms featured worked and unworked objects that were remarkable in their diversity within, and redundancy between, deposits. An important commonality between these caches was that they minimally included objects that were ornaments, ornament debris, and/or raw materials used in ornament production. Through this commonality she argues that buildings were meant to be dressed, much in the same way that bodies were ornamented. Like Lucero's discussion of animation, Chacoan buildings were given an identity and animated through the deposition of beads, pendants, and other materials that provided citations to other bodily practices. Citation was also present in the ways in which small-scale depositional practices replicated the ways in which larger depositional events took place. Small kivas, for example, contained the same kinds of materials as did the largest deposits from great kivas. As she also argues, these continuities of tradition can be traced to the materiality of Ancestral Pueblo memory work into the present day.

People inhabit their worlds in very different ways (Barrett 1999) and create meaning through their residence in different practices. We may get closer to understanding how those differences were expressed by looking at the ways in which memories were created and maintained. Most of us in this volume do not use a phenomenological approach to understand these relationships. Rather, we use materiality as a window to understand the connections between people through time and across space that make each of the societies we study (and social networks within them) different. We try to understand how social memories were constructed in their terms, not our own, creating a cross-cultural study of aesthetics and meaning.

For example, Joyce (this volume) advocates creating a semiotic approach to track these networks between people through time and across space. Like a growing number of other archaeologists (for example, Preucel 2006), she draws on Peircean rather than Saussurean semiotics, arguing that the process of building the pyramid is not the result of meaningful signs (Saussure) but the process of meaning making (Peirce). She uses the example of the malanggan described by Küchler to demonstrate that it is in the linkages or chains between people that meaning is made, not in the fact that they signify something. These images are used in performances that are part of continuing networks through time, recreating memories through their citation to past persons and reshaping them through practices that bridge generations. Their meaning derives from the presence of these connections between people through time.

Webb Keane (2003b, 2005) has made a similar argument for understanding how material items are made meaningful, focusing on the concept of "bundling." The meaning of objects is always dependent on another referent: form is bundled with other associative attributes, and those attributes are responsible for making things meaningful. Although he does not historicize that bundling together of attributes, we may extend this idea to how specific attributes of objects serve as mnemonics, making connections between people, as Joyce's discussion suggests. Many of the other authors in this volume use these kinds of associations to arrive at interpretations of how object meanings were used in memory making. These interpretations may be of individual artifacts, but they may also be of assemblages of objects. Because archaeologists often deal with assemblages, the application of theories to clusters of objects linked by their spatial and temporal properties may hold considerable importance in how we interpret what was meaningful in the past. Nonetheless, although objects within assemblages may refer to each other, for them to be meaningful in the sense of memory work they ultimately need to have associations with people—those who made them in the present and in the past. In short, meaning is a dimension of practice that relates actants to values.

Although most of the authors in this volume do not look at mortuary practices per se, the ways in which genealogies are constructed, the citation to persons in the past, and the heirlooming of objects are all processes that are important parts of ancestor veneration. The chapters by Lucero, Mills, and Nielsen all discuss ways in which ancestors were honored through practices that bridged many generations. Nielsen's chapter most explicitly discusses the dynamic properties of social memory and ancestor veneration, focusing on the late prehistoric or regional development period (900–1400 CE) of the southern Andes. He carefully culls through the ethnographic, ethnohistoric, and archaeological evidence of the relationship between burial towers (*chullpas*) and storage silos and concludes that rather than attempting to typologically distinguish these buildings archaeologists should recognize that chullpas are multifunctional objects involving relationships between people and ancestors. These structures "wove different practices, actors, and contexts of social interaction into a single field structured around the ancestor." Indeed they embodied ancestors and did what ancestors do to "guard the fields and herds, promote their fertility, protect the harvest, bring prosperity to their descendants providing them with food, water, and other (stored) goods, represent the group before outsiders, defend the community and its territory, fight their enemies, [and] inspire political decisions."

RITUAL IS EVERYWHERE

A major outcome of the studies in this volume is that by reconstructing different genealogies of material practices there can be a rethinking of traditional distinctions between ritual and domestic life. The problems with this dialectic have been pointed out in recent years by a number of archaeologists (see especially Bradley 2003, 2005; Brück 1999; Walker 2002). Brück, in particular, critiques the post-Enlightenment concept of ritual as always in opposition to secular life. This dualism was a part of many of the early approaches to depositional practice in that "structured" deposits were seen as the result of ritual, while other, supposedly nonstructured deposits were the result of domestic action. As noted above, adherence to this dichotomy ignored variation in how ritual may have been conceptualized and practiced by past societies. Instead, she argues for an alternative tactic that emphasizes "prehistoric conceptions of effective action" (Brück 1999:314), which may include overlapping spheres of what is considered sacred versus profane and replaces practical with symbolic logic.

Bradley (2003, 2005) and Walker (2002) have made similar arguments, calling for a rethinking of the traditional distinction between sacred and profane and their replacement with the search for alternative systems of logic and value. As Bradley (2003:11) argues, many archaeologists perceive of ritual in functionalist terms as separate from daily life and as something formal in nature. This is why the "structured deposits" argument for ritual action has failed in its ability to discern new systems of value: they were seen as intentional, rational choices within a system of value that reproduced contemporary Western ritual practice. Similarly, other deposits that are less structured were seen as excluding ritual practice.

In this volume all of the authors use the idea that ritual is something to look at through practice, not through a priori ideas about what do or do not constitute ritual deposits. Stahl and Walker, especially, probe this theme in their discussions of how animals were differently valued by the Banda of Africa and Ancestral Puebloans, respectively. Stahl explores the history of Banda people in Ghana between 1400 and 1900 CE, focusing on

the interplay of practices associated with shrines. Building on the ritual theory of Catherine Bell (1992, 1997), Stahl recognizes that to understand ritual it is important to understand it as strategy or practice (ritualizing).
When seen as an evolving process rather than as a type of behavior, ritual
becomes a more malleable phenomenon. Seen in this way, the tantalizing
manner in which ritualizing often transcends rational categories like
sacred/profane, practical/impractical, belief/action becomes more comprehensible. For archaeologists the implication is that the remains of ritualization will not inhere in specific objects or buildings but in the way they
are utilized. To differentiate the ritualization of a range of objects in Banda
society, Stahl tracks the life histories of dogs, pythons, pots, and beads. In
so doing, she does exactly what Bradley has called for: recognition of a continuum of rituals and the possibility of ritual in everyday life. Social memory is implicated in this analysis because of the continuities in tradition that
Stahl so effectively tracks through the long sequence of occupation in the
Banda area.

At the same time that we note that ritual is everywhere, it is clear that
some rituals are performed at scales or with materials that become more
archaeologically accessible than others. Susan Gillespie's chapter looks at
continuities and discontinuities in depositional practices to construct a history of La Venta. She explains the patterning in deposits as the result of
prestige-enhancing competition between elite households. Throughout
much of that history Complex A was a "ritually charged place," which
served as "an arena for negotiating and contesting that hierarchical ordering." She argues that only a powerful ruler could have brought such a long-
term ritual arena to an end. She links the massive deposits of the last phase
not with the abandonment of the site but instead with the emergence of
such a ruling house. Interestingly, the power of this ruler is invoked in a
dramatic event whose memory would replace those of earlier ones as the
sole creation narrative. Further cyclical building activity at the site came to
an end, leading the community to forget the contestable nature of their
past—marking a break in the chain of practices that formed these mounds
in the first place.

CONCLUSIONS

The papers in this volume are examples of the ways in which archaeological studies of materiality contribute to understanding how memory
becomes historicized through linked activities that engage with materials.
Archaeology is the one discipline that provides a long-term perspective on
memory work. Recent research on materiality underscores the ways in

which materials, substances, objects, and so on are important parts of the different activities that people participate in during memory work, whether it is recalling, reshaping, forgetting, inventing, coordinating, or transmitting. Archaeologists have always been interested in material culture, but the intersectional study of materiality and memory through archaeology provides ways in which long-term practices can be appreciated in new ways. To do this we look at depositional practices that create a historicity to the ways in which memories were made. As many of us point out in the chapters that follow, these practices show strong continuities with historic and contemporary traditions. This continuity is made up of chains of repetitions that owe their continuity to particular ways in which memory was transmitted through time and to the meanings ascribed by actors during memory work.

The authors of the contributions to this volume share many concerns. We are interested in linking practices through time—in showing how relationships are created, broken, and recreated through time. One of the points of agreement is that these relationships can be approached materially, because memory work always has a material component. We also agree that what we would like to understand is the diversity of ways that people materialize relationships with the immaterial. There are material dimensions of practice that we can access, but other dimensions may not be as readily accessible. Nonetheless, by working through different scales of practice from the daily sweepings to the construction of monuments, we can begin to build a framework for understanding the range of memory work that was practiced in the past.

2

Practice in and as Deposition

Rosemary A. Joyce

Approaches to archaeological deposition grounded in theories of practice provide a powerful way to transform how we as archaeologists understand the relations of actors in the past to the materialities through which we today explore topics such as rituality, spatiality, and historicity. Central to understanding deposition this way are questions about memory work—remembering, forgetting, and concealing knowledge as secrets—accomplished through practices that relate networks of persons and things over time. Such explorations have transformative potential for archaeology. To realize those potentials, we need to understand what this perspective demands, and what is incompatible with it.

This is not a theoretical project that can be discussed in the abstract. The changes in perspectives involved should infuse all aspects of our practice as archaeologists. I consequently illustrate each of my points with reference to an extended example of how understanding of an archaeological case is transformed by these approaches. The example I draw on comes from my own collaborative research in Honduras on sites dating to the late Early Formative and early Middle Formative periods, ca. 1100–700 BCE.[1]

In dominant models of Mesoamerican culture history, this is the period during which, on the Gulf Coast of Mexico, the first complex polities able to muster labor for large-scale public works took form. Thus, the questions archaeologists working on sites dating to these centuries traditionally address concern the nature of Olmec culture, art, or symbolism and their spread throughout the area (Clark 1994; Flannery and Marcus 2000; Grove 1989, 1997). The sites I work on in Honduras are part of this discourse because specific archaeological features there are among the things traditionally cataloged as evidence of "the Olmec," leading to a long-standing debate about the significance of such "Olmec" features in Honduras, far distant from the heartland of the Olmec archaeological culture on the Gulf Coast of Mexico (Healy 1974; Longyear 1969; Porter 1953; Sharer 1989; Willey 1969). This example thus serves to illustrate how the approaches I advocate shift analysis from sequences of static stages following each other in time to historicized chains of practices through which humans and nonhumans are connected over time in materially substantial ways.

To accomplish this transformation, I suggest we need to engage in a series of shifts of emphasis: to new understandings of materiality as the active medium and product of experience; to a new appreciation of the agency of humans and nonhumans; to a renewed appreciation of the embodiment of practice; and to models of human action that take into account differential knowledgeability, and the ways that knowledge is bound up in relations to persons and things. The approaches taken here require attention, not just to sequence in time, but to *history* understood as something people live and experience.[2]

A necessary condition for these shifts in perspective, in my view, is a move away from a simple structural model in which material things stand as vehicles of cultural meanings, waiting to be decoded and to yield their singular sense. It was from such a perspective that ceramic vessels with carved designs recovered from Honduran sites dating between 1100 and 900 BCE, apparently made locally, could be viewed as signs of "Olmec" identity (Longyear 1969; Porter 1953; Willey 1969). Instead of such a Saussurean model of meaning, archaeologists working on the active historicizing and materializing of practice arguably need a new Peircean semiotic model (Preucel and Bauer 2001). Similar suggestions form part of other contemporary discussions of anthropological approaches to materiality (Keane 2005:187). Nor are they particularly new. Preucel and Bauer (2001:89) cite Singer's (1978:223–224) argument that such an approach can better deal with

> how the different cultural "languages" are related to empirical objects and egos, to individual actors and groups....It is possible to deal with such extra-linguistic relations within the framework

of [Peircean] semiotic theory, because a semiotic anthropology
is a pragmatic anthropology. It contains a theory of how systems
of signs are related to their meanings, as well as to the objects
designated and to the experience and behavior of the sign users.
(original emphasis)

Beginning with an assumption that meanings are created through
practices relating sign-using humans, their actions and experiences, and
nonhumans connected to humans and to each other as referents for signs
and media of signification, even traditional archaeological questions
change form. Understanding practice in deposition and as deposition then
can begin with consideration of how the concrete forms of practices are
materialized and how the repetition of practices is historicized.

MATERIALIZING THE CONCRETE FORMS OF PRACTICES

I begin with a paradox: we must avoid equating materiality with physicality and cannot assume that everything physical constitutes part of materiality (compare Miller 2005). If we take materiality as a dimension of
practice, then (as Josh Pollard suggests) we may want to think of materiality in terms of the legal definition, "that which is material to the case." This
legal definition reminds us that what concern us are the relationships of
people to other materialities and the ways that practices shape and reshape
what matters.

What is material then becomes a matter of context. There may be culturally recognized materialities unseen by us. But we actually do not need
to look so far afield to begin to appreciate the slipperiness of materiality. In
archaeological practice, we routinely identify such things as a past nonhuman agent through materialities of absence. From this perspective, a posthole is material both in its present physicality, as a pattern of soils of
different colors and textures, and as a reference point for inferring past
presences: a piece of wood, selected, shaped, and put in place, perhaps
replaced, perhaps left to decay or removed to another place (Pauketat and
Alt 2005). What concerns us then are not merely presences, but material
that we interpret as signs of action. We are especially concerned with repetitive actions (Joyce and Lopiparo 2005), notably those that archaeologists
have been able to recognize in materialities we label structured deposits
(Richards and Thomas 1984). Such materialities are things whose status as
products of more-or-less intentional actions by more-or-less knowledgeable
actors is defensible at least in part because of the repetition we perceive in

a material register. But repetition is more than simply a methodological advantage; because it involves reproduction of practices over time (including the introduction of changing nuances), repeated practices require us to think in terms of histories.

HISTORICIZING THE REPETITION OF PRACTICES

What we see archaeologically as continuity is the result of an ongoing flow of human practice, the repetition of practices in a chain of performances. I argue that continuity should not be seen as something unproblematic but as the result of extensive social work through which humans maintain their connections over time in networks with nonhumans. Historicizing practice allows us to better describe those moments when materialities change in terms congruent with those we use to describe what went before and thus escape the trap of describing history as stasis punctuated by exceptional incidents of change.

From this perspective, the deep stratigraphic deposits that formed the first 500 or more years of the history of occupation at Puerto Escondido, Honduras (Joyce 2004; Joyce and Henderson 2001, 2002, 2003, 2004), are the materialization of repeated practice, their repetition the evidence of human dispositions and intentions. As the humans occupying this space repeated practices of posthole placement and re-placement, of processing of clay for house walls and the destruction and reconstruction of houses using the same technologies over centuries, they produced the multiple superimposed layers of soils with subtly different characters that we interpret today as signs of their history (Figure 2.1). This is as much materializing practice as the moments when, marked by more dramatic materialities, the humans in this historical network broke with previous practice, burned and razed a standing building, and filled it in as the core of a broad platform where a suite of new practices could be carried out (Figure 2.2). These more marked practices, in turn, are recognizable for us—material to us—among other things because they are also repeated. So, in the case of Puerto Escondido, into the new platform a series of pits intruded, each containing a small, round-sided, incurved-rim bowl. A new practice materialized through a new coordination of humans and nonhumans, formalized through repetition and stylization, it historicized the actors who followed as part of a new chain of linking predecessors and successors.

Archaeologists explore practices primarily through their spatial, material, and temporal dimensions, not primarily through their living performative or discursive dimensions (Joyce and Lopiparo 2005). It may be that another shift we need to make is away from the greater synchrony of Pierre

FIGURE 2.1

Wall of a deep excavation at Puerto Escondido cutting through deposits resulting from repeated episodes of construction, destruction, and reconstruction of perishable buildings dating to 1400–900 BCE. Photograph courtesy of John S. Henderson.

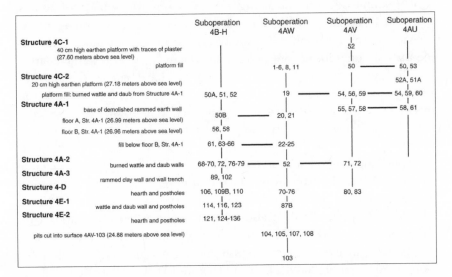

FIGURE 2.2

Reconstruction of the sequence of depositional events at Puerto Escondido, showing the alternation between repeated construction events and innovation marked by the burning of a perishable building and the construction of an earthen platform.

29

Bourdieu's (1977, 1990) influential ethnographic analyses of practice, to something more like the kind of historical and spatial conceptualizations of practices of Michel de Certeau (1984). Archaeologists have a choice to make between approaches to practice that envisage human action quite differently (Joyce and Lopiparo 2005). We can seek to interpret structured deposits like the caches of vessels at Puerto Escondido as evidence of unthinking repetition of actions with preformed symbolic meaning. Or we can understand them as tactics improvised within the bounds of strategies that joined human actors with differential power, tactics with the potential of reforming these networks. What we cannot do, if we wish to pursue this course, is ignore the questions raised about the status of human actors in our pragmatics.

ACTORS, AGENTS, ACTANTS

The kind of actors whose practices we have traditionally been comfortable talking about in archaeology are those select agents who we see represented both indirectly (in the outcomes of their labor and leadership) and directly in things like the human representations that form part of the corpus of "Olmec"-related objects from Honduras (Clark 1997, 2005). "Structured" deposition may seem particularly promising as a site to explore human action because of the promise it makes that here, at least, we can assume someone was acting with intentions, with self-consciousness, and with legitimacy. But as the now voluminous literature on agency in archaeology makes clear, this promise is ultimately no guarantee of evading the core questions about action and effectuality that lie at the heart of the division of the world into subjects (who have agency) and objects (which do not). On the one hand, we can ask, what deposits are *not* structured? On the other, we can ask, if not agency, what do we call the effectuality that so many things—including structured deposits—clearly had on people?

Following Bruno Latour (2005:46–55), we might adopt a wider view of humans and nonhumans as not so very different, as *actants* in networks whose changing articulations become our focus. Without demanding the adoption of a specialized vocabulary that might distance our arguments from those we hope to reach, we can nonetheless follow the lead of a plethora of analysts concerned with the agency of things (Gell 1998; Gosden 2005; Olsen 2003) who insist that we not begin by placing all our emphasis on humans. Returning to the example of those sculptures that appear to constitute prima facie evidence of a more problematic notion of agency restricted to humans (and often, only some humans), we can see

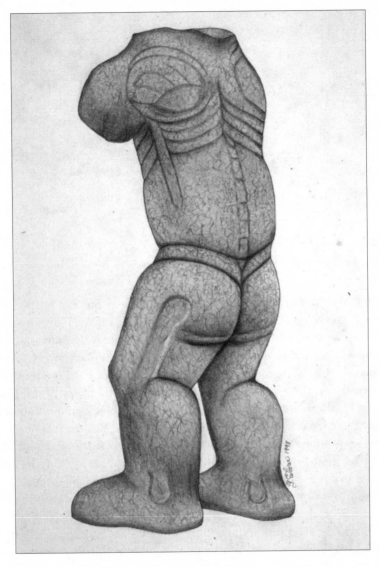

FIGURE 2.3

Three-dimensional, life-size sculpture of anthropomorphic figure, Los Naranjos Monument 4, 125 cm tall. Drawing courtesy of Yolanda Tovar.

that even our understanding of these sculptures is reformulated by considering them as something other than signifiers of a static signified (shaman, ruler, or historical person). A standing figure from Los Naranjos (Figure 2.3) began a history of entanglement with humans when first shaped, but

31

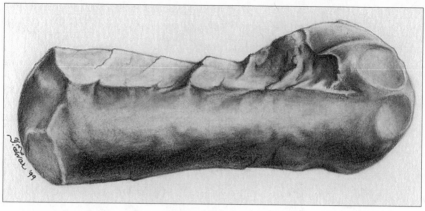

FIGURE 2.4.

Fragment of three-dimensional, life-size anthropomorphic figure, Puerto Escondido Monument 1. Maximum width of crossed legs 73 cm. Drawing courtesy of Yolanda Tovar.

that history did not end there (Joyce and Henderson 2002). Like many such sculptures, this figure was decapitated, and the head, if preserved, was placed somewhere else, creating a dispersed, multilocale network including the human actors who created and modified the sculpture. The body was buried, only to be recovered during the excavation of a modern canal.

Because of the conditions of its discovery, our concept of the history and network formed by this sculpture is much less rich than our knowledge of the network formed by a fragment of sculpture (Figure 2.4) recovered in our excavations at Puerto Escondido (Joyce and Henderson 2002). The recovered piece of worked stone makes up one lower leg of a figure seated in a posture exemplified by many known examples of Olmec stone sculpture from the Gulf Coast of Mexico, also represented at Puerto Escondido by small, hand-modeled ceramic figurines (Joyce 2003a). We could address it primarily as a representation—now, regrettably, fragmentary and thus almost meaningless—of such a seated figure. But this fragmented sculpture, whose surface records not only the marks of production but also the shallow, patterned pockmarks made during its transformation, was recovered in a marked context that points to a wider and more entangled network. Placed in a stone cist of a shape and size to contain human remains, but empty of them, this reshaped stone was buried by a rock fill topped with a small pendant figurine. The conversion of the original life-size stone sculpture into a buried deposit through a sequence of ritualized practices (following Bell 1992) produced a stratification of knowledge reproduced in subsequent generations as memory and forgetting, as secrets and ignorance. We could tell the story entirely in terms of human actors exercising agency—although it becomes much more difficult to identify them as the subjects of representation. Or we can rethink it as an example of the interconnections of humans and things through which the active reconstitution of meanings is foregrounded by the stylization of actions and their inflection in an unexpected, novel way.

From this latter perspective, the existence of these anthropomorphic sculptures connected by visual, spatial, and experiential relations with human beings over time constituted both a potential site of innovation in (inflection of) practice, and a material agent tending to promote certain kinds of practices. The issue is not so simple as whether objects act; as Latour (2005:71) notes in discussing the status of nonhuman actants, the first question to ask is, "Does it make a difference in the course of some other agent's action or not?" The trouble with most of our thinking about nonhumans and humans comes from assuming there are only two ways of making a difference, one proper to human subjects, the other open to nonhuman objects and objectified humans. Instead, we could think about a broader range of ways humans and nonhumans promote action. "In addition to 'determining' and serving as a 'backdrop for human action,' things might authorize, allow, afford, encourage, permit, suggest, influence, block, render possible, forbid, and so on" (Latour 2005:72). Including such nonhuman actors in our models urgently foregrounds questions of intentionality and reflexivity.

INTENTIONALITY AND REFLEXIVITY

Intentionality is always a problem for archaeologists. Imputing motives to past actors whose own rationalizations we cannot ever consult, as ethnographers could, even if we would in the end reject them as forms of false consciousness or misapprehension, can make systemic models that lodge determination somewhere away from inaccessible actors seem attractive. The world would be simpler for archaeologists if people were not reflective, self-directed, at times idiosyncratic, and worst of all constantly engaged in renarrating what they have done and experienced and giving it ever-shifting post hoc coherence. It seems as if it would be simpler if we assumed our human actors were without these kinds of complexities. But in fact, when we substitute actors lacking reflexivity and intentions, our models make only the crudest kind of sense, at the expense of ruling out of consideration many aspects of human experience.

So we need to come to terms with intentionality. Thinking about networks of humans and nonhumans (including animal nonhumans) may go some way toward helping us here. Latour (2005:107) suggests we approach our analyses from the position that "all the actors we are going to deploy might be *associated* in such a way that they *make others do things*" (original emphasis). In one of his central examples, scallops make fisherman do things, just as nets make scallops do things. Tracing the networks created by their associations is a necessary task that cannot be derailed "by the 'obvious objections' that 'things don't talk,' 'fish nets have no passion,' and 'only humans have intentions'" (Latour 2005:107).

Let us take seriously the proposition that the nonhuman objects that form landscapes by their accumulation as stable groups, or by their circulation, in turn shape the actions and experiences of humans. This is not to say that these nonhuman objects intend the effects they create, nor that they reflect on the outcomes of their action and base their subsequent actions on their reflections, any more than all human actions take place intentionally and reflexively. But nor do nonhumans simply passively relay the intentions of human actors. Latour (2005:128) defines good analyses of assemblages of humans and nonhumans as those in which "all the actors *do something* and don't just sit there" so that the accounts "render the movement of the social visible to the reader" (original emphasis). Descriptions that "trace a set of relations" as a network represent "the ability of each actor to *make* other actors do unexpected things" (Latour 2005:129; original emphasis). This formulation engages a different, more productive way to begin to talk about the engagements people in the past had with each other and with nonhuman animals and objects in space and over time.

An example may help make this point clearer. In my writing about early Honduran earthen platforms, I have argued that we misunderstand these platforms when we gloss over their origins as broad, relatively low platforms in preference for the pyramids they later became (Joyce 2004). We take a later stage in the life history of these places as the cause of their construction. Instead, I suggest that the construction process itself gives us a basis to understand some of the expectations their builders could have had of the construction materials. The earliest phases of what eventually became pyramids (at places like Los Naranjos) were broader, more extensive versions of slightly elevated house platforms documented at a larger group of sites (including Puerto Escondido). At a few sites, including Los Naranjos, such early platforms, once in existence, became the kernel of a place with different spatial and material characteristics. Partly this may have been due to the expression by these platforms of unexpected behavior, like the greater durability in the same environment of a broader earthen platform than of a smaller one. These platforms also had the potential to host distinctive practices, like the sequence of burials of pots, and of people, at Puerto Escondido and the burial of at least one person at Los Naranjos. The network we trace does not lead to an end; instead, the nonhuman objects continue to act in concert with the humans in ways that are not entirely determined by any member of the collective. The Los Naranjos platform did not "intend" to grow into a pyramid. It did not reflect on its possible futures. But it did encourage new activities by the people to whom it was connected. And by its actions in hosting new activities—particularly the burial of an individual wearing a massive pair of jade ear flares and a jade belt— it promoted a radically different form of historical consciousness in at least some of those humans, with material consequences.

INSCRIPTION AND DISCURSIVE CONSCIOUSNESS

In common with many other archaeologists I have found the terminology promoted by Paul Connerton (1989) useful for thinking about the kinds of effects materialities can have on historical memory (Joyce 1998; Joyce and Hendon 2000; see also Bradley 1998; Rowlands 1993). Drawing on that vocabulary, we could say that the pyramid at Los Naranjos that developed when human actors interred one person in a memorable ceremony and covered that burial with a greatly expanded platform inscribed in the landscape a particular historical event that could then resonate through other forms of discourse. From this perspective, one of the things we engage when we talk about structured deposits or ritual deposition is a moment or moments of more explicit discourse, for which the material deposits become a continued touchstone.

In a simple semiotic model, the pyramid at Los Naranjos became a signifier of the social ceremony, social identity, and differentials of social status at the time of the original ceremony. A Peircean semiotic perspective transforms this slightly, but significantly: the newly heightened pyramid is not just a signifier, but an index of the labor of the workers; of the presence of those who contributed to the event; of the reconstitution of social relations, of which it was an active part. It may simultaneously be iconic of hierarchy, in the somatic form of high/low contrasts. As a consequence, it can come to be symbolic of the abstractions of hierarchy and difference that become the evident meaning of later pyramids in the region.

We can apply the same concept of inscription, understood from a Peircean semiotic perspective, as an action, not a product of that action; a verb, not a noun, to other materialities from early Honduras. The familiar, quasitextual notion that the incised designs on bowls from early sites throughout the region recorded mythical beings who were characters in spoken traditions rests on seeing the bowls as inscriptions of signifiers of meanings—meanings that were the signified stories told by people living at the time, or of beings understood to exist or to have existed. Instead, we can see the same bowls as processes of meaning making: shaped as food-serving vessels (and some of the examples at Puerto Escondido, at least, demonstrably contained feast foods), these pots carried into the meals in which they were used conventionalized representations of nonnatural zoo-morphic beings. To the extent that the meals where they were used included commentary on these images and the cosmological accounts in which these beings figured, they inscribed interpretations in the discursive consciousness of the participants.

It may well be that, as with many such interpretations, the users of these things were not normally consciously reflecting on this possible commentary. It may even be, as I have elsewhere argued (Joyce 1996), that in Honduras these inscriptions were not understood iconically as referring to the zoomorphs on which they were based, and were most consciously understood as indices of the ceramic artists who made each pot as a unique object. Rather than signaling "Olmec" identity, for some viewers, these images may have signified a local place, person, or corporate group. To the extent that their employment in meals ritualized by their use was the most important conscious association of these and similar vessels, the designs may have inscribed simply the marked nature of the events for which they were made and in which they were displayed. The inaccessibility of the many possible ways that these inscriptions could enter into cycles of memory does not prevent our recognizing their powerful potential as part of memory work.

EMBODIED DISPOSITIONS

Connerton (1989) contrasts inscription with incorporation—bodily memory. That this division is too simple is a point made by everyone who has ever considered the subject. The materialities of Honduras's "Olmec" occupation include some that literally blur the boundary of incorporation and inscription, cylindrical seals and flat stamps used to mark on the living body designs from the same range as are found incised on pottery. These are startlingly clear materializations of bodily discipline, but the creation of embodied dispositions is by no means limited to some select foregrounded set of materials. Arguably, what "structured" deposition or ritualized practice is about, in some sense, is the production of a person oriented socially in a particular way (Bell 1992).

We do not need to take an extreme Foucaultian position to see that humans are socialized to act, evaluate, desire, and persist in particular embodied ways. Our difficulty as analysts in defining which contexts are specially "structured" may stem from a sense that there are moments in the life of any person, social group, or place when the taken-for-granted nature of action is actually in question. Indeed, these moments recur in every human being's life as they make the sometimes difficult transitions to and through social adulthood. The embodied dispositions that are created at the level of a person by their early experiences are in profound ways mediated by their engagement with nonhumans, as much as with other humans. Thus, as Marcel Mauss (1992) taught us, we have a distinctive local, physical style of walking, swimming, running, and generally of bodily practice. Participation in the creation of structured deposits thus created not only the deposits themselves, but also persons with coordinated and specially marked physical experiences.

Our embodied dispositions are not limited to physical sensation. They also include senses of the good, the beautiful, and desirable. These values are another product of social participation, learned through doing. The events during which special spaces and places were created through structured deposition were contexts of marked participatory experience—even where the participatory experience was one of seclusion from an interior secret (a point made by Cesare Poppi in his studies of African secret societies [Poppi 1999]). The power of the coordinated-yet-differentiated participation of humans in striking events, especially events producing inscriptions and incorporated histories, to facilitate new social relations and forms is part of what Bell (1992) understands as the power of ritual.

Enchainment (Chapman 2000a) captures one mode of the relation of humans and nonhumans in networks mediated by materiality. In Chapman's original proposal, enchainment produces relational persons and histories distributed across a network in time and space. From this perspective, we might consider that

> a person and a person's mind are not confined to particular
> spatio-temporal coordinates, but consist of a spread of biograph-
> ical events and memories of events, and a dispersed category of
> material objects, traces, and leavings, which can be attributed to
> a person and which, in aggregate, testify to agency...during a
> biographical career which may, indeed, prolong itself long after
> biological death. The person is thus understood as the sum total
> of the indexes which testify, in life and subsequently, to the bio-
> graphical existence of this or that individual. (Gell 1998:222)

Enchainment is contested and can be erased and recreated. The end of a chain might be considered a form of forgetting; to re-create a chain would be to re-signify the entire network, and thus the persons and things connected by it. We are consequently faced with questions of whose meanings, memories, forgettings, and re-memberings we deal with here.

KNOWLEDGE, MEMORY, PRACTICE

There are methodological implications of the project sketched out above. But far from a generic prescription of how to do this, what happens when this project is adopted is that we come to our sites as the materiality of past practices, at scales from the everyday to the traditional. Depositional practices provide us a way to address the memory work in which, at many times and places, networks of humans engage, in large part by connecting themselves through nonhumans. If the materialities we explore are archives, they are archives understood from the contemporary perspective of Trouillot (1995). There are silences built into the archives, and these gaps themselves are part of the network of humans and nonhumans created by specific materialities. Rereading an archive can reform what is material, and what is not. The memory work engaged in by humans in these networks, whether past or present, is neither seamless nor changeless. Far from conforming to the signifier-signified model, the work of memory (and the work of practice) engages a continual productivity as a person engages with a materiality to form a concept that is historically and materially connected with other persons, things, and concepts:

> People engage with Signs in the world in a regularized way without reflecting on their ambiguity. To Peirce, the many possible meanings of a Sign are not cognized simultaneously, but from one semiotic moment to the next, whether they be internal to one's mental processes...or the engagements of different embodied "knowers." Meanings are not inherently ambiguous, but become so as the same, or different, "knowers" (or, if you prefer, "agents") engage with the Sign...again and again in different contexts. (Preucel and Bauer 2001:93)

One of the many common reference points for discussions of this kind by archaeologists has been the ethnographic work of Susanne Küchler (1987, 1988, 1997) on the *malanggan* of Papua New Guinea. In her most influential articles, she writes about objects made to be destroyed (and thus made available, in huge numbers, for reintegration in global museum collections). These perishable sculptures were created specifically for commemoration of deceased persons, and this gives them an aura for archaeologists that is completely understandable. But we may not have quite explored all the potential significance of this case.

The form of malanggan that is most present in museum collections, and which provided the beginning point of her analysis, was only one of a set of forms through which memory was materialized. The other forms malanggan could take had very different "depositional histories." Some were made to be literally destroyed (not just conceptually removed from the local scene). Perhaps more intriguing, every physical object created is a part of a malanggan, but none actually is the thing itself, nor even a representation of it. The physical objects were expressions of a specific concept owned and controlled by someone, who necessarily authorized the performance of the concept that included, among other outcomes, a physical form. But the important effect of this performance was the connection of humans and nonhumans in a continuing network, and it was in fact the prior existence of such a connection that was a necessary precondition for the citational performance of a malanggan.

We are thus dealing, in this ethnographic case, with the conjunction of knowledge, memory, and practice joining together humans and nonhumans in time and space through specific materialities that were created, used, and disposed of in specifically structured ways. If we take this as a possible model, we might infer that the patterned materialities to which we can draw attention are the likeliest remaining pieces of past networks of knowledge and memory, intentionality and action, personhood and embodied dispositions. Realizing this potential should serve to profoundly transform the meaning of what we routinely do as we tease out the meanings of deposition in practice.

Notes

1. This research, codirected with John S. Henderson of Cornell University, took place under contract with the Instituto Hondureño de Antropología e Historia. I would like to thank Licenciada Carmen Julia Fajardo, former head of investigations of the institute, and Lic. Juan Alberto Durón, head of El Centro Regional del Norte, for their support of this research.

2. This is a direct quote of the formulation proposed by Tim Pauketat during the SAR seminar.

3

Deposition and Material Agency in the Early Neolithic of Southern Britain

Joshua Pollard

In 1984 Colin Richards and Julian Thomas published a seminal analysis of depositional activity at the later Neolithic henge enclosure of Durrington Walls, Wiltshire, southern England (Richards and Thomas 1984). Within that study they presented evidence of the purposeful and patterned discard of pottery, lithic artifacts, animal bone, and other materials across the site (Figure 3.1). The patterns identified could not be accommodated easily within functionalist explanations. Instead, the depositional practices described were considered overtly symbolical, leading Richards and Thomas to argue that they represented the material residue of ritual practice. This accorded well with certain anthropological definitions of ritual that stressed its overtly symbolic, highly formalized, and repetitive content. Their paper stimulated an awareness of the complex nature of deposits in British and European prehistoric contexts and made problematic their interpretation. In the twenty years since there has been widespread recognition of similar "structured deposits" in a variety of later prehistoric contexts (for example, Hill 1995). With reference to the Neolithic (fourth–third millennia BCE), we are now aware of the ubiquitous occurrence of deliberate deposits of artifactual material, animal and human bone from ceremonial monuments, pits associated with occupation events, and a variety of natural topographic features (Thomas 1999a:62–88). Such

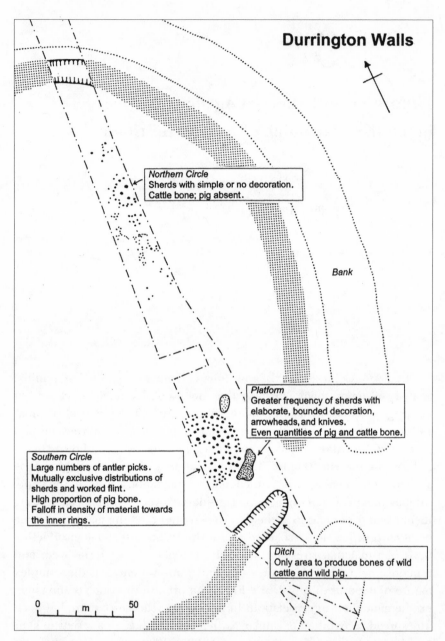

Durrington Walls

Northern Circle
Sherds with simple or no decoration.
Cattle bone; pig absent.

Bank

Platform
Greater frequency of sherds with
elaborate, bounded decoration,
arrowheads, and knives.
Even quantities of pig and cattle bone.

Southern Circle
Large numbers of antler picks.
Mutually exclusive distributions of
sherds and worked flint.
High proportion of pig bone.
Falloff in density of material towards
the inner rings.

Ditch
Only area to produce bones of wild
cattle and wild pig.

0   m   50

FIGURE 3.1

Depositional patterning at Durrington Walls, Wiltshire. Presented in Richards and Thomas
(1984).

deposits vary in scale, format, and content, and must have involved varied participation and circumstance.

The coining of the term "structured deposition," its equation with ritual, and the assumption that this form of practice was somehow categorically different from other forms of deposition (for example, refuse disposal) has since generated problems. Semantics are an issue. "Structured deposits" implies the existence of forms of deposition that are somehow "unstructured." Furthermore, there exists a danger in interpreting all spatial and compositional patterning within deposits that appear "nonfunctional" as representing the outcome of special practices. We should recognize that all deposition will be structured through the constraints worked by the body and physical environment, and because of the patterned nature of habitual practice and the largely unconsidered materialization of culturally specific sets of values. As demonstrated by the ethnoarchaeological work of Ian Hodder (1982) and Henrietta Moore (1986), the routine disposal of refuse—like speech, burial, and the organization of domestic space—reproduces the symbolic categories that constitute culture. At a basic level the compositional and spatial structure identifiable within the routine discard of refuse will vary from one cultural context to another because of differing value regimes attached to refuse, "dirt," and pollution. The result may be archaeological signatures that appear unusual and inexplicable to us in functional terms.

If the patterning of materials at sites like Durrington Walls could represent nothing more than the largely unconsidered materialization of a "symbolic grammar" through routine refuse disposal, then how do we separate out those deposits that are "special" or "ritual" in character? The answer is that we do not, or at least that we exercise caution, since we may be led into another binding dichotomy that bears little relationship to the reality of past "indigenous" experience. "Ritual" is itself a problematic term, and while anthropological definitions may be sought that stress its symbolic content and expression, and its prescribed and repetitive nature, such characteristics are also shared by certain forms of secular action, refuse disposal included. Joanna Brück has cogently argued that the long-standing distinction made by archaeologists and anthropologists between ritual and secular action reflects a post-Enlightenment rationalism: ritual is defined in opposition to those practices in which a means-end relationship can be identified (Brück 1999). She argues that a division of symbolic and secular action is unlikely to have been recognized in the prehistoric past and that we cannot overcome such dichotomous thinking simply by claiming that ritual permeated everyday life. The "practical" and "symbolic" are one

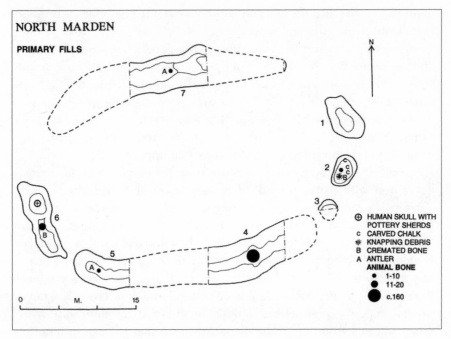

FIGURE 3.2

Deposits in the ditches of the North Marden long barrow, Sussex. Based on information in Drewett (1986).

and the same, and cannot be divorced (Brück 1999:325–326). Instead, a focus on understanding the variable, historically constituted nature of rationality in prehistory is proposed, in which functionality is culturally defined.

Dissolving the ritual:secular dichotomy may be a useful step, since it removes an unnecessary interpretative bind, but we are still left with a realization that some forms of deposition are *qualitatively* different from others. To take a British Neolithic example, the placing of a spread of charcoal in the ditch of the North Marden long barrow, Sussex, into which was set a human skull, surrounded by sherds from four plain bowls (Drewett 1986), represents a different kind of action from the routine disposal of refuse within a settlement midden (Figure 3.2). By virtue of its barrow context and staged performance, the deposition of charcoal, sherds, and skull at North Marden explicitly foregrounds the qualities of materials and their symbolic connections and may have served to fix particular meanings (Thomas 1999b). Rather than attempting to categorize depositional acts, it is more productive to focus on their context and effects. One could think of deposition as embodying a continuum of practices, some routinized and largely unconsidered, others overt performances. At one level the deposition of materials was a habitual action undertaken during the course of daily life, at other times a carefully contrived practice remarkable and memorable because of the objects involved (famed, tainted, or potent) and the spatial and temporal context of its enactment. Those deposits embodying the most formality, for example, in later Neolithic henge monuments and timber circles (Thomas 1996; Pollard 1995), represent an explicit attempt to bring the received qualities, connections, and meanings of objects to the fore. Here explicit reference was made through deposition to cosmological principles of order and particular forms of authority, whether corporal or supernatural.

FROM MEANING TO MATERIALITY

The symbolic and structural archaeology and "textual turn" of the 1980s led to the interpretation of deliberate deposits as material statements and/or codes through which symbolic structures might be read (for example, J. Thomas 1991; Pollard 1995). Deposition was seen as a process by which meaning and message were situated and communicated, objects within deposits acting as signifiers for complex concepts—for example, the relationship between natural and cultural domains (Hodder 1990). With hindsight, the comprehension of object worlds in simple symbolic terms can be seen as limiting, and more nuanced understandings of materiality have developed in which the physicality of things, their biography, ontology, and performative character have taken center stage (Meskell 2005; Miller 2005).

Stimulated by a realization that the characterization of deposits as symbolic statements fails to fully explain their format and context, elsewhere I have drawn attention to the aesthetic qualities of deposition (Pollard 2001). There is undoubtedly a degree of *care* and *respect* afforded to things in Neolithic deposits, implied by the placement of discrete bundles of animal ribs in the ditches of fourth millennium BCE enclosures, the "nesting" of sherds, or the reassembling of butchered cattle in long barrow ditches (Figure 3.3). It is as if the proper treatment of those things mattered, for their sake. Here we are brought to focus on the performative context of deposition and the ontological status of objects, their materiality and agency. A lead can be taken from Alfred Gell's reformulation of an anthropology of art, where the emphasis is shifted from the determination of symbolic content to issues of agency, intention, and causation (Gell 1998). Following such lines, a more active role in shaping social processes can be ascribed to deposits. Before this can be explored further, some consideration should be

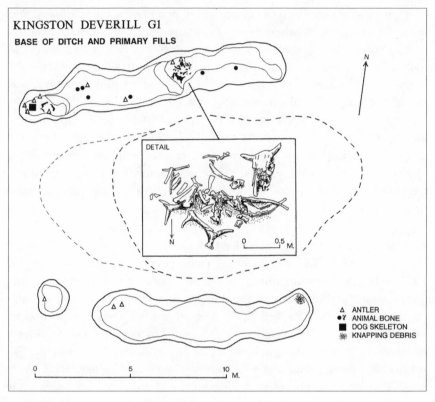

FIGURE 3.3

Reassembled cattle bones and other deposits in the ditches of the Kingston Deverill long barrow, Wiltshire. Based on information in site archive.

given to questions of agency and how human and object lives might be assimilated.

A recent body of literature has sought to demonstrate how people and objects are embroiled in heterogeneous networks that constitute each other. Objects, like people, are delegated identities, responsibilities, and roles, becoming points around which action is constrained and structured (see Latour 1999; Boast 1997; Law and Hassard 1999; Graves-Brown 2000; Jones and Cloke 2002). This is part of a trend within the social sciences to work beyond the problematic dualisms generated by Cartesian philosophies, including that between subjects and objects. One approach is simply to collapse the distinction made between people and things, human and nonhuman domains. Removing subject:object boundaries allows us to see how people and objects are mutually constituted and worked together as hybrid forms (Strathern 1988; Haraway 1991; Fowler 2004) and facilitates an extension of agency—an ability to "act back" and elicit responses—to nonhuman actants.

Such perspectives have resonance with recent archaeological approaches to personhood that have stressed the relational nature of human identities, acknowledging their construction via engagement with complex networks of people, practices, landscapes, animals, and things (Thomas 1999b; Brück 2004; Fowler 2004). John Chapman's seminal study of enchainment and accumulation in the prehistoric Balkans provides a good example (Chapman 2000a). Enchainment here involved the linking together of people through the circulation of fragments of deliberately broken inalienable objects. Located within histories of production and prior ownership, something of a person's identity is seen to travel with the object itself. The distribution of fragments of broken human bone or figurines could therefore become a means of maintaining and cementing social relations. By contrast, accumulation involved the collection of sets of objects that served to integrate different personal identities—"the concentration of community relations" (Chapman 2000a:225). What is of immediate interest is that Chapman's study shows the potential of depositional contexts within graves, settlements, and topographic features for exploring these practices.

For some, such studies do not go far enough, retaining too much of a sociological or person-centered perspective. The clearest exposition is to be found in studies of science and technology that utilize actor network theory (Latour 1999; Law and Hassard 1999), delineating the relational networks that constitute creational processes. The centrality of any particular kind of agency, whether human or material, is subjugated; instead, processes unfold through the work of a multitude or "collective" of "actants." Given the subject's material focus, Olsen (2003) suggests that archaeology has been surprisingly slow to recognize the role of material agency and adopt a similar position in which social and humanist discourses are no longer overprivileged at the expense of things. He calls for a "symmetrical archaeology" in which we approach things as "beings in the world alongside other beings, such as humans, plants and animals" (Olsen 2003:88), while recognizing that things are different from living beings in a relational rather than oppositional sense.

There is the question of how far the distinction between subjects and objects might be collapsed, and where the limits of nonhuman agency might lie (Jones and Cloke 2002:Chapter 3). For Gell things remain as "secondary agents" lacking any intentionality of their own and therefore only capable of operating with human associates (Gell 1998:17). For Gosden objects are "active in the manner of objects not in the manner of people" (Gosden 2001:164). They can elicit particular sensory responses or "effects" that channel social action, sometimes in ways unanticipated, but that does not involve any intentionality on the part of the thing itself. So while people and object worlds are mutually constituted, and agency may be seen as variously distributed, there may be problems with objects being considered de facto as agents, "having lives of their own outside of human constitution" (Meskell 2004:4).

When considering the limits of material agencies, Lynn Meskell is surely correct in stressing that "context is everything" (Meskell 2004:6). Different kinds or degrees of agency may be seen to operate in varied circumstances, some being of more immediate significance than others. At a very basic level, the physical presence of a wall will force people to move around rather than attempt to walk through it; likewise, the presence of a dangerous animal will guide people to take evasive action. Both are instances of nonhuman agency, but of an anecdotal kind. Of more interest are those situations where the emotive or sensory qualities of objects have the capacity to elicit responses that significantly shape or alter human projects in unanticipated ways. These are objects that, like Trobriand canoe-prows, enchant in a spell-like fashion (Gell 1992) or "raise hopes, generate fears, evoke losses, and delight" (Spyer 1998:5). Emotive power is strongest in those things that hold such an "excess" of association as to become threatening or destabilizing. Such is the case of the personal effects of a deceased friend, partner, or relative, which stand as an extension of the dead person and so serve to "presence" the deceased (Hallam and Hockey 2001). However, it is with those objects that are regarded as possessing purposive agency, that are seen to "have life" or be the material form of spirits or deities, that any ontological distinction between subjects and objects dissolves completely. In the world of the fetish and animate object, people may become powerless or secondary agents to the things themselves (Pels 1998).

What implications does such a formulation of materiality have for an archaeology of depositional practices? First, it highlights a need to think of intentional deposits as more than material statements or simple representations. This is not to deny that deposits could be conceived as symbols, material metaphors, or metonyms, situating or presencing meanings within particular contexts. But it does stress that we should remain aware of how embroiled and complex human-object relationships are and how these define the ontological status of objects rather than any essential qualities.

This in turn affects the way that things in their broadest sense (artifacts, animal and human bones, and "natural" materials) can be treated in deposition. By virtue of their participation in complex networks of production, exchange, and use, things might carry with them something of the identity or substance of people, places, and supernatural entities, perhaps becoming hybrid amalgamations of these in the process (Pollard 2004a). This conferred them with an agency—at very least a legacy of associations—that had to be negotiated upon deposition. It might demand care and respect, or a more aggressive removal from circulation in the case of those things regarded as dangerous or malign (consider, for example, the *malanggan* sculptures of New Ireland [Küchler 1992]). Human and artifact lives can be both analogous and coterminous, and the lives of things can end with the lives of people and so require forms of funerary treatment that mirror those afforded people or that are specific to things. By thinking of things as subjects, if of a particular kind, we can begin to comprehend why they were treated in such complex and apparently alien ways at the point of deposition and understand their effective power on those taking part in these activities.

The act of deposition was a performance that drew together different combinations of people and things, often within symbolically charged arenas at critical moments in time (important seasonal festivals, points in the construction and decommissioning of monuments, and so forth). As with funerary rites, it provided a context in which the status and roles of its human and material participants could be highlighted and brought to the fore, where contemplation of their character was very much in evidence. In certain circumstances deposition might be considered an act of display, a process of "abstracting objects from the overall flow of life, so they can be singled out for attention, due to their visual and other aesthetic qualities, or their connections to particular people and events" (Gosden 2004:36). Gosden suggests this abstraction involves separation, "cutting some of the links things have with each other and with people" (Gosden 2004:36), though I would argue that in the context of deposition it also involves creating other links with objects buried alongside and with the places and participants in these projects (compare Holtorf 2004).

The challenge is now to put some of these threads together: to look at how the imbricated relationships of people and things were played out through deposition; how the agency of things was negotiated; as well as issues of display, participation, and memory. This is attempted through a case study of depositional activity at one early Neolithic site in southern England, the Etton enclosure (Figure 3.4).

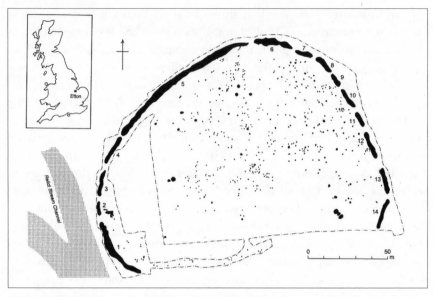

FIGURE 3.4

Site plan of the Etton enclosure, Cambridgeshire. After Pryor (1998).

THE ETTON ENCLOSURE

Ditched enclosures comprise some of the earliest monumental architecture in Britain and northwestern Europe (Oswald et al. 2001). They acted as locales where semimobile populations might periodically aggregate and engage in a range of practices including exchange, feasting, mortuary and ancestor rites, and deposition (Edmonds 1999). Deliberate deposits of material are ubiquitous within enclosure ditches, so much so that we must assume the ditches were created with the dual role of providing a boundary of sorts and acting as receptacles into which material would be buried. Indeed, it is likely that formal deposits enhanced the potency and symbolic efficiency of these earthworks as boundaries. Such is the scale of deposition that it is from these sites that some of the richest assemblages of early Neolithic faunal and artifactual material, and human remains, derive.

The enclosure at Etton was constructed on a gravel floodplain "island" within the Welland Valley, Cambridgeshire (Pryor 1998). It is small and structurally simple by comparison with other monuments of its kind. Constructed in the second quarter of the fourth millennium BCE, it continued to provide a focus for activity into the later Neolithic. Periodic flooding meant it was not occupied year-round, perhaps not even on a regular seasonal basis. The site's valley-bottom location and subsequent covering by alluvium led to high levels of preservation, including the rare survival of organic material within the ditches. This, along with the scale of excavation and the high standards of recording, make it an ideal site with which to study early Neolithic depositional activity. Quantities of animal bone, pottery, worked wood, flint, and other material were found within the ditch segments, almost all of it deliberately deposited. Scattered within the interior were numerous small pits filled with burned material, pottery, and bone, several capped by "special" deposits such as a complete stone axe and quern (grinding) stones. However, it is the deposits within the ditch that I wish to focus on. Every excavated ditch section produced deliberately placed deposits, frequently at the butt-ends fronting causeways, though also as part of linear spreads. Multiple episodes of deposition are evident, with ditch segments frequently recut to receive them. Deposition was therefore an ongoing project, perhaps aimed at reanimating the monument on a periodic basis.

At a macro level there are significant differences in the way that the western and eastern halves of the enclosure were used (Pryor 1998:369–371). The excavator, Francis Pryor, notes that the evidence for ditch recutting was more localized in the western half, where the ditch segments displayed greater heterogeneity in length and treatment. Organic remains (principally wood) were more extensive here, and although this part of the enclosure was more susceptible to flooding, differential preservation alone cannot account for this. It was also in this part of the monument that debris occurred from in situ activities such as wood, bark, and antler working. Ditch segments in the eastern half showed greater uniformity in length and patterns of recutting. Little organic material was present, but more pottery and flint. Highly contrived and arranged deposits—what Pryor refers to as material "statements"—were a notable feature of this part of the monument, particularly along the northern arc of the ditch circuit (Pryor 1998:68).

Similar site-scale patterning in activities and depositional patterns has been noted at other causewayed enclosures, such as Windmill Hill (Whittle et al. 1999), Hambledon Hill (Healy 2004), and Briar Hill (Bamford 1985). It is tempting to see this as resulting from the playing-out of structural schemes, for example, a distinction between socialized and unsocialized domains (for example, Whittle and Pollard 1998), but this ignores the way that gross patterning developed through cumulative depositional actions, many of which were highly varied in their format. Focusing on the "big patterns" may miss how inventive and loosely prescribed depositions were; the microdetail is quite telling. At Etton single or groups of ditch segments were treated in quite distinct ways. This is seen with extensive recutting and the presence of unusual deposits in Segments 1 and 2, otherwise rare on the western part of the site (Pryor 1998:66). Whether this reflects family or kin group "ownership" of single segments, and therefore localized interpretation of "correct practice," is open for discussion, but even within single ditch segments there can be much variation in depositional detail.

Rather than be locked into an analysis of patterning, it may be more constructive to consider the qualities and connections of the material deposited and the treatment afforded it. That deposits were found on the bases of ditch segments, particularly on the west, implies that deposition was integral to the creation of the enclosure and that materials such as pottery, wood, and bone were gathered together for this. In consequence, the primary deposits may be thought of as architectural materials like earth and timber (McFadyen 2003). The material was likely gathered from a range of sources, both near and afar, and carried to the site by the communities involved in creating the earthwork. It would have brought with it a network of connections, a geography of social relations that spilled across the landscape.

Animals and Ancestors

Among the primary deposits were numerous partial animal skeletons, mostly of sheep and pigs, and frequently neonatal or juvenile (Armour-Chelu in Pryor 1998:275–276; Figure 3.5). The presence of these animals provides a way to think about material connections and the agency of deposits. First, the herds from which these animals were drawn represent accumulations in the way defined by John Chapman. They were built up through complex exchanges that were valued for the social connections they facilitated and the histories attached to individual animals and their progenitors. The composition of these herds would have mapped kinship links with the animals themselves (Ray and Thomas 2003). Burying these animals provided a mechanism for building kinship connections into the very fabric of the monument, while their placement at ditch butt-ends perhaps served to articulate and draw together different elements of the monument. Likely regarded as sentient beings whose ontological status was at least relational to people if not occasionally inseparable (Jones and Richards 2003), these animals carried with them identities and agencies of various kinds. Killing, partially dismembering, and then depositing animals that were young, and in some instances newly born, could have been a strategy to draw in something of their raw, generative energy, enhancing the potency of the enclosure.

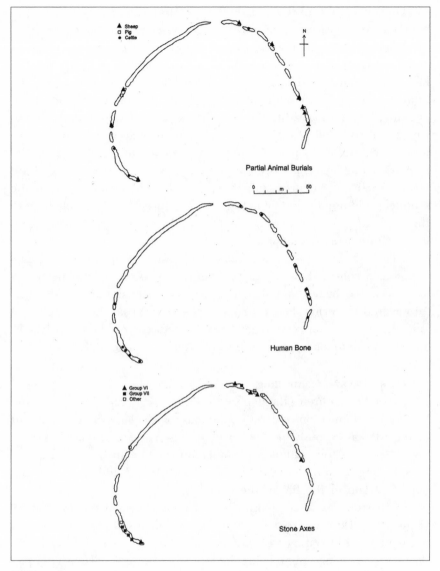

FIGURE 3.5

Animal burials, human bone, and stone axe deposits at Etton. Based on information in Pryor (1998).

The inclusion of human remains within the ditch deposits was perhaps intended to achieve much the same thing. Regarded as a potent resource, human bone was widely circulated during the Neolithic and deposited in a variety of contexts (Thomas 1999a:68, 75). Its inclusion in sites like Etton can be seen as a way of referencing the ancestral dead or, in a more active manner, even locating ancestral spirits themselves, the bones acting as "containers" in which an ancestral essence was deemed to reside. Cranial and postcranial bones were brought in and deposited at various times during the early life of the enclosure. In contrast to animal remains, the human bone displayed signs of breakage, weathering, and even animal gnawing, telling of both its age and history prior to deposition (Amour-Chelu in Pryor 1998:271–272). This "community of ancestors" conceivably was drawn from many places, some quite distant. Once within the enclosure, "demands" may have been placed on the bone to perform important tasks. An active role in protecting the enclosure might be inferred from the sentinel positioning of a skull in Segment 10, upright and looking out into the landscape, and of another in the south end of Segment 6, again upright and facing a causeway.

Following the line that the distinction between people and things was occasionally collapsed, or at least that things could be thought of metaphorically as kinds of beings equivalent to humans and animals, can provide a useful way into exploring the treatment offered to deposits. Like people and animals, at Etton things were gathered/herded, controlled, even "killed," and combined to make new relationships. A few examples will suffice.

Gathering and Controlling

A notable feature of the deposits at Etton and other enclosures is the localized accumulation of certain materials, particularly those that might be regarded as variously "potent," symbolically charged, or special in some way. There are, for example, accumulations of human bone, not necessarily belonging to the same individual, in Segments 1 and 13. Most being deposited late in the life of the enclosure, nearly all the fragments of imported stone axe were placed in two areas: Segments 1 and 6 to 8 (Figure 3.5). Deriving from a number of implements, the fragments from Segment 1 are linked by a common source, Group VII rock from North Wales, the single exception being the butt of a Cumbrian Group VI implement. An unusual symmetry is found with the axe fragments from Segments 6 to 8 on the opposite side of the enclosure, of Group VI rock with the exception of the butt of a Group VII axe. Their stratigraphic position within the ditch fills shows that they were deposited over a period of time. It is likely that the implements traveled along different exchange routes and with them acquired varied histories and biographies. However, at the point of deposition their commonality through shared points of origin was being reassembled, while the inclusion of different kinds of axe in different areas of the ditch may have been an attempt to map out this perceived geography of origin.

Other concentrations of artifacts might be regarded as "caches" (that is, single-event, multiple depositions), though it is unlikely that they were intended to be retrieved. Examples include four unusual notched and scored cattle bones from Segment 9, three fired clay objects from Segment 7, and a pile of fruit stones from the north end of Segment 2. Both the worked cattle bones and fired clay objects have the appearance of "ritual paraphernalia," one of the scored ribs being described as a "tally stick" (Armour-Chelu in Pryor 1998:288), while the clay objects include a phallus-shaped object and ball, linking them to similar carved chalk fertility symbols found on other Neolithic sites (for example, Smith 1965:130–134). These are just the kind of objects that might be regarded as potent, possessing a disruptive "excess" of association (see Hallam and Hockey 2001:117) or "contaminated" by virtue of their employment in rites or ceremonies. All therefore acquired qualities that ascribed them an agency, a power, and required them to be disposed of in a careful manner.

In other ways things were gathered together and controlled. Cattle ribs were bundled and placed at the butt-end of Segment 1. Sherds were found nested together in Segment 6, while in the same area of the ditch, sherds from a different vessel were covered by a slab of stone. Other objects were covered and contained in different ways. A complete quern stone was found inverted at the bottom of a pit cut into Segment 1; leaves and twigs were packed over and around it. All these acts involved people entering the ditch and placing objects in the ground with care and we might assume a certain degree of respect or reverence. These are actions reminiscent of the placing and arrangement of human bodies within graves, though here it is a striking attention afforded to things rather than people.

Killing Things

Control over things occasionally extended to "killing" them through intentional breakage. Querns provide a case in point, and it is striking that so many of those from Etton display evidence of deliberate breakage (Pryor 1998:259), a practice witnessed at other earlier Neolithic sites (Saville 1990:176–178; Bamford 1985:93–94). Given the rarity of complete examples, similar treatment may have been afforded to flint and stone axes (Edmonds in Pryor 1998:268). Again there is precedent. Axes from beneath the contemporary long barrow at Wayland's Smithy, Oxfordshire, displayed fracture patterns consistent with deliberate smashing (Whittle 1991:85), while the majority of flint axes from the enclosure of Carn Brea, Cornwall, showed evidence of burning (Saville in Mercer 1981:138). The practice of breaking and burning axes is widespread in early Neolithic contexts, being well attested in fourth millennium BCE southern Scandinavia (Larsson 2000).

Both Edmonds and Larsson posit a connection between the intentional breakage/"killing" of axes and funerary rituals or other important rites of passage (Edmonds in Pryor 1998:263). This connection may say something about the inalienable character of both axes and querns, and a sense of equivalence between the lives of these objects and those of people. Potentially, both classes of artifact have particular gender associations—axes with men, querns with women—yet as things they may have been conceptualized in very similar ways. Both are objects whose production and use involved comparable technologies of extraction and shaping. Their final form was produced through the application of repeated motor-movements of a similar kind—a process of grinding involving a second stone. Their use also led to eventual diminishment and degradation (an aging). It is not difficult to imagine axes and querns as things thought to have "lives." Because they were the focus of so much labor during their existence, energy being repeatedly transferred from bodies into these tools, they became true inalienable objects, inseparable from their users. It is not inconceivable that upon the death of their human partners it was considered appropriate for these things to undergo the same process of breakage/disarticulation and dispersal as human bodies.

Making New Relationships

The most striking deposits at Etton are highly structured assemblages of different materials arranged along the ditch length. Of an undeniably unusual character, these are perhaps the most difficult of all deposits to interpret. Most combine pottery, stone, and human and animal bone, and are largely limited to the eastern arc of the enclosure. Their format suggests that direct material connections were being made between substances of various kinds through the relative proximity of different objects within deposits. Those within Segments 6 and 7 illustrate this most clearly (Figure 3.6). In the southern end of Segment 6 was a human skull, upright and facing the causeway, against which was placed a red deer antler "baton" and animal bone. Occupying a similar position in Segment 7 was a linear spread comprising a complete upright bowl, bone, an antler comb, then, adjacent, an inverted bowl and inverted, severed fox head.

Human bone was linked to red deer antler and animal bone, pottery to bone and antler. Perhaps these can be read as statements: the inverted

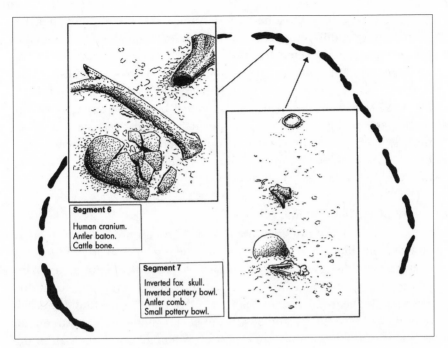

Segment 6
Human cranium.
Antler baton.
Cattle bone.

Segment 7
Inverted fox skull.
Inverted pottery bowl.
Antler comb.
Small pottery bowl.

FIGURE 3.6

Arranged deposits in Segments 6 and 7, Etton. After Pryor (1998).

bowl a skull substitute and so linked to ancestral domains, the fox skull a symbol of the "wild," and the bones of domesticated animals as symbols of subsistence success—a presentation of key concerns in Neolithic social life. Tempting though this is, it again fails to explain the treatment afforded to things and ignores their ontological status. Some materials were placed upright, others (the bowl and fox skull) inverted. Was inversion a process of negation, or was it intended to keep something in, perhaps dangerous essences or supernatural agencies? Bones of fox are uncommon on Neolithic sites, and this may reflect their identification with spiritual agencies of various kinds, and consequent prohibitions on their encounter and hunting (Pollard 2004b). As omnivorous animals, foxes would have had contact with human corpses set out for exposure, perhaps being responsible for some of the gnawing found on human bones. Ingesting human flesh and bone, and so taking on something of the essence of people, probably made them powerful beings in the minds of Neolithic communities. Here deposition of the fox head alongside the bowl and other materials can again be seen as an attempt to control the potency and agency of other, nonhuman, beings.

Other deposits within the eastern circuit of the enclosure took the form of more undifferentiated linear spreads of material, though nonetheless assemblages collected together and deliberately placed within the ditches (Pryor 1998:34–51). The combination of various materials in these deposits served to create new substances and new material relations. Mixing sherds from different vessels, animal bone, and stone tools condensed the multiple identities of the makers and consumers of these objects, their connections and energies. Here deposition facilitated a broader sense of community and material integrity for people who spent much of their time living in dispersed small groups.

Mimicry, Memory, and Citation

Connection and integration also work through processes of mimicry and citation (Jones 2001). Although each ditch segment had its individual character and history of activity, deposits in one segment were occasionally constructed to reference those in others, providing an integrity to an otherwise segmented monument. "Strings" of references are found in small depositional acts: the placing of a round pecked stone in the north end of Segment 9, another round stone (a fossil echinoid?) on a flat slab in the northern end of Segment 8, and a pot placed on a stone at the north end of Segment 7. Sometimes these deposits were linked by analogy of material, on other occasions by functional connections. Thus, a large decorated Mildenhall bowl placed on a birch bark mat at the south end of Segment 1 can be linked to the deposit of a length of twine placed on a similar large sheet of birch bark at the southern end of Segment 2. The bowl had perforated lugs, rare otherwise within the ceramic assemblage from the site, and was made to be suspended, perhaps by the string incorporated in the "partner" deposit.

Depositional citation also worked across time as a form of memory work. Here we are reminded of the importance of material and bodily practices in preserving social memory (Connerton 1989; Kwint 1999). Like exchanges of inalienable goods, depositions forced an evocation of memory, a recalling of the histories and connections of the things deployed and of the places where these performances happened. If we dispel the notion of coincidence, there are some notable compositional references between a number of the primary, mid–fourth millennium BCE deposits at Etton and those enacted during the later stages of the enclosure's life. During the early use of the enclosure, the skulls of two domesticated cattle were placed together in Segment 10, a deposit that is without parallel during this phase. Much later, two aurochs (wild cattle) skulls were deposited in a pit cut into the fills of nearby Segment 12, an act that appears to recall the much earlier event. There is also a striking parallel between the location of the later Neolithic deposition of Group VII axe fragments in the same section of Segment 1 as a primary deposit of a wooden axe handle. Such citations may imply that some early depositions were such critical events, or so central to the enclosure's character, that memory of them was maintained over several centuries and reanimated through the performance of equivalent acts.

CONCLUSION

During the earlier Neolithic of southern Britain, deposition was not a practice simply intended to situate message and meaning—a form of symbolic action. It was a mechanism for exploring the materiality of the world and negotiating the complex and deeply embedded nature of relationships between people, animals, and things. I have suggested that we have to envisage a Neolithic world that people saw as being invested with varying forms of agency, potency, and life forces. Deposition served to control, channel, and pay respect to these various agencies. Through the inventiveness of its practice—a kind of material "play" seen so clearly at sites like Etton—deposition also provided a means of producing knowledge that linked people, places, and nonhuman agents. As such, enclosures might be regarded as "labs" (Turnbull 2000) where the messiness and complexity of the material world was worked through and negotiated. Etton and other monuments like it were spaces that facilitated the gathering of substances as well as the gathering of people. They were spaces for creating and negotiating material relations as well as social relations. Within the "new world" of the early Neolithic, people confronted a material complexity that had to be worked out. Deposition was a practice that enabled this to happen.

4

Founders' Cults and the Archaeology of *Wa-kan-da*

Timothy R. Pauketat

Among these [Siouan] tribes the creation and control of the world and the things thereof are ascribed to "wa-kan-da."...Thus, among many of the tribes the sun is wa-kan-da—not *the* wa-kan-da or *a* wa-kan-da, but simply wa-kan-da; and among the same tribes the moon is wa-kan-da, and so is thunder, lightning, the stars, the winds, the cedar,...the ground or earth, the mythic underworld, [and] the ideal upper-world.

—*W. J. McGee (1897:182)*

It is no insignificant coincidence that the beliefs of eastern Plains Siouan-speaking people pertaining to *wa-kan-da* are consonant with a host of practice-based or phenomenological theories of cultural change. From either point of view, specific people cannot and do not cause change by themselves and, therefore, explanations of history are not to be found in the inferences of their "strategies" or intentions (contra Blanton et al. 1996, among others). In fact, we might conclude that strategies or intentions do not exist in the human mind alone, and agency does not reside solely within individuals (see DeMarrais et al. 2004; Dobres 2000; Meskell 1999).

Agency and intentions are, instead, historically contingent, practiced, engaged, or performed such that they are dispersed across "social fields" or "cultural landscapes" and "distributed" among human bodies, other organisms, objects, substances, spaces, and spirits (see Ashmore 2004; Bourdieu 1977; Gosden 2001; Joyce 2005; Meskell 2005).[1] Agents include seemingly inert things and qualities in addition to human and nonhuman actors (Gell 1998; Latour 1999; Strathern 1988). And all of them may be entangled in the material and spatial dimensions of cultural practices and human experiences.

Now by positioning myself thus, I am not suggesting that cultural change is necessarily gradual or that it is subordinate to the entropy of social fields and cultural landscapes. Rather I am seeking to rethink how we understand major historical shifts and transformations by relocating the "causal powers" of change (in the sense of Harré and Madden 1975). Depending on how agency is divided and distributed, these practices and experiences have the potential to effect pervasive, radical changes to entire cultural landscapes or fields of agentic relationships.

It is a truism that change is a continuous feature of such relational fields. But that change may vary in kind, scale, and degree contingent on the distribution of agentic forces or causal powers. A radical historical change, as I see it, involves a significant redistribution of causal powers within the larger relational fields of human experience, producing an observable nonconformity in human history. Redistributions of this sort stem from rearranging, reframing, or inverting the referents that motivated agency and informed experience. But such referents are, as with agency in general, variously (and "fractally") attributed to bodies, objects, substances, spaces, and spirits (see Barrett 1999; Strathern 1988; Wagner 1991). They include the mysterious life force of Siouan-speaking peoples of the eastern Plains called wa-kan-da, *wa-kon-da*, or simply *wakan* (Bailey 1995; Fletcher and La Flesche 1992; McGee 1897; Powers 1977).

One sort of radical change, where frames of cultural reference (if not also distinct cosmological, institutional, or bodily temporalities) were collapsed and inverted to promote a central person or ruler as a founding ancestor or guardian spirit, may be termed a "founder's cult" (Kammerer and Tannenbaum 2003:4). Just such a cult, I have argued, explains the so-called Mississippian historical disjuncture in the American midcontinent a millennium ago (Pauketat 2004). On the heels of the construction of an American Indian city, Cahokia (at ca. 1050 CE), a founders' cult spawned a series of historically interdigitated movements spread across the Midwest and South. In the Cahokia locality, the radicality of the disjuncture may be observed as population displacements, abrupt shifts in labor and resource allocations, and human sacrifices.

Of course, attributing such radical change to a founder's cult is a shorthand explanation and insufficient to explain the specific causes of the disjuncture. How did founders' cults arise such that entire fields of human experience were altered? The answer, it now seems apparent to me, is to be located in ancient archaeological and depositional practices with the aid of a series of concepts: materiality, citationality, and the enchainment of cultural practices (Butler 1993; Chapman 2000a; Gell 1998; Joyce 2000a;

Meskell 2004, 2005; Strathern 1988). By materiality, I mean the tangible dimensions of cultural practices (Pauketat 2003a). By citation, I mean the way in which practices referenced previous ones (Butler 1993). And by enchainment, I mean the results of such citationality, in which one agentic force becomes associated with that of another (Chapman 2000a:5; Strathern 1988:161).

Using these concepts and based on a careful parsing of depositional practices, I argue that the causes of the Mississippian disjuncture lie in the practices whereby the powers of wa-kan-da—particularly those of the earth and sky—became entangled with human affairs. My attempted untangling examines the structured deposition of earth and sky (or some manifestation thereof) and the memory work of indigenous excavators evident in two historically connected regions in the Midwest: southern Wisconsin and greater Cahokia. After briefly noting some twentieth-century ethnographic background, I will highlight some deposits and excavations, allowing me to argue that the depositional and excavation genealogies in both regions, in different ways, had an aesthetic basis, and that citations of earth and sky were central to how cultural practices were enchained and radically reframed as part of Mississippian founders' cults. The process altered history to such an extent that traces are evident in early twentieth-century ethnographies and in certain contemporary oral traditions of the Mississippian descendants who later migrated into the eastern Plains (Figure 4.1).

BACKGROUND

Various indigenous Plains-Prairie creation stories from the recent Siouan and Caddoan past feature gendered supernatural forces and super-human characters (Dorsey 1997; Hall 1997; McCleary 1997; Radin 1948; Townsend 2004). Among other things, fire, ashes, and light-colored earth seem to have presenced the sun or, more commonly, the sun-carrier or "fire-bringer"—a Thunderer god-man also known as the Morning Star. Dark earth, corn, water, and perhaps refuse signified earth the creator, creation, and the Evening Star or her god-woman cognate most often known as Corn Mother. In some accounts, the Morning Star was said to have been responsible for carrying the sun into this world, an act of daily regeneration. In these or others, the Evening Star or Corn Mother gave the world corn and mothered at least one of two twin heirs apparent, the latter at one point reincarnating the father after retrieving his head or bones from otherworldly "giants" or from the netherworld (for example, Radin 1948).

Fire, earth, water, and certain feathers, tobacco, and paint (made from earthen minerals) were believed to possess agency. They were "spirits" or,

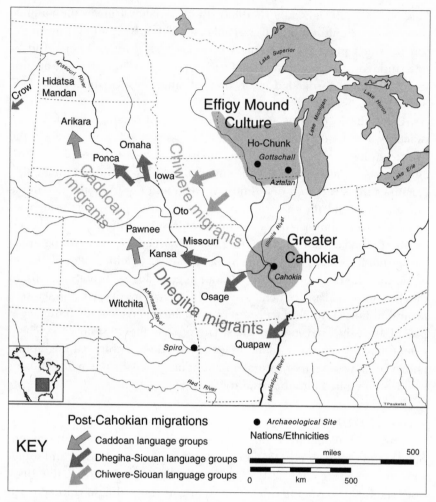

FIGURE 4.1

Select Mississippian archaeological sites and complexes and major post-Cahokian migrations.

in Jason Jackson's (2003) terms, "witnesses" because they could inform the deities what people on earth had been doing (see Bailey 1995; Dorsey 1997; Fletcher and La Flesche 1992; Jackson 2003; Radin 1990; Salzer and Rajnovich 2000; Swanton 1942, 1985, 2001). Men and women made offerings both to earth and fire, or the Evening and Morning Stars, including crops, buckskins, tobacco, and, sometimes, human beings (for example, Weltfish 1977).

Earthen monuments typically commemorated both earth and sky

because, by digging into and piling up earth, people physically embodied notions of life and death and opened a portal between upper and lower worlds (Knight 1989). Stories related the use or manufacture of earth, in one case including crushed human bone, to creation and the masculine hero twins (Buikstra et al. 1998; Hall 1997:18–23). Atop some earthen pyramids sat ancestral temples, with their sacred fires and human bones. And the ashes from those temple fires—which were both fire and earth—were kept with great care by chiefs or priests and used later to bury and build (Swanton 2001).

Of course, such generic cultural practices, as they involved or evoked earth and sky in native North America, were the end products of the very history I seek to explain. And so while I would not suggest that they derive from an unchanging paneastern indigenous belief system,[2] I do suspect that there were aesthetic qualities to earth and fire variously enchained in those depositional practices that were in turn foregrounded as part of the Mississippian disjuncture. These were qualities involving or concerned with physical sensations or emotions rather than pure idealized or cognized beliefs (Gell 1998; Gosden 2001).

Such aesthetic sensibilities were probably closely wedded to the daily practices of Midwestern peoples who routinely dug into the earth to construct semisubterranean houses and storage pits, and who refilled such open receptacles with discarded detritus and dirt in ways that were probably not always or simply expedient (following Pollard 2001, and this volume).[3] Certainly, among indigenous descendants, the cleaning of domestic spaces included the sweeping away of accumulated dirt *and* "evil spirits," ; for instance (Lopinot 1991:51–53; Moerman 1986:241–249). Even today ceremonial grounds are swept outwardly toward the perimeter where they are left as low ring mounds that delineate sacred from profane (see also Waselkov and Braund 1995).

ANTHROSEDS AND EFFIGY MOUNDS

A more extreme example of how earth and fire were used to delineate sacred and profane comes from southern Wisconsin. Hidden at the bottom of a steep ravine in a minor secondary stream valley in southwestern Wisconsin, the Gottschall Rockshelter appears to have been an exclusive ritual shrine wherein, during the pre-Mississippian Woodland period, religious practitioners conducted "ancestor cult" rites (Salzer and Rajnovich 2000). Most significantly, the rites at Gottschall included the painting of supernatural and legendary characters on its rock wall interiors in conjunction with the deposition of artificial soils on its floor.

The artificial soils—dubbed "anthroseds" by Gottschall researchers—were manufactured off-site from the ashes of coniferous wood, sweetgrass, maize grass, crushed bone, powdered limestone, and mussel shells (Gartner 2000). The special dirt was then carried down into the ravine's hidden rockshelter, where it was used to build a bird-effigy mound and repeatedly line and reline the floor of the rockshelter. Occasionally, the specially prepared floor was burned. The artificial earthen layers, burned or not, may have ritually purified the rockshelter interior, sealing off the subsequent performances from earthly pollutants and, perhaps, mediating between the supernatural forces of the sky-world outside from those of the earth or underworld inside the natural rockshelter (Salzer and Rajnovich 2000).

Such practices appear to have started as early as 600 BCE, but were terminated after 1050 CE. Interestingly, the period of anthrosed depositions in the rockshelter correlates with the time when local people also built the well-known effigy mounds of southern Wisconsin, eastern Iowa, and southeastern Minnesota (Birmingham and Eisenberg 2000; Birmingham and Rosebrough 2003). Indeed, an effigy mound group is located quite near the Gottschall site (Salzer and Rajnovich 2000:3). At this mound site and others like it, effigy mounds were built or subsequently used in conjunction with the mortuary rites of otherwise dispersed, semisedentary people. In them archaeologists have found everything from single burials to the disarticulated remains of scores of people (Birmingham and Eisenberg 2000:127).

These mounds were not restricted hidden deposits but communal constructions in prominent locations that depicted thunderbirds, bears, and water spirits (or underworld panthers), anticipating it seems the later Siouan-speaking Ho-Chunk kin groupings "headed by the thunderbird, bear, and water spirit" clans (Birmingham and Eisenberg 2000:118). Apparently, the groups of effigy mounds were built one at a time over a period of years.

> The mounds are rarely layered or stratified. In many cases, there does not appear to have been any special preparation of the ground surface before the mounds were built. Occasionally, however, an intaglio, or "reverse cameo," in the form of the effigy to be constructed was first dug several feet into the ground…[and] left open for a long time.…This sacred area was eventually filled in, sometimes with offerings of specially colored soils, ash, and charcoal. (Birmingham and Eisenberg 2000:125)

Significantly, of 11 excavated intaglios from three specific mound groups, "all were lower-world forms: nine long-tailed water spirits and two bears" (Birmingham and Eisenberg 2000:125–126). Digging into the earth, in this case, referenced generic supernatural forces.

TRANSREGIONAL REDISTRIBUTIONS

Five hundred kilometers to the south, the contemporaneous situation in the greater Cahokia region looks, by comparison, quite different. Prior to the Mississippian period (up to 1050 CE), there were few mounds or other structured deposits. Indeed, by as late as the tenth century near Cahokia, when certain social changes were becoming evident in the region, there was still only minimal earthen construction or commemoration (that is, at least one sand-lined house basin at pre-Mississippian Cahokia and at most a few low platform mounds [see Kelly 1990]). Certain objects, smoking pipes or community gaming stones, were left behind in village court-yards—buried near courtyard posts—but there were no carefully sand-lined burial pits, plastered temple floors, unusual sweepings, layered feasting pits, or alternating fills in earthen mounds that we know of. These all postdate 1050 CE—most immediately so (Pauketat 2004).

Back in Wisconsin, and sometime around that date, the anomalous Red Horn panel—thought to tell the story of a superhuman hero—was painted onto a specially sanded portion of the Gottschall Rockshelter. Nearby, a carved and painted sandstone head (and probably a long-since decayed organic body), also thought to depict the superhuman character Red Horn (the personification of the Morning Star), was buried beneath the earthen floor. And although archaeologists have long assumed that pre-vious Late Woodland–period effigy mounds or a few iconographic clues to this superhuman character exist in southern Wisconsin, there is as much reason to argue that the Gottschall inscriptions mark a transregional redis-tribution of causal powers and a reframing of citational referents.

The reasons include Salzer and Rajnovich's (2000) observation that the realistic artistic style of the Red Horn panel is unprecedented in the region. They also include the widely known "intrusion" of southern Miss-issippian (read, Cahokian) people into Wisconsin at well-known locations such as Aztalan, where novel earthen pyramids, architectural styles, and objects superimpose an earlier landscape of effigy mounds (Goldstein and Richards 1991). Finally, and possibly most significantly, effigy mound con-struction appears to have been terminated at or shortly after 1050 CE in most places (Birmingham and Eisenberg 2000; Stoltman and Christiansen 2000; Theler and Boszhardt 2000). From that point onward, descendants

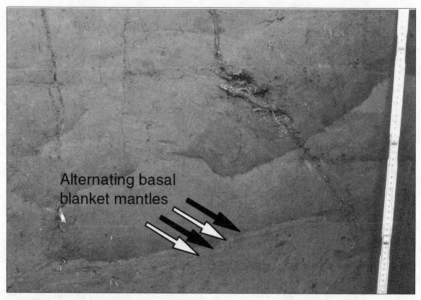

FIGURE 4.2

Profile of alternating basal blanket mantles (overlaid by sod blocks) of the Emerald Mound (11-S-2), Saint Clair County, Illinois.

FIGURE 4.3

Profile of intermediate blanket mantles in the Emerald Mound (11-S-2), Saint Clair County, Illinois.

of the effigy mound builders would have inhabited a landscape of mute monuments and spirits that, through Cahokian or Mississippian places (monuments, architecture, and artwork), cited southern referents.

To the south, the new city of Cahokia was at that time under construction, and the entire greater Cahokia region—including the agricultural hinterland—appears one massive structured deposit. For instance, the many stratified construction fills of greater Cahokia's 200 new pyramids consist of alternating layers of light and dark fills. In some cases, black, clayey "blanket mantles" capped lighter and sandy or silty construction stages, which in turn covered dismantled, oversized pole-and-thatch buildings on earlier stages. Elaborate pole-and-thatch houses and temples were then rebuilt atop the new mantles. Sacred fires therein were lined, relined, and capped with red or black plaster; temple floors were similarly plastered or lined with whitish-yellow and/or dark brown silts and clays (Pauketat 1993, 2000, 2004; Pauketat and Rees 1996). In some cases, as at the Emerald site, a series of sheer fill mantles, some no more than a few millimeters in thickness, may have been laid down in single events. For instance, the basal layers of Emerald Mound feature a sheer centimeter of fill within which are four distinct bands of light- and dark-colored silts in alternation (Figure 4.2). One of the mound's intermediate stages witnessed a similar series of more than a dozen alternating light and dark blanket mantles within a 12-cm-thick deposit (Figure 4.3).

All fills in these and other earthen monuments were virtually free of refuse, even incidental bits of debris. The builders had carefully selected, and possibly processed, the fills in order to obtain the pure qualities. The same is true of the sandy silts used to level Cahokia's 19-ha central plaza at ca. 1050 CE. The paucity of miniscule sherds in those fills suggests that, while borrowed from former residential areas, the plaza sediment was processed by hand, and the larger inclusions were removed (Dalan 1997; Holley et al. 1993; Pauketat et al. 2005). Additional evidence of the processing of fills—associated with red paints or pigments and human remains—derives from features associated with special temples and large, upright marker posts, both often associated in turn with pyramid and plaza surfaces (Pauketat et al. 2005; Pauketat and Rees 1996). In some cases bits of red pigment appear to have been sprinkled into otherwise ordinary construction back dirt.

Such a construction-fill practice recalls the buried remains of Cahokia's large central festivals, where the food wastes of large feasts were mixed with small cedar branchlets (possibly pieces of old brooms) and high densities of other sumptuary items, including tobacco, crystals, shell

FIGURE 4.4

*Profile of an extramural pit adjacent to a temple (Feature 44) at the Pfeffer site (11-S-204),
Saint Clair County, Illinois.*

beads, paint residues, painted pots, special projectile points, cypress wood
chips, craft-production debris, pieces of human skeletons, and the wood
and thatch debris from pole-and-thatch temples and marker posts
(Pauketat and Emerson 1991; Pauketat et al. 2002). Given the alternating
(albeit more irregular) bands of burned white ash and dark, enriched sediments and the basket-loaded construction fills that sealed the pit, the excavator suspected that the entire stratified sequence was itself a structured
deposit (C. Bareis, personal communication 1992). Afterward, at least two
oversized buildings and then a platform mound were built over the site.

There are other "public" or "religious" buildings at rural locations in
the surrounding farmlands that, I suspect, were ancestral temples where
bones of *select* ancestors were kept (Alt 2006; Emerson 1997). Deposits associated with these buildings were structured as alternating bands of burned
and sterile earth and include the same array of sumptuary items, tobacco,
and red cedar along with pits full of axe heads and elaborate carved red-
stone images of deities from Cahokia, including Corn Mother and owl (Alt
2006; Emerson 1997; Pauketat and Alt 2004). These seem associated with
rural temples, such as one example from the Pfeffer town site. Here,
besides a modest 2-to-3-m-high pyramid, the remains of a larger than nor-
mal (4 x 8 m) building were found between the hilltop public space and

Table 4.1

Temple-Depositional Sequence, Feature 44, Pfeffer Site (11-S-204)

Depositional Event	Subdivision	General Fill Description	Interpretation
Construction	—	Yellow and black floor plaster.	Single depositional event.
Special fill	North and west end	6 layers alternating 10YR 3/4 and 4/4 silt and clayey silt.	Single depositional event, or 3 closely spaced events.
Reexcavation and refilling	Phase 1, west end	5–6 layers alternating 10YR 4/4 loam and 4/3 ash or silt.	Repeatedly capped accumulated debris from in-basin fires.
	Phase 1, east end	5 layers of 7.5YR 2.5/ 2–4/3 ashy silt and ash.	Accumulated debris from in-basin fires.
Reexcavation and refilling	Phase 2, east end	10YR 3/2 silt loam, with laminated sand at base.	Portion of basin redug, then refilled after precipitation.
Reexcavation and refilling	Phase 3, west	Burned patch on old floor.	Now, or in earlier phase, this is primary burning location.
	Phase 3, east	7+ layers of 7.5–10YR 4/2–3/2 loamy silt–ashy silt over water-laid loam.	Accumulated debris, slow in-filling, repeated reuse.
Possible reexcavation, final infilling	Phase 4	Homogeneous 10YR 3/2 silty loam filling in west end.	—

the downslope residential area (Kruchten 2000). Its half-meter-deep semi-subterranean floor, all of the more than 60 wall postholes, and five of its extramural pits—one of which contained portions of one subadult individual—had been plastered two or three times with yellow, clayey silt followed by black silt (Figure 4.4).

These characteristics identify the oversized structure as an early Mississippian temple, initially dedicated with a two-layered, yellow and black earthen floor. At some point in the late eleventh century, it was dismantled, commencing a complex depositional sequence that involved at least one and possibly two partial filling events consisting of up to six layers of alternating light and dark or ashy and clayey silts from about 3 to 10 cm in thickness. Subsequently, the basin was reexcavated by people who opened up a large rectangular hole within the former basin, slightly smaller than the original but with the same proportions all the way down to the original hearths on the original yellow and black temple floor. The indigenous reexcavators then burned or cooked something on that floor (on or near the old hearths) before partially or totally refilling the basin once again. This was done in three major episodes—also seen in one of the extramural pits—before the Indian inhabitants finally sealed the temple basin (Table 4.1).

ANCIENT EXCAVATIONS AND MEMORY WORK

The Pfeffer temple was not the only example of an actual pre-Columbian archaeological excavation. There are several possible small-scale excavations at one outlying site, Grossmann, where Susan Alt (2006) has argued that the excavators might have sought to retrieve artifacts, pieces of their own past, for ritual reanimation in the present. Moreover, such digs are even more evident at Cahokia. These include the aforementioned stratified feasting pit and at least two key earthen pyramids. Regarding the feasting pit, there was at least one major aboriginal reexcavation into the various layers of artifact-laden ash, silt, and feasting detritus in the years following the initial depositions. This reexcavation, seen as a gouged-out hole and a steep 60-cm-deep profile wall, was probably coincident with the construction or use of the earlier-noted oversized buildings—possible temples—at ca. 1050–1100 CE (prior to the construction of Mound 51 over this location).

Likewise, there is good evidence of a pre-Columbian excavation into Mound 49 in the middle of Cahokia's Grand Plaza, initially a platform with buildings (again, possible temples) on its various sequential summits. As seen in our own excavations in 1994, a near-vertical profile wall had been cut into an early face of this pyramid, probably not long after the monument's initial 1050 CE construction (Pauketat and Rees 1996). And these original Cahokian excavators seem to have situated their nearly 1-m-high profile wall to expose 10 flat-lying layers of alternating sand, charcoal, and light and dark packed-clay construction fills (Figure 4.5). The construction history of this particular mound might have ended with a "ridge-top" earthen cap, one of nearly a dozen such ridge-top mounds known from the greater Cahokia region, making it similar to yet another Cahokia monument rich in evidence of structured deposition and indigenous excavation: the well-known Mound 72 (Fowler 1997; Fowler et al. 1999).

The history of Mound 72 appears to have begun with the decommissioning of a single ancestral temple, or charnel house, followed by the removal of a large wooden post nearby sometime shortly after 1050 CE. In

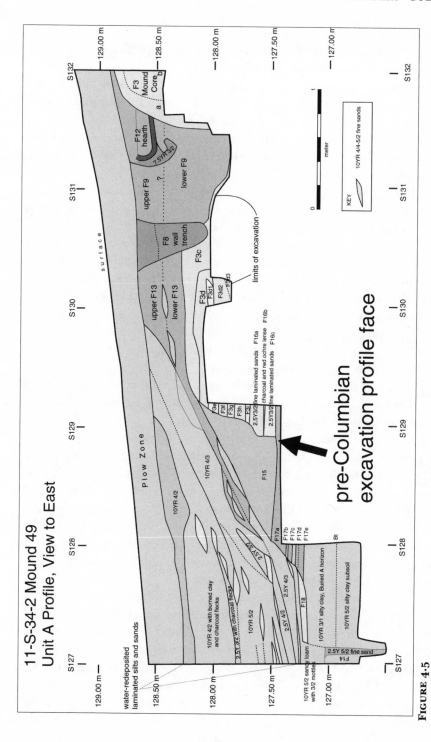

11-S-34-2 Mound 49
Unit A Profile, View to East

pre-Columbian
excavation profile face

KEY

10YR 4/4-5/2 fine sands

0   meter   1

FIGURE 4.5

Profile of Mound 49, lower levels (Unit A) at Cahokia (11-S-34-2). The aboriginal profile cut through Feature 3 fills; both were later covered by Feature 15 fill.

73

these earliest events, piled human bones or corpses were buried over the top of the removed architecture, presumably commemorations of specific persons or houses (following Gillespie 2001). Subsequent to these tightly spaced events, a series of mortuary interments in trenches (or "death pits") were made and then covered with mound fill, each fill unit initially comprising a separate small mound later subsumed by one final ridge-top mound. Along the way, the various little mounds and mound enlargements appear specially shaped or oriented to mark the locations of the bodies beneath them (Fowler et al. 1999).

The central Mound 72 interment, made sometime before 1100 CE, consisted of the corpses of two men, one on and one under a thunderbird-shaped cape or "mat or blanket" studded with 20,000 shell beads (Fowler et al. 1999:132). Near them were accoutrements (arrows, gaming pieces, beads, crystals) laid over the bodies of retainers, all of which may be pieces of a Morning Star/Evening Star creation story, told or retold here via mortuary theater. Elsewhere, I have argued that this mortuary theater was probably not just about the dead, but probably starred, as it were, one or more living cult-heirs, themselves "reincarnated" founders emerging from the events that took place in the land of the dead (Pauketat 2005). The bodies of the "twin" men (likely impersonators of the superhuman Thunderers) appear oriented to reference the summer solstice sunset and the winter solstice sunrise, while subsequent interments appear to cite the placement of these two men (see Fowler et al. 1999).[4]

In this particular theatrical performance, the deposition of earth—in conjunction with other materials—was an integral component of a liturgical sequence. Bodies of honored and executed men and women were laid on prepared surfaces of earth or in white-sand and pelt- or mat-lined death pits, all covered over or filled with dark silty and clayey earth and then capped by the small mounds. Now, not only did the small mounds mark the location of the burials beneath and cite the twin Thunderer men, but there are at least three pre-Columbian excavations timed, it appears, to one or another of the major mortuary interments.

The first involved someone excavating down through the small mound that covered the charnel house over the top of and then into the fills of the removed temple post pit in order to bury 22 sacrificed women (Features 204–205). The second consisted of a rectangular excavation through this same early mound down to a premound mass grave of 19 young women in order to deposit commemorative caches of artifacts: a pile of 36,000 shell beads, another heap of 451 chipped-stone projectile points, six smashed ceramic pots, and "several hundred bone projectile points" (Ahler

1999:105). The composition of the assemblage and the orientation of the excavated pit toward the twin-Thunderer burial may mean that this pit was excavated, filled, and then buried at or near the time of the interment of those two men. Sometime later a third excavation was made down through the small mound that covered the twin men and their retainers until the bones and accoutrements of those retainers were located. Then three more individuals were laid at orthogonal angles atop the retainers beneath them.

The three aboriginal excavations into Mound 72 are reminiscent of the Pfeffer temple to the extent that the apparent goals of the indigenous excavators included relocating, commemorating, or reanimating the buried remains below. In the case of Mound 72, each act was concluded with the interment of more bodies. In the case of the Pfeffer temple, the excavation was followed by the building of fires on the old temple floor and, subsequently, the reburial of that floor.

Although it remains unclear in the Mound 72 case (pending a reanalysis of the field records), another goal of the native diggers in all of the other cases, including the Pfeffer temple, seems to have been to reinspect or document the stratigraphy in the exposed profile walls. Each reexcavation of the Pfeffer temple fills, the sub–Mound 51 feasting pit, or the lower layers of Mound 49 afforded the native excavators an opportunity to examine the alternating light and dark layers of earth. Such an inspection might have served to remind themselves or others of what had been deposited or experienced in previous years, quite likely within their own lifetimes at this place. Or it might have been intended to redistribute the powers of the earth buried there by reincorporating them into the agentic world above. In any case, the depositions and excavations established a history of that place for the people who lived or attended the gatherings there. A cursory review of the placement, superpositioning, and potential profile cuts exposed by indigenous excavators elsewhere at Cahokia, East Saint Louis, and elsewhere leads me to wonder if earth-historical knowledge was gathered as a matter of course during many of the subterranean excavations of ordinary pits, post pits, or house basins (see Collins 1990; Pauketat 1998; Pauketat, ed. 2005; Pauketat and Alt 2005).

DISCUSSION

Clearly, excavation and earth-moving had been a fact of daily life for many peoples up and down the Mississippi Valley for centuries before 1050 CE. So, without detailing this long history and without engaging in direct-historical analogies (that imply all people understood the different soils to mean the same thing), there is reason to argue that the aesthetic qualities of earth—say, clean, pure sands versus dark, organic clays—evoked memories or associations of place for the diggers or observers. Most likely, the memories and associations differed between people, particularly widely separated people like those in southern Wisconsin versus greater Cahokia. They were place-contingent.

On the surface, the intaglios under effigy mounds and the layered fills and manufactured sediments in the Gottschall Rockshelter might seem comparable to the alternating fills in greater Cahokia's temples, mortuary deposits, feasting pits, plazas, and earthen pyramids. And yet the termination of earthen practices in Wisconsin at 1050 CE coincident with the efflorescence of them in greater Cahokia seems to indicate that there was something inconsistent between the two. That is, they were *not* both expressions of some generic Midwestern belief system or ideology. In fact, when combined with the evidence of Cahokian "intrusions" into southern Wisconsin and with the evidence of large-scale immigration into greater Cahokia around 1050 CE (Alt 2002, 2006; Pauketat 2003b; Pauketat and Alt 2003), it is difficult not to argue that the only thing shared between the various peoples in either area was a very general aesthetic understanding that different dirts had different associations.

It may be no coincidence that the most elaborate depositional practices and indigenous excavations known in the greater Cahokia region, discussed above, date to the founding phase of Cahokia, when the degree of the region's centrality is matched only by the cultural diversity of its regional population. Likewise, it may also be no coincidence that, around Cahokia, these practices do not seem to have been exclusive or private. Quite the opposite: the depositional practices around Cahokia were very much "incorporated" via the bodies of many living earthmovers and the corpses of the sacrificial dead (Connerton 1989). Likewise, the aboriginal excavations of mound and pit fills might also have been open to the public, as it were, at least to an extent sufficient to affirm the veracity of the interpretations espoused by the diggers.

By the same token, the earthen citationality of Wisconsin's effigy mound builders might well have been inconsistent with the new Cahokia-Mississippian narrative, painted on the Gottschall Rockshelter wall and, not coincidentally, embodied by intruders or converted locals residing at a series of likely Cahokian outposts or missions in southern Wisconsin (see Stoltman 2000). From that point of view, the end of effigy mound construction was a consequence of the decoupling of the old practices from their referents and their enchainment to the new referents, those of a foreign founder's cult centered at a distant place (Cahokia) where the powers of wa-kan-da were being gathered. The effect was to dissolve effigy mound building in Wisconsin.

Importantly, the gathering of the dispersed agentic powers in greater Cahokia would have been realized through the depositional practices of earth and sky (and, in southern Wisconsin, through the cessation of those depositional practices and the concomitant silencing of certain ancestors). Structured deposition, aided by the occasional native excavation, was in this way the materiality of the agentic redistribution or enchainment process. Earth and sky were gathered by Cahokians by citing the sky (the sun, fire, and unseen thunderbirds) and the earth (and the forces of the netherworld), both drawing on everyone's aesthetic sensibilities, to construct an invariant earthen order.

It should be no surprise that almost all of the structured deposits of the pre-Columbian American Midwest were in some way celebrations or commemorations of ancestors, and that the liturgical reconfiguration of depositional practices that appeared as a Mississippian disjuncture at 1050 CE were, likewise, invariably associated in some way with ancestral temples. The temples, temple-related feasts, central posts, and the earthen pyramids gathered the dispersed agentic forces of wa-kan-da into a common order with a decidedly sedimentary logic. The new Cahokian ancestors were inscribed on the wall of Gottschall in an agentic medium—paint— and remembered via the redundant and intensive depositional practices of greater Cahokia and its outposts, aided by native excavations that exposed the apparent sedimentary truths that they or their parents or grandparents had themselves buried in the ground.

CONCLUSION

Oddly, the lesson of this transregional case study in dirt archaeology may contradict an accepted sedimentary theory of human agency. It has been assumed based on well-worn notions of "habitus" or "bodily discipline" that certain memories were merely "sedimented" in bodies through "incorporating practices," constituting an "embodied knowing" where bodies wrote, according to de Certeau (1984:93), "without being able to read" (see Bourdieu 1977; Connerton 1989; Foucault 1979; for example, Bradley 1998; Hodder and Cessford 2004). However, such a theoretical perspective might understate the aesthetics of depositional practice and overstate the strategic actions or ideologies of elite founders. That is, people likely had some aesthetic sensibilities about good and bad, rich or poor, and clean or dirty earth that they would have knowingly referenced with each laborious depositional practice. Thus, the citation, in its pure Butlerian sense, would have been made from a point of knowledgeability (rather than Certeauian ignorance), making ordinary people and the earth itself participants in a rapid and large-scale historical process.

We might better understand the radical shift in causal powers behind the alternatively amplified or silenced depositional practices of the trans-regional Mississippian phenomenon by thinking about citationality and enchainment in terms of John Barrett's (1999:259) "geography of being." Local inhabitants after 1050 CE—in southern Wisconsin or greater Cahokia —may have been "able to find a place for themselves by reference to their own biography" even as they recognized a newly "fixed" place, Cahokia, and cited it accordingly and knowingly. The Mississippian case, of course, points out that a geography-of-being was simultaneously a genealogy-of-being with a proactive sedimentary logic that entangled persons, places, and things with "the creation and control of the world and the things thereof." Thereafter, vast agentic fields were radically reframed, as the agency of bodies, objects, substances, spaces, and spirits was dispropor-tionately redistributed to the living god-men and god-women of the earth and sky who now inhabited the land and watched peoples through earth and fire.

Acknowledgments

Funding for the research highlighted here was provided by the National Science Foundation (SBR-9996169 and SBR-9305404), the National Geographic Society (Grant 6319-98), the Wenner-Gren Foundation (Grant 5625), the Cahokia Mounds Museum Society, the Illinois Transportation Archaeological Research Program, and the University of Illinois. I am sincerely grateful to Barbara Mills and William Walker, who pulled together a wonderful group in Santa Fe, Washington DC, and Exeter that proved to be exceptionally productive and enjoyable. Much of the success of this vol-ume is also to be credited to the wonderful environment of the School for Advanced Research in Santa Fe, thanks to James Brooks and George Gumerman. Finally, I am indebted to Susan Alt, Thomas Emerson, Robert Hall, Tim McCleary, and two anony-mous reviewers for their critical comments on earlier versions of this paper and related ruminations. The final product is, of course, my own responsibility, even though this paper seemed at times to confront me as an agent in its own right.

Notes

1. Much like Foucault's (1979) notion of power.

2. The tenets of such a normative, cultural-historical approach still underlie many contemporary archaeological interpretations in eastern North America owing to

the continued use of the "direct historical approach" and cultural taxonomic systems developed in the 1930s.

3. A thorough review of domestic earthmoving, subterranean practices, and structured deposition in the American midcontinent is well beyond the present paper's scope. I suspect that careful, planned disposal events, where fills were thought-fully rather than expediently deposited, exist at many Late Woodland, Mississippian, and Plains village sites (see Emerson et al. 2000; Pauketat 2004; Wood 1998).

4. Another commemoration of the winter solstice sunrise is well known from Cahokia. After the "woodhenge" had been removed at around 1200 CE, and several more decades had passed, an incised beaker decorated with a motif evocative of the "woodhenge" and the winter solstice position was burned and buried in a small hearth. That hearth—inside a Moorehead-phase house (1200–1275 CE)—itself superimposed the post pit where the woodhenge's winter solstice post had stood decades earlier (compare Pauketat 1998; Wittry 1996). Two generations later, this family apparently remembered the precise location!

5

Remembering while Forgetting

Depositional Practices and
Social Memory at Chaco

Barbara J. Mills

A central paradox of the study of social memory is that memories are made during a process that includes forgetting. The relationship of memory to its counterpart has been part of the Western philosophical tradition for millennia. As Adrian Forty (1999:16) points out, the ancient Greeks located the springs of Lethe (Forgetfulness) and Mnemosyne (Memory) next to each other so that one could drink from the first before the other. European philosophers from Proust to Heidegger have also recognized that "remembering is only possible on the basis of forgetting" (Forty 1999:12–13).

Susanne Küchler (1999, 2002) has persuasively shown that the interdependence of remembering and forgetting is not limited to Western society. Rather than a literal forgetting, her work deals with the practices that surround the memorialization of people, events, and places through the sacrifice of objects. Her work on *malanggan*, objects made for funerals that encapsulate social histories and are intentionally destroyed representations of the deceased, shows how memorialization occurs as part of rituals of sacrifice. Like Zuni War Gods, or Ahayu:da, malanggan are forms that construct memories through their production and destruction, not through their preservation.

In this chapter I argue that forgetting is an important part of memory work, one that has been frequently used in the past. I outline several different ways in which forgetting contributes to memory work and then illustrate a few of these examples through a recontextualization of archaeological collections from Chaco Canyon, New Mexico.

FORGETTING AS PART OF MEMORY WORK

The practices that surround forgetting as part of memory work are widely divergent. One form of forgetting is through secrecy. Items may be secreted out of sight as part of different ritual practices such as the dedication and commemoration of structures. Social memories are constructed during the interactions between ritual participants and objects with particular qualities and origins as part of the commemorative performance. Although out of sight, sometimes permanently, the location of those objects may be remembered for long periods of time. Similarly, objects that are either deposited or destroyed during mortuary rituals, like malanggan, represent another form of forgetting while, at the same time, they are part of the creation of chains or networks of people through things in the present (Chapman 2000a).

Other forms of forgetting transform and even deconstruct memories. For example, memory may be transformed through the imperfect reproduction or recollection of past practices, including what are called copying errors in the transmission literature (Mandler and Johnson 1977; Shennan 2002). Many of these so-called errors are now seen as potentially beneficial in the literature on cognitive psychology, because there are few who would choose to become like the character in Jorge Luis Borges's tale, "Funes the Memorious," who remembers every detail but cannot abstract or generalize (Gigerenzer 2005).

A more active deconstruction of memory may occur through the ritual retirement of objects no longer useful but too powerful and inalienable to be discarded like other objects (Mills 2004). Another manifestation of the active deconstruction of memory is the deconsecration of ritual spaces through burning, selective removal of architectural elements, and/or filling (Creel and Anyon 2003; Walker et al. 2000). In these cases, objects or spaces are filled, destroyed, or otherwise removed from circulation and use because they are considered too powerful to be preserved in situ once their use in specific contexts has ended.

The transformation of memory may have a more overt political or nationalistic motive. Memories may be transformed or reshaped as part of the invention of tradition (Hobsbawm 1983), in which new practices are replaced by others but are claimed to have great time depth to legitimize extant political forces. The transformation may be even more politically charged, as in the deconstruction of buildings, monuments, and groups of people, intended to end the reproduction of specific social memories and replace them with others, as seen with the Bamiyan Buddhas—examples of "past mastering" or "negative heritage" (Meskell 2002). Ironically, these examples of deconstruction often have results opposite to those intended. Through destruction, including the entombment of buildings, the defacing of statues and other monuments, and genocide, those who have attempted to erase the past make their marks more materially visible (especially archaeologically) and socially contested.

These examples illustrate how forgetting is an important part of memory work, along with recalling, reshaping, inventing, and coordinating. Memory is a social practice (Halbwachs 1992), and it links people and things through time in the process of shaping history. Part of the study of memory must also look at how those links are transformed, broken, and replaced. To complement ways in which social memories have been constructed and reproduced through practice (Bourdieu 1977; Bourdieu and Wacquant 1992), I look at how these memories are reshaped through a variety of depositional practices that incorporate the placement of objects in spaces that were sequestered or sealed as well as those that were intentionally destroyed and/or removed from circulation for at least a portion of their biographies (Meskell 2004).

At Chaco Canyon the deposition of items took place in architectural spaces of different sizes and forms. These differences in the spatiality of memory work are one way that archaeologists can approach memory and materiality as they were constructed within different social networks. Different social groups inscribed their memories within these spaces as part of the performance of commemorative ceremonies, the storage of objects used in ritual performances, and the marking of spaces used for multiple interments. Chacoans also erased earlier structures, retired objects and spaces used in collective ceremonies, and removed objects from earlier deposits as part of the active transformation of social memories that illustrates how the multiple trajectories of forgetting are active parts of memory work.

DEPOSITIONAL PRACTICES AND SOCIAL MEMORY AT CHACO

Discussions of the materiality of depositional practices are far less common than one might think, given that Chaco is considered a "rituality" (Yoffee 2001) or a place of "high devotational expression" (Renfrew 2001). Although several recent studies have called artifact deposits at Chaco "votive," "ritual," or "sacred" in some way, most of them do not talk about variation in the practices that produced these deposits. There has been little comparison of the overall content of different deposits in terms of who deposited them, in what contexts they were deposited, and how these practices were part of the materiality of Chacoan life. Analysts have specialized in particular material classes, and as a result we have excellent overviews of turquoise (Mathien 2001, 2003), wooden objects (Vivian et al. 1978), architecture (Lekson 2007; Van Dyke 2004), ceramics (Crown and Wills 2003; Toll 2001), chipped stone (Cameron 2001), and animal burials (Hill 2000; Kovacik 1998) but very little on different materials with shared contexts of deposition beyond the density of their spatial locations (Neitzel 2003a). Yet at sites within the canyon, people inscribed their memories within different architectural spaces as part of the performance of commemorative ceremonies, the storage of objects used in ritual performances, and the marking of spaces used for multiple interments. Chacoans also erased earlier structures, retired objects and spaces used in collective rituals, and removed objects from earlier deposits as part of the active transformation of social memories in ways that illustrate how forgetting is an active part of memory work. The strategies and practices (de Certeau 1984) of memory work resulted in the deposition of large amounts of objects in architectural spaces at Chaco, especially at Chaco Canyon sites dating to the tenth through twelfth centuries. The peak use of Chaco by Ancestral Puebloans was shorter than a century, from 1030 to 1100 CE, sometimes called the Classic Bonito phase. Many of the practices seen in Chaco can be traced to contemporary Pueblo society—evidence of the efficacy of Puebloan ways of remembering while forgetting (for example, Kuwanwisiwma 2004).

Previous research on social memory at Chaco includes Kovacik's (1998) analysis of faunal materials and Van Dyke's (2003, 2004) interpretations of great house architecture. Kovacik compared the distribution of fauna in small site structures dating from 500 to 1180 CE, finding that there were continuities in the deposition of carnivores and bird of prey elements within architectural spaces. He argued that this was evidence of social memory over a long period of time, maintained through the renewal of buildings and the deposition of elements within floors and in the rafters. His analysis is important in that it also demonstrates that these practices bridged significant breaks in the occupational sequence of individual sites leading to the interpretation of continuities over multiple generations. Van Dyke's work (2003, 2004) underscores how memory, meaning, and large-scale architectural constructions at Chaco were interrelated through the visible impact of buildings, their symmetry, and their locations on the landscape. Her work on the Late Bonito phase (1100–1140 CE), particularly, shows how great houses were transformed at the end of the canyon's occupation, and she argues that this is evidence of social memory at work. My analysis complements the above works on memory at Chaco. Like Kovacik, I focus on the depositional contexts and continuities of materials and their contexts, but I expand his approach to include a variety of materials. Like Van Dyke, I focus largely on great houses, but I look at how memory work inheres within architecture rather than how the buildings were perceived within the Chaco social and physical landscape.

Architectural contexts at Chaco include rectangular pueblo rooms, which are masonry rooms usually constructed in room blocks, and round rooms that were at least partially if not fully used for ritual practices (Lekson 1986, 2007). The latter include room block kivas, tower kivas, courtyard kivas, and great kivas. Room block kivas, round rooms that were constructed inside of pueblo rooms, are generally smaller than courtyard kivas. Tower kivas are room block kivas that were elevated through multistory construction. Courtyard kivas, larger round rooms within plaza spaces rather than room blocks, are intermediate in size between round rooms and great kivas. Great kivas, the largest circular structures, may be in the plazas of pueblos or isolated, such as the great kiva at Casa Rinconada. They are identified on the basis of a specific constellation of floor features and their larger size; they are greater than 10 m and usually closer to 15–20 m in diameter. Courtyard kivas and great kivas were semisubterranean, room block kivas were both subterranean and first-floor kivas, and tower kivas were elevated to two or three stories. Each of these spaces was constructed by members of different social groups who participated in different social fields. Each of the spaces also structured subsequent social interactions in terms of who and how many people could participate and view ceremonial events.

In looking at deposits at Chaco, I focus on offerings in several spatial contexts. The first are offerings in ritual structures of different sizes. I use these to look at how social memories are made through the deposition of objects in architectural features that mark different moments in the use of these spaces, especially their construction and termination. These are examples of memory work through the practice of secrecy in which things that are hidden acquire value through the acts of gathering them together and placing them in architectural cavities (Hendon 2000; Piot 1993). Secrecy is an important principle among contemporary Pueblos (Brandt 1980) and has clear historical continuities with Ancestral Pueblo material practices. I then look at deposits in Chaco great house rooms that are examples of the ritual retirements of objects used in Pueblo ceremonialism. These may be associated with the retirements of specific rooms or spaces within the pueblo but are more certainly the retirements of ceremonial objects, including altar pieces, staffs of office, and other objects that were intentionally buried and/or left behind, many of which were left in their ritual storerooms. I use these objects to illustrate how, through the active process of forgetting, they were used in the memory work of those who lived in and visited Chacoan great houses.

DEDICATING AND DRESSING THE HOUSE

The use of ornaments as offerings has a long history in the Southwest, but nowhere does it appear in the concentration and quantities present at Chaco during the Classic Bonito phase. Dedicatory and termination offerings in great kivas, court kivas, and room block kivas are overwhelmingly composed of finished ornaments and the debris from ornament working. Each of these ritual structures was used by different social networks of varying sizes and based on different principles of recruitment and degrees of inclusiveness. The deposits found in these structures illuminate the ways in which ornaments played a central role in commemorative performances and the construction of social memories on different scales at Chaco.

Although they occur over a broad area of the Southwest in various forms, circular roofed great kivas are closely associated with Bonito Phase architecture at Chaco Canyon (Vivian and Reiter 1960). They have a long history, dating at least to the Basketmaker III period (ca. 550–750 CE) at Chaco. Most are found at Chaco great houses, but a few are isolated from pueblos, such as the Casa Rinconada and Kin Nahasbas great kivas in Chaco Canyon (Figure 5.1).

Based on their size, great kivas were used by large segments of the community and may even have been places shared by members of multiple communities (Adler and Wilshusen 1990). Although they were not big enough to house the entire Chaco Canyon population, much less all of Chaco's nearby outliers, it is clear that they drew people from multiple social networks. As the largest structures constructed for ritual use, they are one of the most prominent forms of monumental architecture in the canyon. Their regular features, which became highly standardized during the Classic period (Van Dyke 2003), suggest a liturgical order to the performance of ritual. Because of their high visibility, their construction and reconstruction were points at which social memories were created for large segments of the community, whether or not they actually participated in the building events themselves.

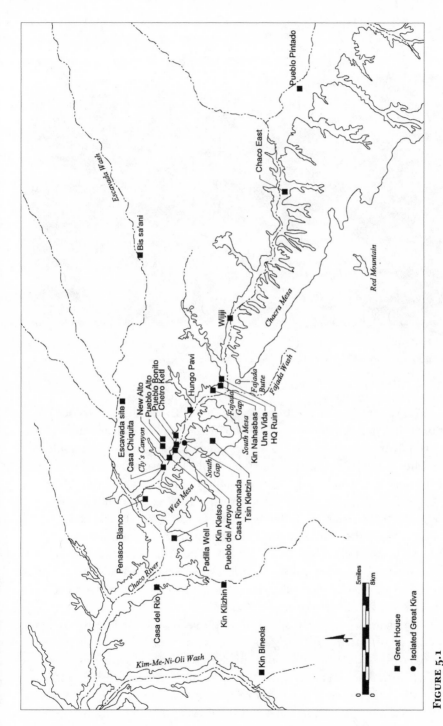

Figure 5.1
Chaco Canyon sites. Chaco Archives.

FIGURE 5.2

Great Kiva II (below Great Kiva I), Chetro Ketl. After Hewett (1936).

The Chetro Ketl Great Kiva II, lying under Great Kiva I, provides one of the best examples of the materiality of dedicatory and termination/closing rituals at Chaco. This great kiva was constructed at the southern side of the Chetro Ketl plaza, where many of the late constructed rooms at the pueblo had been built (Lekson 1983:253). Ten niches were built into the lower wall of the structure, each measuring 15 x 25 cm and 45 cm deep (Hewett 1936; Vivian and Reiter 1960; Figure 5.2). The niches were planned by the builders based on their regular layout and incorporation within the initial construction of the wall. The entire construction of the wall appears to have been done over a relatively short period with no visible breaks in the circular wall. During the mid-1000s CE, Great Kiva II was reconstructed and expanded into Great Kiva I.

The niches in the Chetro Ketl Great Kiva II have stone lintels, like fenestration but with no opening to the exterior, which suggest they were intended to remain open for part of the use of the structure. However, when excavated by archaeologists, they were filled with masonry that was in a slightly different style from that of the surrounding stonework. Before being closed with masonry, each niche was also filled with long strands of

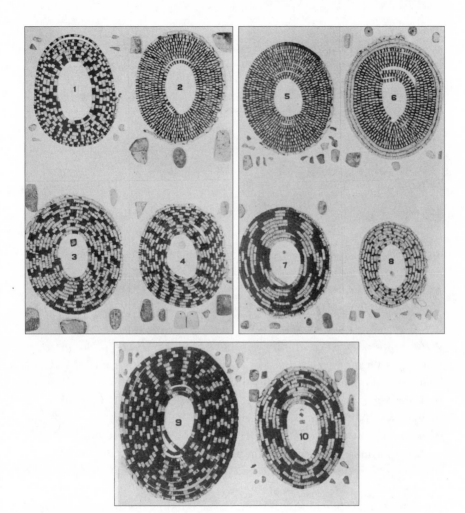

FIGURE 5.3
Contents of wall niches, Great Kiva II. After Hewett (1936).

black and white beads and multiple turquoise pendants (Hewett 1936:90–
92; Figure 5.3). The niches were sealed so that the stones were flush with
the rest of the wall, and once the wall was plastered, the niches would have
been completely out of sight—a symbolic forgetting that illustrates the
importance of secreting away as a practice in Ancestral Pueblo memory work.

There are striking repetitions in these offerings. First, not only are they
of the same materials, but the color, sizes, and forms of the beads are also
highly regular. This repetition suggests a standardization or even habitual-
ization in the acquisition and production of these objects in addition to

TABLE 5.1

Contents of Niches in Chetro Ketl Great Kiva II

Niche	Number of Beads	Length of Strand of Beads (m)	Number of Pieces of Turquoise
1	1,724	3.8	8
2	1,538	3.2	5
3	1,797	4.3	5
4	1,940	3.6	9
5	1,770	3.7	13
6	1,745	4.	8
7	1,831	3.8	7
8	983	2.1	1
9	2,265	5.2	10
10	1,861	3.	16
Total	17,454	36.7	100

Modified from Hewett (1936:89).

their deposition. Second, the strands of beads are quite long; when restrung, they range from 2 to 5 m in length and include from 983 to 2,265 beads each (Table 5.1). Thus, it is likely that these strands were not made by a single person but represent the products of multiple hands within the network that participated in the termination of the lower kiva and the construction and dedication of the overlying kiva in the mid-1000s.

The secreting or hiding of these necklaces was preceded by the construction of a series of social memories surrounding the life history of the objects, including their procurement, production, and finally their placement in niches. The closure of such a large building, its intentional filling, and then the construction of yet another great kiva in the same place would have been a memorable series of events for the community. Thus, even if the community members had not all witnessed the closure of the niches, because of the scale of the offerings and the amount of labor required to produce the objects, partially fill the lower structure, and construct an even more massive building and roof on top, the effort would have been one in which memory and materiality closely intersected.

Several other forms of offerings in the Chetro Ketl Great Kiva II were found in basal deposits lying below the pits for the massive upright roofing posts, in rectangular masonry floor vaults, and on the benches between remodeling episodes. Large stone disks were made for each of the four large postholes, also called seating pits (Vivian and Reiter 1960:Figure 15).

One of these, the northeast seating pit, contained four large disks, which had been placed over four alternating layers of lignite and adobe (Vivian and Reiter 1960:Figure 16). One-third meter below the lower adobe layer, excavation of a test pit revealed the remains of a leather bag containing turquoise. When the northwest seating pit was excavated, a similar offering was found.

The Chetro Ketl GK I/II east vault had a clean layer of sand above a flagstone floor. In this fill were deposited "numerous potsherds, turquoise fragments, 'anthracite' and calcite beads (singly), two pendants, and fragments of malachite-painted wood. Similar material was recorded from the west vault" (Vivian and Reiter 1960:36). These deposits were probably associated with GK II because of their depth and location near the base. When Chetro Ketl GK II was remodeled to construct Great Kiva I, 97 to 112 cm of fill were deposited, along with the raising of the walls of the floor features, construction of a new exterior wall and bench, and the removal and reconstruction of the massive roof. In the fill were found other deposits, including three coiled strands of beads, one uncoiled strand, and several other ornaments (Vivian and Reiter 1960:37). The bench also contained an offering of beads, although descriptions are not detailed. Like the offerings in the niches, these offerings served as both a closing of the earlier structure and dedication of the new one.

The objects placed in other great kivas appear to be primarily dedicatory offerings, and most are ornaments (Table 5.2). These include strings of shell, jet, and turquoise beads and pendants. Clearly, the construction of these buildings was one of the most important events to mark by depositing objects in parts of the building prior to their completion. As at Chetro Ketl the strands of beads were ways of ensuring that these structures would be ritually dressed throughout their lives.

Although items related to ornaments are more common, another pattern is repeated at smaller scales in other ritual structures. Kiva Q, a great kiva at Pueblo Bonito, contained a remarkably diverse assemblage of bone, slate, turquoise, and shell beads along with unworked minerals, fossils, pebbles, expertly crafted bifaces and flakes, sandstone jar covers, bone and ground stone tools, fragments of ceramic vessels, a fragment of a cloud blower, concretions, seeds, insect parts, and parts of the paws of a mountain lion, a bear, and a dog (Figure 5.4; Table 5.3). These items represent the widespread networks that Chaco residents were engaged in, with goods coming from as far as the Gulf of California (for example, olivella beads). Some of these objects were highly valued for their rarity and acquisition in distant places, as Helms (1993) has discussed in the context of Central

TABLE 5.2
Ritual Deposits in Chacoan Great Kivas

Site	Kiva	Feature/Context	Objects	Offering Type	Date (CE)	Reference
Chetro Ketl	Great Kiva II	Northeast seating pit	Leather bag with pulverized turquoise.	Dedicatory	Mid-late 1000s	Vivian and Reiter (1960)
Chetro Ketl	Great Kiva II	Northwest seating pit	Turquoise.	Dedicatory	Mid-late 1000s	Vivian and Reiter (1960)
Chetro Ketl	Great Kiva II	East vault	Sherds, turquoise fragments, jet and calcite beads, 2 pendants, and malachite-painted wood.	Dedicatory	Mid-late 1000s	Vivian and Reiter (1960)
Chetro Ketl	Great Kiva II	Niches 1–10	Jet and white shell bead necklaces, turquoise pendants.	Termination /renewal	Late 1000s	Hewett (1936); Vivian and Reiter (1960)
Chetro Ketl	Great Kiva I/II	Floor fill	4 strands of beads and other ornaments.	Termination /renewal	Late 1000s	Vivian and Reiter (1960)
Chetro Ketl	Great Kiva I	Bench	Beads.	Dedicatory	Late 1000s	Vivian and Reiter (1960)
Casa Rinconada	Great Kiva	Upper floor (south of firebox)	Sherds, 2 copper bells, 328 white (shell?) beads (probably strung).	Termination /renewal	Late 1000s	Vivian and Reiter (1960:24)
Casa Rinconada	Great Kiva	Subfloor trench (south of firebox)	Copper bell fragment.	Termination /renewal	Late 1000s	Vivian and Reiter (1960:24)
Aztec	Great Kiva	Western vault, pit	Worked turquoise (several), shell beads.	Dedicatory	1000s?	Morris (1921:133)
Aztec	Great Kiva	Western vault, pit	Shaped copper sphere, turquoise fragments.	Dedicatory	1000s?	Morris (1921:133)
Aztec	Great Kiva	Between floor resurfacings	Broken pottery vessels, turquoise from mosaic, strand of olivella shell beads with turquoise pendant.	Termination /renewal	1100s?	Morris (1921:126)
Pueblo Bonito	Kiva Q	Wall niche	Plant remains, shell ornaments and debris, fauna (black bear, dog, and mountain lion), chert and obsidian projectile points, chert knives, ground stone, worked bone (see Table 5.3 for detailed list).	Dedicatory	1040s (probable, earliest), possibly as late as the 1100–1150s (Windes 2003)	Judd (1954:323, Plate 90)

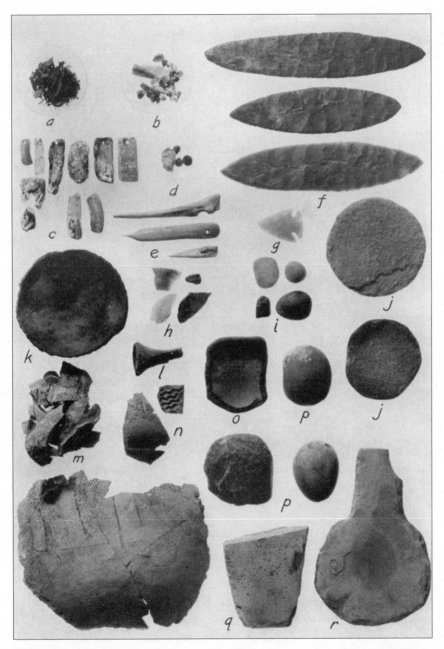

FIGURE 5.4
Contents of niche in Kiva Q, a great kiva at Pueblo Bonito (see Table 5.3). After Judd
(1954:Plate 90).

Table 5.3

Objects from Kiva Q (Great Kiva) at Pueblo Bonito

Number of Objects	Description	Illustration (Judd 1954: Plate 90)	Number of Objects	Description	Illustration (Judd 1954: Plate 90)
Numerous shreds	Juniper and rush	a	1	Sandstone worked concretion	o
3	Abalone shell scraps	a	3	Quartzite hammers	p
1	Twined fabric, possible sandal	a	1	Sandstone muller fragment	q
1	Chert arrowhead	b	1	Sandstone palette	r
2	Obsidian arrowheads	b	1	Turquoise pendant, fragment	—
1	Claystone tessera	b			
4	Turquoise tesserae	b	2	Turquoise discoidal beads	—
9	Abalone shell pendants	c	6	Turquoise bead blanks	—
1	Quartz crystal	d	7	Turquoise worked fragments	—
3	Azurite pellets	d	6	Turquoise matrix fragments	—
3	Bone awls	e	2	Bone discoidal beads	—
2	Chert (brown) blades	f	1	Slate discoidal bead	—
1	Quartzite blade	f	2	Olivellas, spires removed	—
1	Chert knife blade	g	1	Squash seed	—
2	Chert spalls (flakes)	e	4	Wild grape seeds (*Vitis arizonica*)	—
2	Quartzite spalls (flakes)	e			
2	Quartz pebbles	i	1	Unidentified seed fragment	—
2	Quartzite pebbles	i	1	Spine of western locust (*Robinia neomexicana*)	—
2	Sandstone jar covers	j			
1	Base of indented corrugated cooking jar	k	2	Mountain lion (*Felis concolor*) claws	—
1	Bowl of cloud blower	l	178	Black bear (*Euarctos americanus*) digital bones and claws	—
1	Fragments of 2 black-on-white jars with hachure	m			
1	Fragment of 1 black-on-white bowl	n	28	Dog (*Canis familiaris*) digital bones and claws	—

America. But these objects and others may also have been selected for their physical or aesthetic properties (Hosler 1994; Pollard 2001; Pollard and Ruggles 2001)—as in the conundrum of a rock that looks like a shell in the case of the many fossils. Unlike the distant objects in Central America, these were not used within a prestige-goods economy, but in ritual consumption. They may be better viewed as a "gathering together" (Bradley 1990, 1998) of objects from multiple sources, marking what Pollard (this volume) calls a geography of social relationships or what Chapman (2000a) calls enchainment, linking people together through time.

Court kivas overlap in size with great kivas but do not have the same floor features. They do show a similar range of materials in dedicatory offerings (Tables 5.4 and 5.5), such as the one from Kiva D at Pueblo Bonito, where a white *Laevicardium* shell was nested inside a masonry box below the floor. Within the shell were worked and unworked shell and minerals, including four species of colorful shells along with azurite, turquoise, and hematite minerals. All were either finished ornaments or materials used in ornament production and from different areas of the Southwest. The selection of these materials is striking, as is the citation to all six of the colors used in historically documented Pueblo directional symbolism (for example, Cushing 1883; see also DeBoer 2005). The use of color as a geographical mnemonic linked people to places—an example of the spatiality of memory work.

Even the smallest ceremonial rooms had dedicatory offerings, but surprisingly, these room block kivas showed remarkable redundancy in their contents. Roofs in the Chacoan style room block kivas were built criblike, beginning on low pilasters. Each of the pilasters contained a short log in which offerings were placed before the roof was constructed. A small hollow was made in the pilaster logs, the offerings were placed inside, and then the receptacles were capped with sandstone or wood lids. The offerings, such as those from Room 161 at Pueblo Bonito, are primarily beads, production debris, or unworked turquoise. Each pilaster contained only a handful's worth, but they are highly similar from pilaster to pilaster and from room block kiva to room block kiva throughout the site.

These different architectural spaces at Chaco are where performances were shared and "different forms of community" (Joyce and Hendon 2000) were made into historical facts. Each of the structures was used by a different network of people. The relationship of spatial proxemics to ceremonial performance might initially suggest that depositional practices in smaller spaces should be more variable than those that took place in larger spaces, but the Chaco room block kivas go against this expectation. Like the redundancy in the features themselves, the offerings are highly standardized from structure to structure. They illustrate a shared habitus—and a shared understanding and performance of what should be done in the construction of social memories associated with the dedication and termination of ritual structures that crosscut their membership. Like the practice of constructing the highly redundant forms of the structures themselves, including their internal arrangement of features, the practice of placing objects within architectural cavities was formalized through repeated construction and dedication. The frequency of building and

TABLE 5-4
Ritual Deposits in Court Kivas

Site	Kiva	Feature	Objects	Offering Type	Date (CE)	Reference
Chetro Ketl	Court kiva	Floor pit (sipapu?)	Unworked and worked turquoise, two white quartz pebbles, two brachiopods, several small bird bones, limestone polishing stone.	Dedicatory	Early 1000s	Vivian and Reiter (1960)
Pueblo Bonito	Kiva D	Masonry box in floor	*Glycymeris* bracelets and fragments, hematite cylinder, *olivella* shell, unworked and worked azurite, figure-8 shell beads, *Haliotis* shell, worked turquoise, worked *spondylus* shell.	Dedicatory	1000s?	Judd (1954:Plate 89); Judd (1964:184–186)
Pueblo Bonito	Kiva R	Pilasters and/or ceiling (2 deposits)	Bill of redhead duck (*Nyoca americana*); bone, shell, turquoise beads; broken pendants; shell bracelets (*Glycymeris* sp.).	Dedicatory	1000s?	Judd (1964:191–193); Judd (1954:322)
Pueblo Bonito	Kiva R	Wall niche	Shell trumpet (*Murex* sp.), black-on-white bowl.	Ritual retirement	1000s?	Judd (1964:192); Judd (1954:Plate 82, a and b)
Pueblo del Arroyo	Kiva C	Pilasters 1–8	*Olivella* shell beads, turquoise beads and pendants, unworked turquoise and shell (see Table 5.5 for a more complete list).	Dedicatory	Mid-late 1000s (tree-ring date of 1067 + x)	Judd (1959:60–62)
Pueblo del Arroyo	Kiva C	Fill above bench	Prairie falcon (*Falco mexicanus*).	Termination?	Late 1000s	Judd (1959:63–64)

TABLE 5.5

Contents of Offerings in Pilasters, Kiva C (Court Kiva), Pueblo del Arroyo

Pilaster No.	Number of Objects	Description
1	30	*Olivella* shell beads and fragments
	27	Oblong and figure-8 beads and fragments
	9	Discoidal beads and fragments
	10	Turquoise fragments
	1	Sandstone cover
2	12	Oblong and figure-8 beads
	2	Discoidal beads
	1	Turquoise pendant fragment
3	20	*Olivella* beads and fragments
	11	Oblong and figure-8 beads
	7	Abalone shell fragments
	3	Turquoise fragments
	1	Rib fragment, deer or antelope
4	2	Discoidal beads
	1	Turquoise pendant
5	18	*Olivella* beads and fragments
	26	Oblong and figure-8 beads and fragments
	6	Discoidal beads
	5	Abalone shell fragments
	2	Turquoise pendants and fragment
	3	Turquoise fragments
	1	"Cylindrical shell (?) bead, cross-drilled"
6	16	*Olivella* beads and fragments
	32	Oblong and figure-8 beads and fragments
	9	Discoidal beads and fragments
	1	Chama bead fragment
	2	Shell fragments
	4	Turquoise pendants and fragments
	6	Turquoise fragments
7	13	*Olivella* beads and fragments
	13	Oblong and figure-8 beads and fragments
	1	Discoidal bead
	1	Turquoise pendant fragment
8	5	*Olivella* beads
	70	Oblong and figure-8 beads and fragments
	7	Discoidal beads and fragments
	1	Oval shell bead fragment
	8	Discoidal turquoise beads
	7	Discoidal turquoise bead fragments
	4	Turquoise pendants and fragments
	1	Turquoise tessara
	47	Turquoise chips

From Judd (1959:61–62).

rebuilding of these structures made these ritual practices canonical, a process in which strategies channelized practices (de Certeau 1984).

Although small in numbers, the contents of the room block kiva dedicatory offerings are like shorthand references to the larger deposits found in the court kivas and great kivas. In the case of the room block kivas, the performance of placing materials in the pilasters was a citation to the construction and dedication of larger structures—as well as previous structures of the same kind—linking people to different sites of memory within the canyon. Those sites of memory were other structures within the same building, such as Pueblo Bonito, but also other round structures within the canyon and its outlying great house communities.

The linkages between ornaments in ceremonial structures are also citations to what was considered the proper way to adorn a body, animating the ritual structure. Many strands of beads are depicted as hanging on kiva walls in later Pueblo IV–period murals, such as at Pottery Mound's Kiva 2 (Hibben 1975:Figure 17), attesting to the long-lived importance of ornaments in Pueblo ceremonial life and their use in dressing ceremonial rooms. In contemporary Pueblo society, jewelry is worn by individuals, but especially large pieces adorn kachinas. Jewelry is also worn by houses in Pueblo society. At Zuni, when dedicating a new house at Shalako, it is important to cover the walls with textiles and to hang the house's interior with jewelry. This makes the house beautiful and gives the house its identity.

These practices, seen in contemporary Pueblo society, can be traced to the numerous offerings containing shell, turquoise, jet, and other ornaments in Chaco Canyon buildings. Collectively, they show the importance of certain structures and afford glimpses of the materiality of Chacoan ritual practice. Ceremonial houses were adorned and made ready for use by depositing or "forgetting" ornaments in caches that marked the dedication and renewal of structures. Like the New Guinea malanggan, strands of beads and other ornaments were "produced to be discarded" (Strathern 2001:259) in Chacoan kivas. However, unlike the malanggan, they were secreted away rather than destroyed.

The entire process from production through deposition involved the producers in the process of memory construction. This process began with the planning and conception of the deposits that would be included, and continued with the acquisition of materials, the working of the stone or shell, the carrying of the beads to places where they were deposited, and their placement in kiva features that were then sealed off from view. Because of their association with ritual production, unworked turquoise, shell, and other materials, and the debris of production, were treated as equals of the finished products—not merely leftover bits or pieces, but part of the materiality of ritual practice. Although the presence of production debris is often interpreted as evidence of where the production took place, when the debris is found in sealed spaces within structures, it is clear that these spaces were not exactly where the materials were transformed into finished products, but where highly valued objects were placed because they were considered to be as valuable or inalienable as the finished objects. Their close association with other incorporative activities of memory construction was part of their consubstantiality, conferring value through the linkages made as parts of rituals of dedication.

THE MEMORIALIZATION OF PEOPLE AND PLACES

A second set of deposits at Chaco illustrates additional ways in which memory and materiality were linked through depositional practice. A significant number of artifacts recovered from Pueblo Bonito and Chetro Ketl were used in ceremonial contexts but intentionally placed in rooms and then left behind when the occupants moved out. Many of them are preserved because the rooms had been intentionally sealed, while others were preserved because of their placement deep within the buildings.

Some of these room assemblages also contained mortuary deposits, which, as Nancy Akins noted, occur in two major clusters within Pueblo Bonito (Akins 2003; Neitzel 2003a, 2003b). Because human remains were present in nearby rooms, many of these objects have been interpreted as mortuary deposits. However, these deposits represent a range of depositional practices, some of which include the memorialization of ancestors. Other deposits more clearly were the result of other kinds of practices, such as the ritual retirement of powerful objects, the termination of ritual societies, and perhaps even the termination of the buildings themselves.[1] To distinguish among these different pathways, I look at some of the most well-known of the "caches" at Pueblo Bonito and Chetro Ketl to point out different ways that certain people, social groups, and perhaps a larger collective of Chaco were memorialized through the discard of large numbers of inalienable objects during moments of forgetting.[2]

The closing off of spaces associated with the death of a ritual leader is not unknown in Pueblo societies historically or today. For example, there is a room in Zuni Pueblo that was sealed upon the death of a particularly prominent religious leader. He had used the room as his retreat—a place to go to prepare for his participation in different ceremonies. What is particularly interesting about these closed-off spaces is that many people remember where they are long after the room has been sealed. One room near the retreat, completely sealed, was recently reopened when extensive renovations were done in the village. The intact roof was dated to the late 1690s, almost immediately after the Pueblo Revolt ended in 1692. Although this example was relatively recent, there are other similar spaces that had been in the collective memory of residents of Zuni Pueblo from previous room closures. These examples show that room spaces in early established parts of long-occupied pueblos are often the spaces that are considered to be most sacred, especially when associated with specific persons, and may resonate in the social memories of a pueblo's residents.

In addition to these rooms, historic and contemporary pueblos contain other rooms where inalienable items used in individual and corporate rituals are stored (Beaglehole 1937; Mills 2000). While individually owned items are usually buried with the deceased, collectively owned items are passed down from one generation to another through flexible kinship networks that ensure the perpetuation of the religious society. These networks are often retained within specific lineages, and thus certain ceremonial objects may be associated with particular houses over several generations. Senior male members of the house are responsible for their guardianship, but senior female members may ceremonially feed them. The participation of household members in different societies as well as the relative ranking of different societies reproduces household status. Those households responsible for the maintenance of key ceremonial objects accrue considerable prestige. In this sense, storage is a situated practice (Hendon 2000) that contributes to social memory within the confines of designated spaces.

In multistoried pueblo buildings, such as Zuni Pueblo, ceremonial storage rooms are typically less accessible and located in back of living and other domestic rooms. In part this is because of the way that pueblo architectural additions are constructed with new living rooms on the exterior of the room block, but also because it is important to limit access to these rooms. Visitors and even some members of the household cannot view these objects because they are considered too dangerous. Some objects are considered to be so powerful that they are stored in ceramic vessels in these rooms (Mills 2004). Altar pieces of different ritual sodalities, such as medicine societies, are also stored in these rooms and then reassembled in ceremonial rooms when in use. These objects are not discarded but restored and repainted when needed. They are not generally buried with individuals because they are not individually owned. In Pueblo society, these are among the best examples of inalienable possessions (Weiner 1992) because they cannot be bought or sold; they belong to the group and are inherited to ensure the continuity of the society. Again, it would be unusual for these items to enter the archaeological record at all.

Given the ways in which collectively owned inalienable possessions are passed down in historic and contemporary Pueblo society, it is therefore surprising to see such large numbers of these items at Chaco. The quantity of material that by anyone's criteria can be called ritual or inalienable objects at Chaco Canyon sites far exceeds that from any other area of the Southwest. Collectively owned ceremonial objects such as altar pieces are present, but rare, from most other archaeological contexts across the entire Ancestral Pueblo area (Mills 2004).

The most spectacular of those at Chaco is a cache of wooden ritual artifacts found in a second-story room at the back of Chetro Ketl (Vivian et al. 1978). They were serendipitously found much later than Hewett's School of American Research/University of New Mexico excavations at the site, and only because a large area of the pueblo was undercut by a flood in the mid-twentieth century and required stabilization. Covering the floor of one room were hundreds of fragments of painted wood. Many of them had been broken, but when pieced together they are primarily parts of altars, headdresses, and wooden staffs and wands.

Besides the Chetro Ketl cache, it is clear that Pueblo Bonito has more objects that appear to have been ritually retired than any other site in the canyon, if not the rest of the Southwest. In contrast to all other great houses, Pueblo Bonito seems even more unusual than it did when the original excavators, Neil Judd (1954, 1964) and George Pepper (1920), reported their findings.

Besides the cache of objects that appears to have been ritually retired in Room 93 at Chetro Ketl, many other examples from Pueblo Bonito suggest the retirement of collectively owned objects. Two of these rooms, Rooms 10 and 13, contained the remains of many objects that are not clearly associated with individuals, including objects used in ornament and tool production, altar pieces, and whole and fragmentary shell trumpets (Pepper 1920:54–57, 67–69). Altar pieces and shell trumpets suggest use by a group, rather than an individual, and the large number of objects apparently intentionally broken in Room 10 is particularly interesting. Rooms 10 and 13 are both in the earliest-constructed portion of Pueblo Bonito, which dates to the 890s CE (Windes 2003:Figure 3.4). However, both were apparently left open and used for at least another 300 years before the final residents left.

Room 32, also in the north-central portion of Pueblo Bonito, contained over 300 wooden staffs, a wooden "design" board, many personal

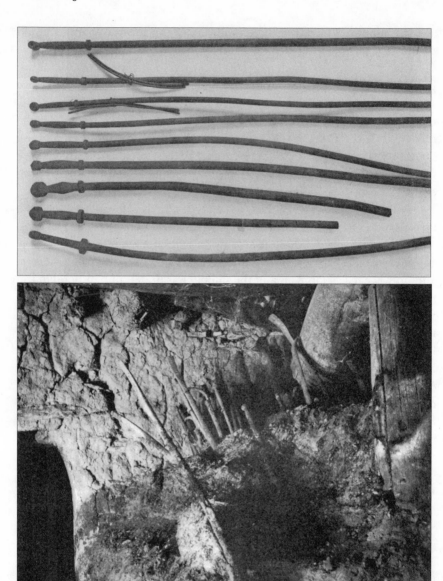

FIGURE 5.5
Wooden sticks from Room 32, Pueblo Bonito. After Pepper (1920:Figures 52 and 53).

ornaments, and whole vessels (Pepper 1920:129–163; Plog 2003; Figure
5.5). Although wooden staffs of office have been interpreted as individually
owned, they are usually present archaeologically only in small numbers,
and all are from mortuary contexts, such as the Magician's Burial near

Flagstaff (McGregor 1943). At least one burial is present in this room, associated with a cloth-covered cactus stalk that resembles a badge of office. The staffs, also considered to be badges of office in historic Pueblo society, were found in a different portion of the room, however, and their numbers are out of proportion with the single burial. One would expect one or a few staffs with an individual, like the Magician's Burial. Instead, the staffs seem to represent the collective insignia of office of many members of a ritual society—not just one. In addition, the painted wooden board is a probable altar piece and would be considered to be collectively owned according to historic Pueblo practices. The room in which these objects were left was constructed and used between 1150 and 1250. The last use would have been during the Late Bonito period (and even into the post-Bonito period), when very few rooms were still in use at Pueblo Bonito.

Room 32 is adjacent to Room 33, a room with multiple burials that contained more objects than any other room at Pueblo Bonito (Neitzel 2003a). Together with Rooms 53 and 56 they are considered to be the north burial cluster, containing 24–28 different individuals (Akins 2003:Table 8.1, Figure 8.1). The number of human remains and the large number of ritual items suggested to Akins that these were the burials of highly ranked individuals with ascribed statuses based on ritual positions within the Pueblo Bonito hierarchy. The close biological affinity of the remains suggested to her some degree of familial relatedness, one that was different from the biological grouping in the west burial cluster. A recent reanalysis of the excavation notes by Heitman and Plog (2006) shows that there are both primary and secondary burials in Room 33. The ritual retirement of these items suggests the memorialization of these individuals and the place, and, as they argue, evidence of a "house society" (in the sense of Joyce and Gillespie 2000; see also Heitman and Plog 2005). The practice of placing objects in these rooms may have been a link to the founding families of Pueblo Bonito (such as discussed by Pauketat for the Southeast, this volume), whose remains were curated and redeposited in one of the oldest portions of the pueblo as part of the practice of ancestor veneration (see also Nielsen, this volume).

The cache of cylinder jars from Room 28 at Pueblo Bonito more clearly falls into the category of ritual retirement unassociated with human remains (Figure 5.6). This room was constructed early in the building's history and has later tree-ring dates of 1071 and 1116 (http://www.chaco archive.org/docs/dendrochronology.xls, accessed March 6, 2006). According to Windes (2003), the room remained in use until as late as 1150 to 1250 (and therefore into the post-Bonito period). In addition to the

FIGURE 5.6
Cache of cylinder jars in Room 28, Pueblo Bonito. After Pepper (1920:Figure 43).

cylinder jars were sandstone jar covers, fragments of *Murex* shell trumpets, hammered copper, ceramic bowls and jars, ornaments, and many other objects (Pepper 1920:129–163). Of those vessels that were painted, the decoration was in a style that has been dated to 1040 to 1125 CE (Toll 1990:285).

Crown and Wills (2003) observe that many of the cylinder jars were refurbished and compare these vessels to kivas during the Bonito phase. They interpret the intentional reslipping, repainting, and refiring of cylinder jars as symbolic of their use within rituals of renewal, similar to the way that ritual structures were renewed:

> By renewing these vessels through time, Chacoans maintained their continuity with the past while giving the vessels a new appearance. The hidden layers of designs probably added to the power of the latest design. Renewed by labor, imagination, slip, paint, and fuel, the vessels became repositories of collective memory and historical continuity between past and present. (Crown and Wills 2003:525)

Moreover, they draw on the idea that these pottery and kiva renewal rituals were ways in which identity was being maintained during a period of rapid change and population influx. These are examples of acts of forgetting through the painting over of ceramic surfaces and the rebuilding of structures that are closely associated with the production of ritual memories at different social scales.

As Toll (2001:63) has noted, the cylinder jars were made by many different producers and were probably brought to Chaco from different communities as representations of "membership in the community of communities" at Chaco during ritual pilgrimages. Unlike other caches of inalienable objects from Pueblo Bonito that were placed within interior rooms, Room 28 is adjacent to the western plaza. When these jars were taken out of the room, they would have been highly visible, and the room's proximity to the plaza and the number of jars suggest that their use was in this open space rather than in the room itself. Although other ritual caches at the site marked the termination of particular societies, memorialized the death of prominent leaders in lineages that maintained important ritual societies, or were part of a depositional practice associated with the maintenance of the "house," the use and deposition of the cylinder jars was a unique expression of Ancestral Pueblo materiality. The use of these vessels continued until the early twelfth-century reorganization, perhaps terminated by Pueblo Bonito's last ceremonial community, consisting of a dwindling population in the late 1100s.

REMEMBERING WHILE FORGETTING IN THE PUEBLO WORLD

Objects found at Chaco had entangled histories (N. Thomas 1991)— associated with specific persons and their ritual offices, and used in multiple social fields. The deposition of large numbers of objects used in ritualizing practices, whether they were left in architectural cavities within ritual structures, interred with ritual leaders, or left behind in ritual storage rooms, was ceremonial discard on a grand order. These objects were placed out of sight during practices of dedication, renewal, memorialization, ritual retirement, and structure termination. Dedicatory and renewal practices were mostly in round rooms, used by ceremonial groups of different sizes. Objects used in ceremonial practices were stored in rectangular mortuary rooms and ritual storerooms within the pueblo. Burial clusters were used over long periods of time, some as long as 200 years or more, as the cumulative repositories of ritual items associated with specific areas of the site and with specific social groups. Still other objects were deposited in ritual storerooms during the life of the site when the pueblos' residents moved to other sites and/or the societies no longer were extant. Variation in the kinds of materials left in these storerooms, and in the different locations and accessibility of these rooms, suggests their use in different forms of ceremonial practice and what was considered to be of value to those who deposited them.

These forms of practice also illustrate the range of ways in which forgetting was a part of Chacoan memory work. Objects that were set into architectural spaces and then sealed, such as in kiva niches and pilasters, were placed out of sight and "forgotten" as part of the practice of secrecy. They memorialized the structures and were part of the materiality of Chaco ritual in ways that have been well described by Connerton (1989) as the process of inscription. The meters of shell beads that were placed in some of these spaces, such as the great kiva at Chetro Ketl, were once highly visual artifacts that inscribed the value of the structures in the memories of those who participated and would have been remembered in subsequent ritual performances, despite being no longer visible. Smaller ritual structures received fewer and less visually performative objects, but even the smallest kivas contained shell, turquoise, and other materials that ornamented the foundations of the roof and the spaces in which altars were erected.

The intentional placement of large quantities of collectively owned objects with and near the members of high-ranking lineages at Pueblo Bonito also marks moments of remembering while forgetting. In this case, personal objects were placed with the deceased to reaffirm the position of their descendents. In other cases, collectively owned ritual objects either reached a point where they could not be renewed, or the societies in which they were used were no longer extant. Their ritual retirement was through discard in spaces considered different from more mundane locations. The stacking of hundreds of ceremonial staffs of office in the corner of one of the adjacent rooms was a way of marking the importance of those who were buried there. They would have been seen, and perhaps even used, by family members each time the room was accessed in new acts of deposition and burial in the adjacent room. These crypts and the objects that they contained were places long remembered in the history of the site as evidenced by the repeated deposition of objects and people in the same areas of the site over many generations.

Another kind of forgetting was the intentional leaving behind of objects used in collective rituals, not in burial chambers, but in their storage rooms. No other site in the Southwest has as many of these rooms as Pueblo Bonito, nor so many deposits of inalienable objects. The cache at the nearby site of Chetro Ketl is exceptional for that site; together the remains from Chetro Ketl and Pueblo Bonito represent numerous cases of ritual retirement of ceremonial objects. I doubt that the presence of these objects was quickly forgotten by the sites' residents. Much as the empty rooms at Zuni were still remembered for several generations, even though sealed off and in some cases deeply buried within a mound of more recent rooms, the placement of powerful objects in these rooms would have ensured they were remembered by the pueblos' residents for many generations. The fact that many of these objects were interpreted by their excavators as intentionally broken before the rooms were naturally filled with sand and the walls of the structures collapsed is particularly intriguing in light of what we know about the end of the Pax Chaco and the sudden reorganization of Chaco society that led to its depopulation by the middle of the twelfth century. The breakage of these items may have been a "past mastering" on the part of those who were the last to leave or later visitors eager to rewrite the history of Chaco before it was buried.

A final form of forgetting may not have involved the residential population at all. At the end of Pueblo Bonito's use, residents from other sites and perhaps even outside the canyon continued to use the plaza and many of the kivas that ring the plaza. At least one ritual storage room was associated with this late use, in which objects that have no obvious precedents or antecedents—the ceramic cylinder jars—were brought out to be used in the plaza or in the plaza kivas. The objects marked the participation of multiple groups in the memory work of a larger community. Their final placement in a storage room commemorated this participation and the building itself. When these rituals were terminated, the objects were left behind as material manifestations of ritual engagements that were not needed in the next place, memorializing the building itself. Together, the deposits of dedication and termination illustrate the active ways in which people engaged with objects and how remembering and forgetting were part of the memory work of past and present societies.

Although the specific locations may not have remained part of Pueblo social memory, the practices at Chaco were reproduced by Pueblo society members at later sites throughout the Southwest. Painted wood, the deposition of turquoise, the use of shell and other materials from far-off places, and color symbolism are still important parts of Pueblo ritual practices today. In this way, they fit with Connerton's other process of social memory construction—incorporation. They became fundamental parts of ceremonial ritual practice through repeated social practices at multiple scales and were replicated at other settlements across the Ancestral Pueblo landscape.

The practices that I have described are part of long traditions of material practices within the Southwest. The memory of Chaco also resides in the historical narratives of contemporary Native Americans in the Southwest. As

Leigh Kuwanwisiwma (2004) recounts, Chaco Canyon is the place called Yupköyvi to the Hopi. Not all clans trace their migration pathways from or through Chaco. Of those that do, there is a history of clan order and particularly memorable places where ceremonies were performed. This history, recounted over 800 years later, demonstrates the efficacy of Pueblo ways of remembering while forgetting, and how the Chacoan past became the present.

Acknowledgments

Many thanks to the American Museum of Natural History, and especially David Hurst Thomas, Lori Pendleton Thomas, and Anibal Rodriguez for facilitating my study of the Pueblo Bonito materials excavated by George Pepper. Very helpful comments were provided by my fellow seminarians at SAR and by T. J. Ferguson, Julia Hendon, Steve Plog, Bob Preucel, Ruth Van Dyke, and Chip Wills. I also appreciate invitations from Stanford University and the University of California at Berkeley to present this work and to talk to colleagues and students about the ideas presented in this chapter.

Notes

1. The retirement of ritual structures could also be approached in this way through the analysis of animal sacrifices found in the fill and in features. Hill (2000) compiles some of this data across the Southwest, and Creel and Anyon (2003) discuss this for Mimbres structures. Because of the lack of screening and the excavation methods used at Chaco for the earliest and most extensive excavations, the presence of these kinds of termination rituals are more difficult to identify, though they may be accessible through detailed analysis of the field notes.

2. I use the term "moments" recognizing that this term does not reflect the continuous phenomena that practice really is. However, many archaeological deposits do represent events rather than the kinds of depositional practices that would produce a more continuous record.

6

History in Practice

Ritual Deposition at La Venta Complex A

Susan D. Gillespie

Archaeologists need constant reminders of the biases impacting their interpretations, including from such mundane technologies as mapmaking and illustration (for example, Bradley 1997). Even with well-established conventions for depicting three-dimensional space in two dimensions, opportunities for erroneous readings abound. But beyond difficulties in our graphic systems of representation are more profound biases concerning what the artifacts and features we map and draw signify to us. In normative and processual archaeologies, archaeological remains have been considered to represent actions reflective of preexisting beliefs, values, and customs, or to result from adaptive and cultural processes (Joyce, this volume). In contrast, a practice perspective (Bourdieu 1977; Giddens 1984) focuses on actions not as the outcomes or representations of processes but as those processes themselves (for example, Pauketat 2001:85). The ontology and value of objects is dependent on their performative contexts and engagements with human actors, and not solely on their physical qualities (Mills, Pollard, this volume). Process generates form, rather than the reverse (Ingold 1995:58). Beliefs and values are instantiated in social interactions, all of which involve some degree of materiality (Gosden 1999:120; Thomas 1999b:71). Thus, instead of being reduced to an "archaeological record," in this perspective materiality is investigated as the media for and outcome of social action (Barrett 2001:153).

Much of this rethinking of representation—in terms of both our maps and our notions of the archaeological record—has come about through the study of ancient landscapes. Landscapes are "systems of reference" that make human action "intelligible in terms of other past and future acts" (Thomas 2001:174; see Ingold's [1993] "taskscape"). Although each generation is born into a landscape, their practices reproduce it via their "inhabitation" of it (Barrett 1999; Ingold's [1995] "dwelling perspective"). What the archaeologist may see and draw as a static arrangement of structures and features on a Cartesian grid, often meant to be viewed from an omniscient "god's eye" perspective, was a dynamic, lived landscape to the inhabitants, who shaped it by their actions even as those actions were shaped by the landscape. In an "archaeology of inhabitation...the material no longer simply represents the consequence of processes which we need to discover but becomes instead the historically constituted and necessary conditions of a world inhabited, interpreted, and acted upon" (Barrett 1999:257).

The site of La Venta, Mexico, exemplifies how this shift in focus toward examining the historically constituted world—in terms of landscape as a system of references for the intelligibility of practices—can provide a radically different perspective on the past. Complex A, La Venta's famous ceremonial precinct excavated over 50 years ago, is known to archaeological audiences as a series of images that have achieved iconic status because they are continually reproduced in publications, forming "an important part of the way we know" the site (Jones 2001:338). These images include a single site plan of the architecture, abstract mosaic faces made of serpentine blocks, caches of jade and serpentine celts arranged in cruciform shapes, and an assortment of anthropomorphic figurines positioned to form a tableau (Offering 4). The value of the objects deposited at La Venta has been assessed archaeologically in terms of such static factors as the raw material, distance from source locations, quantity, and inherent symbolic meanings.

To the archaeological mind-set, these synchronic representations have overshadowed the complex processes of ritual deposition in Complex A that, transpiring over several centuries, produced those forms. Moving beyond these passive images to understand the practices that shaped that sacred place reveals new insights on social processes, particularly the role of memory and forgetting in forging the intersubjectivity of people and the landscape, and of the present with the past.

LA VENTA AS A STUDY OF REPRESENTATIONS

La Venta, situated near the Gulf Coast in Tabasco state, was one of the most important primate centers of the Formative period Olmec culture in Mesoamerica. Its principal period of occupation was the Middle Formative (ca. 900–400 BC uncalibrated). The area designated Complex A is just north of the great earthen pyramid that dominates La Venta's large civic-ceremonial zone. It consists of a walled precinct (the "Ceremonial Court") with low clay and adobe-brick platforms both within and adjacent to that enclosure. Complex A was excavated in the 1940s (Stirling 1940, 1943a, 1943b; Drucker 1952) and again in 1955 with a major project directed by Drucker and Heizer (Drucker et al. 1959). The area was badly disturbed by development projects and looting after 1955 (Drucker and Heizer 1965: 62–63), and little else has been excavated at La Venta (González Lauck 1996). The Complex A excavations therefore continue to dominate under-standings of La Venta and the Olmecs more generally (for example, Diehl 2004; Evans 2004).

The formal plan of Complex A exhibits unusual bilateral symmetry not found at the rest of the site (Diehl 1981:78; Figure 6.1). The Ceremonial Court has three interior low platforms—the Northeast, Northwest, and South-Central—and its southern boundary is marked by the Southeast and Southwest platforms. Four lateral mounds are equidistant from a north-south ("centerline") axis that runs through the center of the South-Central Platform, the court itself, and Mounds A-2 and A-3, respectively north and south of the court. The same centerline also bisects the great pyramid (Mound C-1) at the southern edge of Complex A. In 1942 and 1943 trench-ing that north-south line revealed a great number of exotic buried objects, including those found in what appeared to be rich graves (Drucker 1952:Figure 14).

Figure 6.1 is the sole published plan view of all the architecture, fea-tures, and buried objects found through 1955 (Drucker et al. 1959:Figure 4 [Figure 3 is a simplified version of Figure 4, and the frontispiece is a per-spective drawing]). What cannot be determined from this plan view is the long span of use of Complex A and the changes it underwent over several centuries: how the mounds were gradually enlarged with thin resurfacings of colored clay, the court floor was built up with tons of clay and sand, pits were dug—some of them massive—and thousands of crafted exotic objects were buried in them and sometimes later removed. The different episodes of construction and later modification are conflated in this one drawing. Mounds A-2 and A-3 were eroded, rounded knolls in the 1940s, and they were so mapped, although their original form was rectilinear. In contrast,

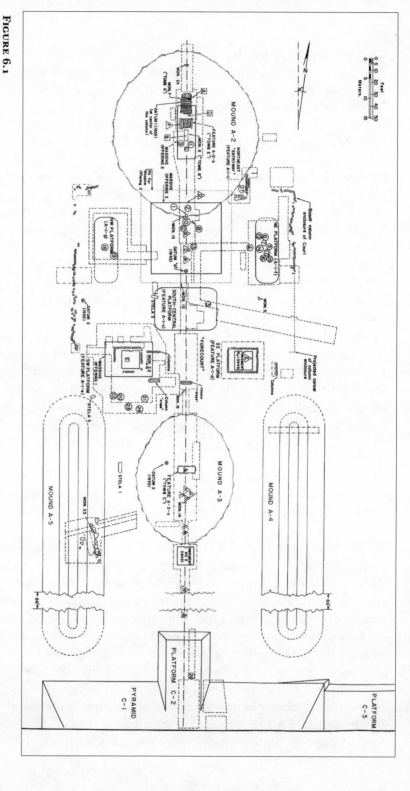

FIGURE 6.1

Plan of La Venta Complex A, indicating the locations of all offerings and excavations (Drucker et al. 1959:Figure 4). Dashed lines indicate excavation units in 1942–1943 and 1955. Symbols for offerings are based on year of discovery: square for 1942, triangle for 1943, circle for 1955. Government Printing Office, Washington, DC.

some platforms were subsurface, buried under drift sand, and their dimensions were reconstructed by trenching. Since 1959 renderings of Complex A have virtually always reproduced this plan, showing the mounds at these different points in time, two in their eroded condition alongside other architecture in pristine condition.[1] With this representation, Complex A was flattened in time.

One reason for creating a single surface plan map was that the excavators used trenches rather than clearing operations, a procedure not conducive to level-by-level plan views, which would have shown changes to the Ceremonial Court over time. To serve the latter purpose, the excavators published profile views of their trenches. These should have provided the important information on the history of this ritual landscape, given that Drucker and Heizer (Drucker and Heizer 1965; Drucker et al. 1959) distinguished four successive building phases (I–IV) for the Ceremonial Court. Although they were considered exemplary at the time (for example, Coe 1960:119; MacNeish 1960:296), these drawings have been difficult to interpret. The profiles were published at different scales, the horizontal and vertical scales are usually not the same in a single drawing, and many drawings lack datums or other reference points (Coe and Stuckenrath 1964:4; Figure 6.2). Because some details are schematic, especially the thin layers of clay on the platforms and floor that were rarely accurately recorded (Heizer 1964:46), it is impossible to line up one drawing with the next in the same trench. The different strata are not labeled according to construction phase; that information is buried in the text.

However, the flattening of La Venta cannot be blamed on graphic conventions alone. A fundamental premise of the excavators' understanding of Complex A is the continuity over centuries of a formal plan for the architecture and buried offerings oriented to the centerline axis (Drucker 1981; Drucker and Heizer 1965). Drucker and Heizer concluded that La Venta was a "one-period site that exhibits four successive building periods" (Heizer 1959:178). They assumed that through all its phases, construction did not deviate from the design principles of the original conception, dominated by a north-south orientation (Drucker and Heizer 1965:41; Drucker et al. 1959:124). Such persistence in ritual practices lent a general sense of sameness to what they presumed were centuries of occupation (Drucker and Heizer 1965:64).

Political organization was similarly assumed to be static, with either priests (Heizer 1960, 1961, 1962) or a long-lived dynasty of secular rulers (Drucker 1981) exerting strong control of the populace during the entire use-life of Complex A. Only in its last phase, IV, were "large tombs and sar-

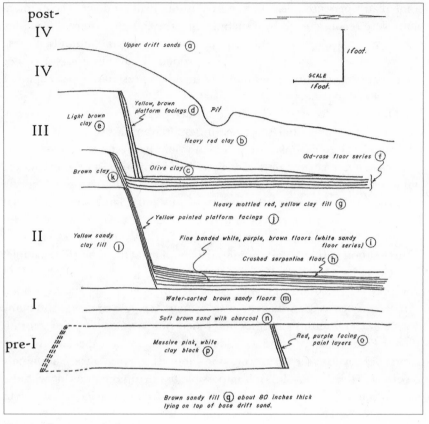

FIGURE 6.2

North-south profile of the Northwest Platform, 1955 excavations (Drucker et al. 1959:Figure 20). Phase designations have been added. Government Printing Office, Washington, DC.

cophagi" (Heizer 1960:220) placed in Complex A, suggesting a "top-heavy" social structure that could not or would not be supported by the general population. This political development was believed to have precipitated the abandonment of the Ceremonial Court and La Venta itself after Phase IV (Drucker et al. 1959:127).

There is an interplay of remembering and forgetting embedded in the archaeological interpretations of La Venta, although these processes are rarely explicitly acknowledged (see Mills, this volume). The "staggering" effort and cost (Diehl 2004:74) evident in La Venta's buried wealth has been considered an "incredible waste" of exotic, finely crafted items (Coe 1968:61, 63) dedicated to the veneration of enigmatic gods. Three large abstract faces made of hundreds of worked serpentine blocks were laid in pits and almost immediately covered with clay, as if part of "a cult, or secret, burial of the spirit of the totemic gods" (Piña Chan 1989:176). Drucker and Heizer (1956:367, 370) mused: "As baffling as any single fact about the Olmec is the passion they had for burying their most treasured structures and possessions...apparently almost as soon as they were completed.... Were they mad?" The common opinion is one of waste and conspicuous consumption associated with rendering the objects invisible—hence forgotten (if truly "wasted")—but it is paradoxically juxtaposed with notions of secrecy and exclusivity, which imply unequally shared memories.

While altogether these actions were thought to manifest possible collective insanity, order and systemic control have also been assumed in the interpretations of La Venta. Drucker (1981:30) believed that a state-level society with centralized political authority is evident in the ability to accomplish "long-term projects, such as the four-century progressive construction of the A, B, and C complexes at La Venta, adhering all the while to the centerline orientation." This scenario implies recourse to a dominant memory of orthodox principles of ritual deposition, along with a profound desire to make the present continuous or equivalent with the past.

Memory must also have played a role in Offering 4, an arrangement of small stone anthropomorphic figurines set against a line of upright celts that create a backdrop for the scene. The excavators believed that the offering, once covered with clay, was later dug up partway, exposing the figurine heads enough to be "inspected" by certain persons. The stratigraphy suggests that a small pit was excavated directly from above the buried objects and then refilled (Drucker and Heizer 1956:367; Drucker and Heizer 1965:61; Drucker et al. 1959:152–161). Some archaeologists believe records must have been kept or surface markers placed to remind the caretakers of Complex A of the locations of certain buried caches (Coe 1968:66; Drucker and Heizer 1956:367, 374; Drucker et al. 1959:132)—that is, presuming that human memory would have been insufficient and forgetting was not an option.

Drucker and Heizer's two important conclusions from the 1955 project can therefore be summarized as follows: first, Complex A was built according to a formal plan that remained unchanged for centuries due to the control of a single dominating authority; and second, the clay platforms with their buried offerings were produced by the continuous actions of elite caretakers, who engaged in regular practices of ritual deposition over many generations, resulting in four distinct building phases. However, the second interpretation, having to do with performance, should call into question the likelihood of the first, which is premised upon certain representations. Drucker and Heizer (1965:64) emphasized the sameness and symmetry of ritual depositional practices in Complex A over time—an "obvious continuity" from Phases I to IV—against critics who wanted to claim that only the last phase was truly "Olmec" (Drucker and Heizer 1965:65). Nevertheless, the evidence they reported reveals asymmetry in the early construction phases that, though slight, may have eventually resulted in a profound change in the court's plan over time, possibly as the result of contestation and conflict, despite what looks like adherence to a centerline orientation dictated from the very beginning.

In contrast with the static images and unchanging quality assumed for La Venta, I take a diachronic approach to the Complex A data to consider how practices of ritual deposition built a sacred landscape that shaped its caretakers even as their actions transformed that place. My purpose is not to criticize the pioneering archaeologists of La Venta; on the contrary, I hope to rescue some of their findings, which have been disregarded. I utilize an interpretive perspective that considers the consequences over time of the performance of ritual practices, the role played by materiality and social memory in these practices, and their enactment within a dynamic orienting landscape. This approach implicates consequences for social organization and political strategies of the builders of Complex A (as did Heizer and Drucker's interpretations) and how those strategies may have changed through time, despite the dearth of archaeological evidence on domestic activities and residences at La Venta. Treating ritual as a context for both reproduction and transformation of sociopolitical relations (Stahl, this volume), I suggest that the Complex A landscape played an agentive role in La Venta society as sociopolitical organization may have changed in concert with, and as a consequence of, the processes of building this ceremonial precinct.

A BIOGRAPHICAL SKETCH OF THE CEREMONIAL COURT

A diachronic perspective can be achieved via a biography of the Ceremonial Court and its associated mounds, based on the premise that "as people and objects gather time, movement and change, they are constantly transformed, and these transformations of person and object are tied up with each other" (Gosden and Marshall 1999:169). Complex A was continually modified by the importation and deposition of clay, sand, and stone as well as finished artifacts, such as stone figurines, celts, pottery, and serpentine blocks. These items and materials were brought together in new contexts within this setting through highly formalized and repetitive practices that thereby would have transformed social relations and identities.

The focus is on the Ceremonial Court because Drucker and Heizer (1965:40) demonstrated it was the premier architectural structure of Complex A. The court and its associated platforms were built and modified by the deposition of specially prepared earth; discrete episodes of digging through those deposits to cache or remove artifacts; engineering for surface-water control; sweeping; refurbishment; and ceremonial offerings (including burned offerings), among other activities, carried on without significant interruption for a considerable period of time. Drucker and Heizer's four construction phases were not designed to reflect modifications to the individual mounds but only major changes to the court as a whole (Drucker and Heizer 1965:45). Their phases were based on the alternation of rare instances of digging great pits for "massive offerings" (MOs) of layers of hundreds of serpentine blocks with the more routinized painting of thin, colored clay layers on the court floor and platforms. In their interpretation, each new construction phase (after the first) was initiated by the placement of a massive offering in a great pit (MOs 1 and 4 in Phase II, MO 3 in Phase III, and MOs 2 and 5 in Phase IV). The offerings were rapidly covered with prepared clay fill, and the court floor was more gradually raised with a phase-specific series of distinctive layers (the water-sorted floors in Phase I, the white-sandy floors in Phase II, and the old-rose floors in Phase III). For Phase IV only a covering of red clay fill remained.

The major architectural constructions assigned by Drucker and Heizer to each phase are summarized in Table 6.1 and form the basis of the phase-by-phase plan views in Figures 6.3–6.6. Table 6.2 describes the offerings by phase. This biographical sketch is preliminary: it relies on the incomplete and partly schematized published excavation drawings and treats Complex A in isolation from the rest of the site. Plan drawings are purposely crude approximations to give a general sense of change in the structures and offerings over time and do not indicate accurate dimensions or surface appearances of the structures. Change through time is treated as relative because the radiocarbon dates (1000–600 BC uncalibrated) have proven controversial and do not support the four-century sequence (one century per phase) originally interpreted by Drucker and Heizer.[2]

Indeed, the integrity of the four construction phases was challenged early on by Coe and Stuckenrath (1964:6), who claimed that any rule of bilateral symmetry of Complex A is a product of the maps and interpretations of the archaeologists but not supported by the stratigraphic evidence. They exposed the different construction histories of the Northwest and Northeast platforms: the Northwest seems to postdate the Northeast Platform, but it also seems to have remains of pre–Phase I structures underneath it

TABLE 6.1

Construction Events by Phase

Phase	New Architecture	Floor Series	Massive Offerings and Other Features
Pre-I	Remnants of painted platforms or floors under area of Mound A-2 and Northwest Platform.	N.A.	—
I	Clay enclosure wall. Mound A-2. Northeast Platform. South-Central Platform. Northwest Platform? (or Phase II). Mound A-3.	Water-sorted floors.	Leveling of court area (removal and filling).
II	Southwest Platform. Southeast Platform (presumed); both platforms built of adobe brick with basalt facing blocks.	White, sandy floors.	MOs 1, 4. Adobe brickwork with basalt facing blocks placed next to clay enclosure wall.
III	—	Old-rose floors.	MO 3. Raising of court floor with fill. Some platforms greatly enlarged.
IV	Mound A-5. Mound A-4 (presumed).	If there had been a floor series, it was completely eroded.	MO 2. MO 5? "Tombs" A, B, C, D, E. Red clay "cap" throughout court, Mound A-2, to the south (Mounds A-4 and A-5). Basalt columns alogn wall, and atop Southwest and Southeast platforms placed red clay. Use of limestone and sandstone.
Post-IV	Filling in of drift sand.	N.A.	Pits and pottery offerings. Sculptures?

(see fig. 6.2; a "pre–Phase I" court was rebuffed by Drucker and Heizer [1965:42]). Yet "these structures contribute heavily to the appearance in Complex A of bisymmetrical layout with implied coordinated growth of balanced or twin structures" (Coe and Stuckenrath 1964:6). Despite the interpretation of coevality and a consistent formal arrangement, Coe and

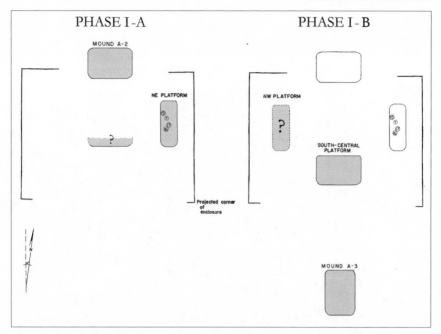

FIGURE 6.3

Sketch map of Phases Ia and Ib architecture and offerings. Based on information from profiles and plan map in Drucker et al. (1959), reoriented with north at top. Here and in Figures 6.4–6.6, locations, shapes, and sizes of platforms are approximate, and shaded areas indicate new architecture or massive offerings.

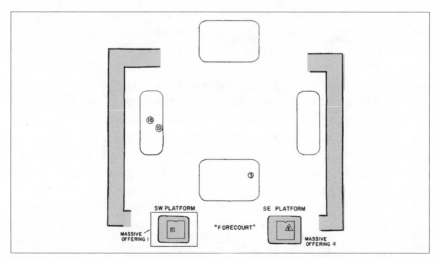

FIGURE 6.4

Sketch map of Phase II architecture and offerings. Based on information from profiles and plan map in Drucker et al. (1959).

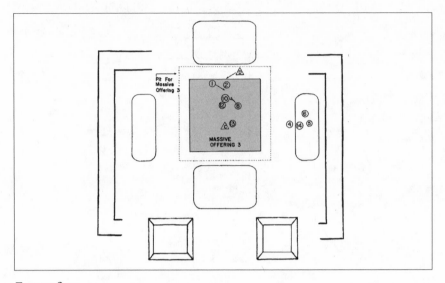

FIGURE 6.5

Sketch map of Phase III architecture and offerings. Based on information from profiles and plan map in Drucker et al. (1959).

Stuckenrath (1964:6) suspected that "the various surface structures comprising the Complex evolved in disjointed, independent fashion," such that the final appearance of a balanced plan was only the result of "a quite asymmetric earlier development" (Coe and Stuckenrath 1964:35). In other words, symmetry was produced out of a sequence of building activities, with later structures erected in response to earlier ones, and need not be explained as the execution of a preexisting plan.[3]

In reply to Coe and Stuckenrath, Drucker and Heizer (1965) acknowledged that they could not date the Northwest Platform to Phase I; it might have been Phase II. They recognized that the Northeast Platform had more offerings and may have had a different function than the Northwest, which was likely built later as its architectural complement only after the Northeast Platform was fully functioning (Drucker and Heizer 1965:44). They further admitted that exactly the same earthen materials were not laid down everywhere throughout a single court floor series—the "individual floors often thinned out and were replaced by another of different color and thickness," something not recorded in detail (Drucker and Heizer 1965:46). They attributed variations in the number of floor layers within the same series in various parts of the court to wear or erosion and their repair (Drucker and Heizer 1965:46). In addition, the three floor series vary in both their materials and the colors used, indicating important

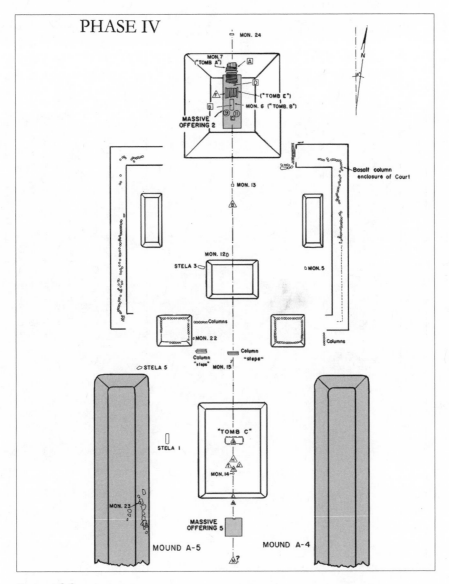

FIGURE 6.6

Sketch map of Phase IV architecture and offerings. Based on information from profiles and plan map in Drucker et al. (1959).

temporal differences in the use of the court.

Phase IV presents its own difficulties. Tons of prepared red clay were brought in to raise the level of the floor and cover all the platforms, including Mound A-2 and Mounds A-3, A-4, and A-5, south of the court. The red

TABLE 6.2

Offerings by Phase

Number	Location	Contents
Phase I:		
7	Northeast Platform.	Jade items on a layer of orange clay and cinnabar (pseudoburial).
15	Northeast Platform, under Offering 6.	Single pottery bowl, inverted.
16	Northeast Platform.	Single vessel, like No. 17, no pit associated.
17	Northeast Platform.	Single vessel, like No. 16, same situation.
Phase II:		
3	East half of South-Central Platform.	Large number of jade and other costume ornaments and small objects in bed of cinnabar (probable pseudoburial), disturbed by bulldozer.
18?	In shallow pit intruded into Phase I levels at center of Northwest Platform.	Pottery vessel in a pit (see No. 19).
19?	In shallow pit intruded into Phase I levels at center of Northwest Platform.	Pottery vessel in a pit, 13 cm above and 69 cm south of No. 18 in same pit.
MO 1	Southwest Platform.	Stacks of serpentine under mosaic mask.
1942-E	Southwest Platform, in fill over MO 1.	6 serpentine celts; possibly 2 arms of incomplete or incompletely cleared cruciform arrangement.
1943-E	Southeast Platform.	20 celts and a concave mirror in cruciform arrangement.
MO 4	Southeast Platform.	Serpentine mosaic mask like MO 1, not excavated below mask but likely has stacks of serpentine.
Phase III:		
1	Centerline of site, beneath Monument 13.	20 large serpentine pseudocelts in 3 rows.
2	Centerline of site.	2 layers of 51 celts of jade, serpentine; 5 decorated with incised designs.
2a	Centerline, just northeast and outside of pit of Offering 2.	5 celts, placed prior to making pit for No. 2.
4	West of center of Northeast Platform under court floor.	Grouping of 16 figurines and 6 (cut) celts.
5	Northeast Platform.	Pottery, with earspools and beads laid out between 2 rows of 4 small stones (pseudoburial).
6	Northeast Platform (see Offering 15).	2 earspool assemblies, pendants, and beads laid out as if on a body (pseudoburial).
8	Centerline, in fill under old-rose floor series.	3 groups of celts in a row transverse to the centerline.
10	Centerline, in fill overlying MO 3.	38 serpentine and jade celts in a cruciform pattern, 13 cm above the uppermost layer of serpentine blocks.
12	Centerline, in fill overlying MO 3.	2 round masses, one green malachite and the other red cinnabar; no objects.
13	Just east of centerline above MO 3.	2 celtlike serpentine objects, set upright, spaced 69 cm apart (possibly part of offering uncovered in 1943).

...?	South-Central Platform and court, centerline above MO 3.	2 pottery vessels.
MO 3	South-Central Platform and court.	6 layers of serpentine blocks, not fully exposed.
1943-D	Mound A-2 and area to south, centerline.	6 serpentine celts.
Phase IV:		
9	11.7 cm west of centerline, in fill overlying MO 2, in Mound A-2 just southwest of coffer.	Paired with No. 11: 1 concave mirror (magnetite) and 9 jade and serpentine celts in 3 rows.
11	11.7 cm east of centerline, in fill overlying MO 2, in Mound A-2 just southeast of coffer.	Paired with No. 9: 1 concave mirror (ilmenite), 9 jade and serpentine celts in 3 rows, 907 jade beads.
1942-A	Mound A-2.	Tomb A/Monument 7 (basalt column tomb) contents; separated into 2 groups with bundle burials.
1942-B	Mound A-2, just south of Tomb A.	Monument 6 (sandstone coffer) contents (Tomb B) (pseudoburial).
1942-C	Mound A-2, on centerline just south of coffer (1942-B).	37 celts in cruciform arrangement.
1942-D	Mound A-2, in between Tomb E and Tomb A.	2 jade earspools, 1 figurine fragment, 6 jade beads, 28 cylindrical and disk jade beads (pseudoburial).
1943-B?	Mound A-2 area, centerline above MO 3.	12 serpentine celts, no particular orientation.
1943-F	Mound A-2, beneath pile of basalt columns (Tomb E) between Tomb A and coffer.	Celts, earspools, and other ornaments, jade skull, concave mirror, many beads (pseudoburial).
MO 2	Mound A-2.	Pit with single layer (?) of serpentine blocks.
1943-G	Mound A-3, Feature A-3-a, Tomb C.	Contents of cist pseudoburial: celts, ornaments, figurine, etc.
1943-H	Mound A-3, between Tomb C and Monument 14.	2 serpentine celts.
1943-I	Mound A-3, between Tomb C and Monument 14.	Sandstone vessel.
1943-J	Mound A-3, between Tomb C and Monument 14.	Small jade mosaic plaque?
1943-K	Mound A-3, between Tomb C and Monument 14.	Amber pendant.
1943-L	Mound A-3, Tomb D contents.	Small pseudoburial: pottery vessel plus adornments.
1943-M	Mound A-3, just south of 1943-L.	4 serpentine figurines.
MO 5?	South of Mound A-3; dating uncertain.	Incomplete mosaic mask; possibly on layers of serpentine but not excavated below.
Phase IV or Post–Phase IV:		
1943-N	On centerline south of MO 5.	253 serpentine "celts" and 1 concave mirror.
1943-O	On centerline north of Platform C-2.	4–5 pottery vessels in drift sands at north flank of pyramid.
Post–Phase IV:		
20–27	—	Pottery vessels found singly and in concentrations in the drift sands after Complex A was no longer being maintained.
1943-A	Ceremonial Court, between South-Central Platform and Mound A-2.	Several pottery vessels found in upper drift sands.

Based on Drucker et al. (1959:133–191, 218–226, Table 1, Appendix 1); Drucker and Heizer (1965:59).

clay is comparable to that used in earlier filling episodes, although extreme in terms of extent of coverage (Drucker and Heizer 1965:49). It may have been meant to be leveled and finished (Drucker and Heizer 1965:48); however, no traces of a superimposed floor series were found, and the red clay was eroded prior to being covered with the airborne sand that pummels the site during rainstorms. The excavators considered this cessation of maintenance as evidence of the abandonment of La Venta itself, at least for a period of time (Drucker et al. 1959:246; see Berger et al. 1967:9). Others, however, have suggested that occupation continued at La Venta into the Late Formative, based on post–Phase IV deposits of pottery in the accumulating drift sand in Complex A (for example, Coe 1960:120; Lowe 1989:Table 4.1). An alternative hypothesis to site abandonment is that for the first time in centuries, major ritual attention shifted away from the Ceremonial Court in Complex A to a different locale within a still vibrant and powerful center.

HISTORY IN PRACTICE

This brief biography of the Ceremonial Court can be considered in relation to the emerging subjectivities of persons for whom it formed a salient nexus of sociospatial relationships. Complex A provided a nonquotidian arena for the negotiation of personal and corporate group identities within a referential framework that was structured by fundamental cosmological principles, as seen in the persistent spatial patterning of acts of deposition. However, architectural transformation of Complex A is also evident through its life span, implicating transformations in La Venta society.

What kinds of practices motivated these particular architectural forms and spatial patterns? Surprisingly, the functions of the Complex A architecture have never been systematically interpreted except to fall back on the conventional use of platforms as substructures for perishable buildings (Diehl 2004:68), for which there is no evidence at Complex A. However, there are other ritual structures in the Mesoamerican inventory that can serve as analogues, namely, foundation caches and altars. Both are conceived as cosmic replicas, and both are involved in the interaction of people with spirits—for example, ancestors, earth lords, winds, guardians, and celestial denizens.

Dwyer (1996) suggests that the degree to which he calls the "visible and invisible worlds" are either coextensive or spatially separated varies with the scale of social complexity. As complexity increases, the invisible world (spirits) tends to be bounded off from the visible (the routine actions of daily life), confined to certain places. It could be argued that the ritual activities in Complex A were intended to spatially constrain interactions with the invisible world of particular spirits, to circumscribe them in this singular locus. Furthermore, much of what was put in that place was literally "invisible" to mortals, at least, and not just spatially segregated. However, that the massive offerings and jade costume objects were buried rather than displayed should not be taken to indicate their relative unimportance in political life compared, for example, to the exposed stone carvings at La Venta, nor should it be relegated to acts of conspicuous consumption. The invisibility of the buried constructions may have been a sign of their potency, and the processes of making the offerings and rendering them invisible may have generated more political resonance than their display, engendering remembering rather than forgetting (see Mills, this volume).

Foundation caches in Mesoamerica typically reference cosmic totality via the patterned use of objects or materials that signify cosmic levels or segments—the sky, earth, sea, and underworld. As such, they connote myths of cosmic origins, inscribed into the landscape and rendered experiential (see Pauketat, this volume). Foundation caches among the neighboring (and later) Maya were typically placed at the original building of a structure and also at each renovation, usually on the centerline (Joyce 1992; Mathews and Garber 2004). Without having access to this subsequent literature, Drucker and Heizer surmised the importance of the massive offerings, three of which are on the centerline, as initiating a major remodification of the Ceremonial Court. As foundation caches, the massive offerings sanctified that entire enclosure in an act of "world renewal." Caches are part of the architecture (Joyce 1992:497); thus, the belowground architecture in Complex A dwarfed that which was aboveground.

The second functional analogue—the altar—shares similarities with the foundation cache but is formally opposed in being visible and aboveground. Altars, as still built today by ritual specialists in Mesoamerica, are also iconic models of cosmic totality. They are made according to recognizable principles, but in their making they concretize and memorialize abstract theological notions and do not simply mimic orthodox design plans (Sandstrom 2003:51). Rectangular forms—tables and benches—are commonly employed to reference the four directions of the horizon (Vogt 1993:11). Although in the Mesoamerican worldview the entire landscape is believed to be imbued with animating power, the altar is necessary as a material place to serve as a "seat of exchange" between living peoples and spirits, a focal point for the presentation of offerings to spirits in requests for favors (Sandstrom 2003:61).

The Ceremonial Court can therefore be seen as a great altar, its rectangular shape defined by a prominent wall from its inception, and its associated platforms were positioned according to a quadripartite spatial design referencing the earth's surface (see Figure 6.5). The individual platforms also functioned as altars, thereby metonymically referencing the whole space, but they could take on different symbolism—as the archaeology shows that they did—which changed over time. The episodes of painting thin clay floors following the burial of the massive foundation caches could also have formed a series of commemoration events, dedicated to the episodes of world creation materialized by the massive offerings, forming institutionalized acts of remembrance.

The platforms, as altars made of earthen materials, were likely dedicated to spirit denizens associated with the earth, including ancestors. Like the Andean *chullpas* described by Nielsen (this volume), the altars, which were continually enlarged, may have become "monumental embodiments" of those spirits, endowed with agentive capacities. They would have invoked the presence of ancestors and other guardian spirits in the daily lives—and the everyday politics—of the people of La Venta.

Although the archaeological emphasis on buried offerings has given rise to notions of a cult of secrecy, commentators who make such judgments do not take into account the performance of ritual actions and the deeply felt social memories they entailed. Too much scholarly emphasis has been put on the symbolic meanings or high cost of the buried objects of Complex A, and too little on the performative contexts from which human–human and human–object relationships emerge (see Pollard, this volume). The massive offerings would have taken a considerable amount of time to prepare and accomplish, even if the digging and filling of the pits were done more rapidly. By participating in the construction of the foundation caches—from the logistics of planning trips to acquire and stockpile the serpentine, which was cut and shaped in workshops; to the laborious digging of the pits and removal (to somewhere else) of the now sanctified earth they contained; to the collection and preparation of the clay fill; and so forth—numerous corporate groups and titled individuals created connections and "sedimented" them quite literally in cosmically sanctioned ways at a sacred locale known to everyone, even if usually accessible to only a few.

Much of this activity would have occurred in the presence of large crowds of active participants and audiences, even if the final deposition were witnessed by a smaller select group, such that inclusivity rather than exclusivity would have prevailed. The logistical requirements of feeding and housing guests would also have absorbed considerable resources and labor. The social memories created by these actions would have forged a linkage among those who participated (following Küchler 1993), even after the impetus for their coming together had been finished and the caches rendered invisible under the platforms or court floor. Those memories would have become the stuff of legend, part of the oral histories maintained and retold by every social group whose living members—and later ancestors—had taken part in these great events.

Drucker (1981:31) imagined La Venta as a state-level society whose "control structure would center on one individual, scion of a royal lineage, whose immediate subordinates would be a hierarchy of hereditary nobles." He based his scenario on the presumed maintenance of the ceremonial plan of Complex A over centuries, with its requisite need for the control of the labor of thousands, and not from the discoveries of palaces and elite residences or even the dwellings of commoners. Nevertheless, the archaeological evidence from Complex A holds open the likelihood that there were multiple groups of ritual caretakers, whose performances would have invoked competing memories rather than a unitary line of transmission of past knowledge.

At certain times those groups acted in concert, as when creating the massive foundation caches and resurfacing the entire court floor. However, even concerted actions reveal variability. The two serpentine mosaic faces buried under the Southeast and Southwest platforms were "*almost* the exact counterpart(s)" of each other (Drucker et al. 1959:93, emphasis added) but had minor differences. The number of stones used to make them varies, as do the colors of sand that fill the facial cavities (Drucker 1952:56–59; Drucker et al. 1959:93–94). The placement of the serpentine chunks in layers under the mosaic in the Southwest Platform also showed variation, including one area of one row with carefully worked blocks (Drucker et al. 1959:96–97), possibly set there by a distinct work crew. Furthermore, as noted above, the individual platforms had different construction histories with different quantities and types of offerings. As noted above, in Phases II and III the colors of the painted floors and the numbers of floor layers varied from one part of the court to another, as if deposited by different groups at different times.

Although such variation in the deposition of materials, including asymmetry between the eastern and western platforms, may have resulted from symbolic differences maintained by a single ruling authority, I suggest that through much of its history the apex of La Venta's sociopolitical hierarchy consisted of several chiefly "houses" (in the sense of corporate groups; Gillespie 1999) with proprietary claims to different sections of Complex A. Pauketat (this volume) notes that among peoples of the southeast United

States, the use of certain colors or activities such as fire-keeping were the prerogatives of specific corporate groups, whose ritual coordination in the making of earthen deposits forged social networks.[4] Participation of different groups in rituals within the Ceremonial Court would thereby have created a "geography of social relations" (Pollard, this volume). It would also have been a performative means to assert house membership, which (based on ethnographic analogy) was likely contested. Houses could have maintained access to different sources of clay as their property and may also have had their own attached artisans with distinct craft technologies. By collecting and working materials from certain locales for ritual use in the court, houses would have continually asserted their rights to that property.

Some of the places indexed by deposition in the Ceremonial Court were near localities visited by La Ventans themselves, the sources of the clays and sands. In contrast, the stone came from far distant places, requiring the mobilization and organization of a large number of people to travel and acquire the serpentine, basalt, sandstone, schist, and limestone, lugging the stones overland or rafting them on the rivers. Jade from Guatemala and magnetite from Oaxaca may have been obtained through down-the-line exchanges, referencing unseen locales. The figurines, celts, earspools, and other objects made from exotic materials were likely exchanged and heirloomed, encoded with the identities and histories of their owners to create a chain of social relations ("enchainment," following Chapman 2000a:171). Those personas and histories were "gathered" (in the sense of Heidegger 1977) along with the prepared earth, at the places where they were interred, creating novel intersubjective relationships of places, persons, and materials.

Interestingly, the Phase III Offering 4 figurines—the largest figurine cache found—exhibited considerable difference in technical skill, quality of the raw material, and apparent age of the individuals portrayed. Some of the figures were worn, had old breaks, or lacked part of a limb. Four of the upright celts that form a stage-setting for the scene were cut to that shape from older objects (Drucker et al. 1959:160–161). Drucker et al. (1959:161) thus suggested that the cache "was assembled from figurines that had been made in times past." These were heirlooms, referencing different owners but all put together in a miniature tableau. The tableau is sometimes interpreted as representing a historical event, but even if not, the figurines may have created a gathering of identities (corporate or individual) at the central (east-west) axis of the Northeast Platform. This kind of act has been called "accumulation" by Chapman (2000b:171), indicating "a new type of relationship between persons and objects which was in tension with traditional, enchained relationships."

Coordinating ritual activities according to spatial orientations within Complex A would have become one of the mechanisms (along with marriage exchange, descent, and possibly warfare) for organizing relationships and rankings among the chiefly houses. Complex A would have been an arena for negotiating and contesting that hierarchical ordering, as house identity and prestige were materialized in fairly regular fashion within this ritually charged place. As a sacred locale, the court (and thus its caretakers) was associated with creation stories that served to define sociocosmic categories and legitimize social hierarchies. Those definitions could themselves have been held out for scrutiny and questioning, moved out of the realm of doxa and into the "universe of discourse" (Bourdieu 1977:168) as a consequence of their concretization in the ephemeral ritual performances and the more enduring architecture of Complex A.

At a minimum, important differences between the east and west sides of the court in its early history are seen in variations between the Northeast and Northwest Platforms in Phase I, and the Southeast and Southwest Platforms (two adobe-brick mounds built over the massive offerings of serpentine) in Phase II. In pan-Mesoamerican cosmology, east and west are the fundamental directions, marked most obviously by the rising and setting of the sun, the basis for a cyclical rhythm of time. East is the more important direction, and at Complex A the Northeast Platform is earlier, with more offerings, than the Northwest. This fundamental cosmic distinction, with its embedded hierarchical ordering, was likely integrated with social differences recognized between the houses that maintained the altar-platforms on the east and west sides of the centerline. The salient relationships among the chiefly houses may have been metaphysically mediated by the cosmic symbolism manifest in their altars and more pragmatically negotiated through the rituals carried out in the Ceremonial Court.

Phase III in Drucker and Heizer's scheme began with MO 3, the largest of the five massive offerings and the first to be placed on the centerline. Precious objects buried in the clay fill above the serpentine blocks that make up the offering were also all placed along the centerline for the first time, although additional elaborate offerings in the Northeast Platform, including the tableau of figurines (Offering 4), were also dated to this phase. The rapid construction and refilling of the massive offering constituted an important shift in the use of space in the Ceremonial Court and correlatively, I suggest, in the relationships of the chiefly houses who maintained Complex A. The east-west symmetry of the Phase I–II structures seems to have created the open space between them that was subsequently co-opted, possibly by the house(s) associated with the Northeast Platform.

Moreover, when the La Ventans dug through the court floor for that massive offering, the accumulated linear history, which they themselves had sedimented into this sacred landscape as layers of clay, would have become self-evident, possibly contributing to an innovated understanding of time and duration.

Just before the initiation of Phase IV, Offering 4, on the western edge of the Northeast Platform, was opened for "inspection" (Drucker et al. 1959:154). But all of the Phase IV offerings were placed along the center-line, and with one exception were now positioned north and south of the court, in Mounds A-2 and A-3, which had no known earlier caches. These included two massive offerings (one cutting through Mound A-2, the other south of Mound A-3) and several features labeled as Tombs A–E. The transition of offering placement from east to west within the court to the north-south axis outside the court was complete. No Phase IV offerings were discovered in the other platforms.

This structural transformation in the materialized spatial orientations in Complex A could be evidence of a corresponding shift in the hierarchy and relationships of chiefly houses at La Venta, having to do with the materialization of "history" in a new context and an expansion of extralocal relationships beyond La Venta. The Phase III–IV ceramics show a significant widening of La Venta's external connections (Lowe 1978:366). It is also in Phase IV that new types of imported stone materials were incorporated into Complex A features—the great columnar basalt pieces, limestone, sandstone, and greenschist (Drucker et al. 1959:126).

Drucker and Heizer had commented on the elaborate graves and tomb constructions of Phase IV as indicative of more powerful leaders, per-haps so overbearing that they toppled La Venta's political organization. Tomb A in Mound A-2 was constructed of basalt columns arranged as if to form a house of stone "logs," while nearby Tomb B was a great limestone sarcophagus with carving on its outer surface making it appear to be the body of a saurian. Tomb C in Mound A-3 was lined with sandstone slabs, but Tombs D and E lacked stone constructions.

What was missing from most of these "tombs" was human bone. Wedel (in Drucker 1952:64), who excavated in 1943, referred to his finds as "grave-like deposits" in which fine costume items such as earspools and beads were "so arranged as to suggest grave furniture but without the slightest accom-panying trace of bone or tooth enamel." Stirling, who led the 1942 expedi-tion that uncovered Tombs A and B, was convinced that skeletal remains could not survive in the tropical soils (Stirling 1943a:323–325; Stirling and Stirling 1942:637), an opinion that was later widely repeated. However,

Drucker and Heizer (1965:56) subsequently apologized for their use of terms such as "tombs" and "graves," reiterating that only Tomb A contained human skeletal remains as two bundle burials (Drucker et al. 1959:162). They further dismissed the notion that bone would have completely perished based on Drucker's prior experience of finding bone in the region. Furthermore, the positioning of the artifacts in the pseudoburials is such that the objects could not have been found as they were if they had actually adorned a decaying corpse—they are sometimes too perfectly placed (Drucker et al. 1959:162).

Drucker and Heizer (1965:58) concluded that there was a pattern of surrogate burials at Complex A, starting in Phase I and continuing through Phase III, primarily in the Northeast Platform. What these features have in common is an assortment of costume items of greenstone and other precious materials on a prepared layer of cinnabar or similar material, an ore or color that may have had mortuary significance. Joyce (1987, 1999, 2000b) analyzed the ornaments in these pseudoburials—assuming that they stood for personages whether or not there was a body—and suggested that they may represent gendered persons. For the preliterate Olmec, such costume ornaments "can be viewed as quasi-textual elements, with messages to be read" (Joyce 1987). They evidence "inscribed practices" (following Connerton 1989), contributing to social memory in ways that transcend the temporal and spatial limitations of ephemeral performances. The burials (real or pseudo) are the materializations of individual persons, indexically signaled not by bodies but by precious objects, inalienable house property that likely referenced named or titled ancestors. This is a materialization of a memory, real or innovated, but it just as likely entailed forgetting, because only certain individuals would have been rendered visible through their costume ornaments, while others were not.

Drucker and Heizer had suggested that the rich tombs appearing in Phase IV signaled a major change in La Venta's political hierarchy, which may have become too top-heavy for the populace to bear. In fact, pseudoburials date back to Phase I (Offering 7), all but one of them in the Northeast Platform, so the Phase IV features can be seen as a continuation of a venerable tradition. However, the linear arrangement of multiple surrogate burials in Phase IV north and south of the Ceremonial Court, which by then was possibly closed off to further buried caches, is new, indicating a transformation of the earlier practice. It hints strongly of the narration of a pedigree or genealogy as a dynastic history. These interments thus constitute an extremely important "moment" in the production of history, the "fact assembly" involved in making an "archive" (following Trouillot 1995:26).

It is possible that earlier offerings had been placed along the center-line in Phases I and II but were removed for the massive offerings made during Phases III and IV (Drucker 1981:36). If so, such an act of oblitera-tion would have been one of the "silences" common in historical produc-tion, a strategic forgetting as a result of "the differential exercise of power that makes some narratives possible and silences others" (Trouillot 1995:25). The pseudoburials in particular, and all of the Ceremonial Court more generally, were "signs in history," objects or patterns of action that "become involved in social life as loci of historical intentionality *because* of their function as representational vehicles. These objects are frequently considered to be concrete embodiments or repositories of the past they record, that is, to be endowed with the essentialized or reified property of historicity" (Parmentier 1987:11–12, original emphasis).

Historical narratives "are always produced in history" (Trouillot 1995: 22), and the production of this specific narrative (with its later emenda-tions) must take into account the prior history of inhabitation of Complex A. The La Venta elites performed their history, literally putting their "ancestors" as indexed by house valuables into the otherworld/othertime dimension that Complex A had become over generations. And in Phase IV they did so on the centerline as part of the last major "world creation" event enacted at that place, when the final massive foundation caches (MO 2 and MO 5) were positioned in association with Mounds A-2 and A-3—the locales of the Phase IV pseudoburials. Certain house ancestors became incorporated into the cosmogony, materially sedimented within the sacred narrative of the establishment of cosmic order and the distribution of cos-mic power to demigods and heroes. The landscape was therefore inscribed with a slightly different creation story (as happened at Cahokia [see Pauketat, this volume]). However, this was not a universalizing recounting of foundation events. Instead, it devolved out of the mythic past into a more narrow recent history that belonged to what had by then become the paramount house of La Venta—"a narrative of inclusions and exclusions" in Chapman's (2000b:172) phrase—as an act of self-definition, possibly of a new social category.

In the scenario sketched here, the ritual deposition practices that built Complex A over a number of generations were part of a strategy for nego-tiating and contesting sociosacred relationships and defining identities and categories of persons in the process. These activities had been carried on generally uninterrupted, incorporating several episodes of "world renewal" that redefined the entire court in the process. Those episodes allowed for a return to the past and the regenesis of the invisible world, to create transformed memories in forging links between past and present. Complex A was a place of transformation, allowing for the emergence of new relationships and social fields.

By Phase IV, however, a single paramount house may have performed and inscribed its own history in ways not open to other chiefly houses, contenders for their rank. This house (with or without its allies) monopolized the most sacred and controlled location in their world: its ancestors now flanked the north and south ends of the Ceremonial Court. Its history may subsequently have become a "world history" for La Venta, because "history is made isomorphic with the hierarchy of chiefly persons" (Heckenberger 2005:285; Sahlins 1985). Multiple collective memories and the memory work of ritual deposition of past generations would have been trumped by the ownership and privileged recitation of house histories in what had become a different setting. This effort would have been part of a "forgetting campaign" to redirect the memory of ancestors for political purposes, like that of the Inkas described by Nielsen (this volume). It is therefore quite probable that with the application of the thick red clay cap, which covered all the altar-platforms and Tomb A, and into which a few more surrogate burials were laid, Complex A was closed to ritual resurfacings, to the refurbishment of altars to contact spirits. The founding history inscribed there was not to be disturbed. Basalt columns were erected to raise the height of the court wall (although they never completely encircled it). Complex A was left to erode and fill with drift sand.

One suspects that only powerful rulers could have accomplished the cessation of such long-standing traditions, to enforce "a rupture between past and present," which is how we think of history (Hoskins 1993:307). Importantly, La Venta may have continued for some time as a primate center. Several stone sculptures, including a large stela that depicts elite persons, were placed atop the red clay stratum in Complex A. They are similar to monuments positioned in Complex B, south of the great pyramid (Mound C) that hid Complex A from view. Complex A had become invisible (just like its buried caches), but it was not forgotten. Its hidden history would have been implicated in the controlled contexts of ceremonies in the plaza of Complex B. The political positioning and cosmic sanctioning of later paramounts was dependent in part on the prior history that had been produced in Complex A, maintained as memories of the royal and noble houses. This was the legacy bequeathed by the earlier generations of the Complex A caretakers, but they could not have anticipated that outcome when they first engaged in those ritual labors and performances.

I am thus presenting a scenario of a new orientation to the temporal qualities of landscape like that proposed by Barrett (1999) for Stonehenge and its environs between the Neolithic and the Iron Age. In the earlier use of Complex A's Ceremonial Court, the landscape was transformed by repetitive actions as a form of inhabitation to "evoke or revitalize the ever-present ancestral and spiritual order embedded in that same landscape. The actions of construction, and the inhabitation of these places, thus overlay the sacred structure of the landscape in such a way that the past and present effectively existed alongside each other" within that locale, as Barrett (1999:261) described for Stonehenge. However, in the process of shaping the landscape, a distinction was created between the past—the origins of cosmic and social order—and the present, facilitated in the British and Mexican cases by the "construction of a linear representation of time which projected back to a time of origins" (Barrett 1999:261). In Britain this was the unintended consequence of the inclusion of graves of warrior-chiefs into mounds to which more graves were added, creating a lineal sequence of the dead in the landscape, a "human past distinct from the present" (Barrett 1999:261). The mythic past of the earlier landscape with its monumental ancestral forms was now no longer part of the routine temporal horizon of the people who lived there, so those monuments were no longer subjected to modifications or renovations. The landscape presented its living inhabitants with a very different system of referents than before, and society was transformed in the process.

CONCLUSION

Despite its tremendous importance in Formative and later Mesoamerican prehistory, and notwithstanding evidence of its lengthy occupation, La Venta has been treated as a single-period site. The reasons for the failure to properly consider the history (and not just the chronology) of Complex A range from confusing graphic representations to archaeological agendas that put greater emphasis on continuity than change. The diachronic perspective pursued here, examining the biography of Complex A's Ceremonial Court, has treated this landscape and the people who built it in terms of intersubjective practices of inhabitation in space and time. Performance and the interplay of remembering and forgetting among multiple groups with both coordinated and competing agendas come to the fore. Minor variations and discontinuities originally observed and recorded by the excavators were thereby given more significance. Attention to variation, to the actions and perspectives of different categories of people, and to the internal origins of social change are among the advantages of practice theory (Brumfiel 2000). All of these factors provide clues to how the Complex

A landscape, as a system of orientation, could have been modified over time, even as the La Ventans adhered to fundamental cosmological principles and reproduced customary practices through commemorative acts. Such orienting structures "do not simply constrain agents but allow them to act in ways that frequently lead to their transformation" (Rowlands and Kristiansen 1998:23).

What has previously been neglected at La Venta is not so much the evidence of change at Complex A but the potential for understanding the development of social differentiation and political hierarchy, entwined with the rise of new categories of social persons in a value-laden landscape built from generations of depositional practices. A shift in the placement and types of ritual depositional activities must have been influenced by the preexisting materialization of orienting principles. As Barrett (1999:257) observed, "each generation [has to] confront its own archaeology as the material remains of its past piled up before it." Deposits and constructions in the later phases (III and IV), which emphasize the north-south centerline, were integrated into and dependent upon the prior landscape created in the earlier phases (I and II), when an asymmetrical east-west axis was more apparent. The bilateral symmetry so produced may have opened the central space for the north-south axis between them. As with Pauketat's (2000) "tragic commoners" at Cahokia, the unintended consequences of earlier actions created a landscape of power that could be appropriated for innovated purposes.

When building is enduring, and the same practices are repeatedly performed for generations, the system of reference may become doxic (Bourdieu 1977:164) or taken for granted, a component of "practical knowledge" (Giddens 1984:4, 22; see Joyce, this volume). But Barrett (2001:154) suggested that archaeologists pay attention to "moments when practitioners stood apart from the world of their actions and looked in upon that world discursively. They objectified certain conditions as a strategy for acting upon them." Such moments would have included salient occasions "when political authorities sought to extend their authority, to objectify, and thus to act upon, the lives of others" (Barrett 2001:154).

In the latter period of use of Complex A, I suggest, one or more chiefly houses may have done just that in appropriating this ritually charged place to materialize its own history, including highly elaborate pseudoburials of revered ancestors in a linear arrangement. The archaeological evidence suggests that after centuries of continuous use, Complex A was closed to further modifications, so that the history inscribed into that sacred earth could not be further changed, even as the site may have flourished for some time. This profound structural transformation in the linking of history to an innovated manifestation of political authority cannot be fully explained by reference only to internal factors peculiar to La Venta: La Venta's external connections had considerable impacts that are also manifest in Complex A. Nevertheless, the La Venta excavations of 50 years ago can continue to yield insights into how internal and external factors stimulating change were played out among La Venta's chiefly houses through practices of ritual deposition, the invocation of social memory, and the consequences of their accumulated actions in history.

Notes

1. A later rendering of Complex A (Heizer et al. 1968) attempted to correct this misperception, showing all the platforms as rectilinear, but it is equally problematic and has not been accepted.

2. Space limitations preclude discussion of the dating of Complex A. See Drucker et al. (1957), Drucker et al. (1959:264–267), and Drucker and Heizer (1965) for the 1955 dates; and Berger et al. (1967:5) and Heizer et al. (1968) for dates from the short 1967 and 1968 field seasons. For critiques, see Coe and Stuckenrath (1964:8ff.), Graham and Johnson (1979:3), Grove (1997:72–73), and Heizer (1964:49–50).

3. An additional problem is the South-Central Platform, which seems to have been placed farther north in Phase I and was repositioned to the south in Phase II (Drucker et al. 1959:Figure 9). Based on these discrepancies, I divided Phase I into two subphases in my plan views (Figure 6.3).

4. Pauketat (this volume) describes the typical pattern at Mississippian centers of alternating light and dark colors of clay or earth that have been carefully selected and processed to eliminate impurities. The same practices characterize the ritual deposition at Complex A.

7

Practice and Nonhuman Social Actors

The Afterlife Histories of Witches and Dogs in the American Southwest

William H. Walker

Does the structure of archaeological deposits record practices of human and nonhuman members of society? Do material traces of interactions between people and supernatural social actors exist (for example, ghosts, witches, spirits)? I argue that expanding our understanding of society to include such actors is useful for the archaeological study of religion because it facilitates identification of artifact patterning. This perspective is inspired primarily by the work of Robin Horton (1993 [1960]) and by more recent scholars wrestling with the limitations of anthropocentric approaches to society (for example, Gell 1998; Latour 1993; Schiffer and Miller 1999) and their consequences for archaeological taxonomy (for example, Boast 1997; Meskell 2004:41–58; Olsen 2003; Pollard 2001).

In the ancient pueblos of the American Southwest, human skeletal assemblages and skulls associated with violence (Table 7.1) that do not resemble typical funerary deposits occur primarily in ceremonial contexts, particularly pithouses and kivas, which are both subterranean ritual buildings (see Bullock 1998; Martin 1997; Turner and Turner 1999). These deposits of human remains appear to be part of a broader pattern of ceremonial deposits in these kinds of structures (Walker 1998, 2005). They are analogous to what Neolithic archaeologists commonly refer to as "structured deposits" or "formal deposits" (Bradley 2000; Hill 1995; Mills 2004; Pollard 1995; Richards and Thomas 1984; J. Thomas 1991), and what I have

TABLE 7.1
Contexts of Anomalous Human Skeletal Remains

Time (CE)	Pit Structures	Row %	Kivas	Row %	Towers	Row %	Surface Structures	Row %	Extramural Features	Row %	Total
BM II (<500)	3	50.0	0	0.0	0	0.0	0	0.0	3	50.0	6
BM III (500–700)	5	100.0	0	0.0	0	0.0	0	0.0	0	0.0	5
P I (700–900)	19	67.9	0	0.0	0	0.0	7	25.0	2	7.1	28
P II (900–1150)	16	21.9	22	30.1	1	1.4	28	38.4	6	8.2	73
P III (1150–1300)	11	9.6	38	33.3	23	20.2	32	28.1	10	8.8	114
P IV (1300–1540)	0	0.0	11	52.4	0	0.0	3	14.3	7	33.3	21
P V (>1540)	0	0.0	2	66.7	0	0.0	0	0.0	1	33.3	3
Unknown	0	0.0	0	0.0	0	0.0	0	0.0	3	100.0	3
Total	54	21.3	73	28.9	24	9.5	70	27.7	32	12.6	253

described as ritual deposits (Walker 1995, 2002). Based on analogies to known Pueblo cultures, these architectural contexts or features within them were places of interaction with an underworld inhabited by spirits and deities. The structure of these deposits appears to be a result of such interactions.

Ceremonial ordering of deposits in Southwestern pithouses (500 BCE –900 CE) and later in kivas (900–1700 CE) makes sense given that pithouses were the precursors of kivas. In fact, the evolution of pithouses into kivas tracks an important temporal change in Pueblo religious practices (Walker and Lucero 2000). In earlier ancestral farming villages, ceremonial and domestic activities centered on pithouses. With the development of surface architecture, habitation and storage activities moved aboveground, and the subterranean pithouses were transformed into the more formalized locations of ceremonial activity found in later prehistoric and historic kivas.

In a paper written almost a decade ago, I interpreted these remains as those of persecuted witches (Walker 1998). One unsympathetic critic ridiculed that effort, noting that according to my logic I could also conclude that dogs found in similar contexts were also witches. In hindsight, I wish I had recognized that possibility as clearly as he did. Implicit then, and explicit now, my understanding of society includes people and a range of nonhuman social actors, including dogs. Indeed, it was particularly prescient to mention dogs in the discussion of prehistoric witchcraft evidence. In the American Southwest and elsewhere, canines often appear in contexts similar to those of humans. They are given their own funerary rites and are deposited in human burials (for example, Carlson 1963:11; Guernsey and Kidder 1921:15; Hall 1944; Lister 1964:9; Olszewski et al. 1984:143; Roberts 1939:Figure 44). Interestingly, dogs purposefully buried in architectural settings are recovered most frequently from pithouses and kivas.

The suggestion that a dog might have been treated as a witch or in some other social role is supported in ethnographies and seems to correspond to archaeological patterning. I argue in this chapter that dogs, like people, probably had multiple social roles in prehistoric Pueblo societies, including as witches, guardians, and pets. Therefore, when we encounter their remains in kivas and pithouses, it would be reasonable to ask: is this a witch executed at the threshold of the underworld, or perhaps a faithful dog protector sacrificed to stand spiritual watch and prevent witches from crawling up from below?

In groping with these data and other deposits that appear to have resulted from the interaction of people and nonhuman actors, I was stuck by Bradley's (2000:122–127) comments about structured deposits in natural places. To paraphrase him, these deposits mark or highlight the origins of objects, their histories, and the significance of particular places. They also bring together and keep apart certain classes of objects. Finally, these attributes of their organization (their structuring) may result from the enactment of narratives, such as might attend practices associated with the memory work of oral traditions.

Such narrative practices seem to have been at work in the Pueblo Southwest for a long time. To imagine and interpret them, I begin my first section with a discussion of anthropocentrism, practice theory, and the study of religion. I then highlight how the merger of a practice perspective with a nonanthropocentric approach to society leads to archaeologically useful ways of reconceptualizing oral tradition. A practice orientation, for example, allows me to simultaneously understand oral tradition as a form of Pueblo history making, and therefore, at least in part, as an explanation of the history that gets made.

When considered a form of practice, oral tradition becomes more than abstract narratives. In practice, people's relationships with objects (artifacts, architecture, other people) often animate objects and shape the histories of both, including their material traces in archaeological deposits. Understanding the symmetry between the lives of people, artifacts, and buildings (in the sense of Latour 1994) is central to archaeological study of prehistoric religion. If we redefine religion as that aspect of practice that extends the boundaries of society to include social relationships with what people perceive to be nonhuman social agents (in the sense of Horton 1993), then it is possible to imagine that many animated objects, including axes, grinding stones, homes, ceremonial buildings, and animals, were past societal agents. Social relationships in such an expanded understanding of society would include processes of collective and individual remembering, memorializing, and forgetting (Küchler 1999), and find expression in material objects. Not surprisingly, therefore, archaeological artifact patterning could reflect interactions with spirits that referenced past oral traditions and contributed to future interactions.

To explore these relationships between social memories and practice, in the next section of the paper I consider the role of dogs and witches in the oral traditions and practices of ethnographically known Pueblo societies. Both are important social actors associated with death, the underworld, and creation. I conclude with an interpretation that explains the placement of witches and dogs in kivas and pithouses. While recognizing the possibility that some could be witches, I also argue that some could be guardians associated with protecting the living from forces of death.

Underlying both interpretations is the argument that it is reasonable to conclude that these Pueblo dogs, like people and witches, emerged into this world from the world beneath this one, and that their deposition in kivas, pithouses, and other subterranean contexts represents the practice of transferring their souls between the two realms.

ANTHROPOCENTRISM, SOCIETY, AND RELIGION

If we define society by people's practices, then we should include spirits and other animate forces as social actors. Human practices in the present, as well as memories of practices past, involve relations with material objects such as buildings, artifacts, and dogs that are often perceived as both animate and possessing agency. Social theory, as a tool for perceiving human interaction, is always a work in progress that strives for more precision and accuracy. A recent and positive example has been the exploration of the causal roles played by material things (including artifacts and architecture) in the study of society and technology (for example, Gell 1998; Latour 1993, 1994, 2005; Schiffer and Miller 1999). Of particular interest are theorists focused on assigning agency to nonhuman agents or actors (Latour 1993:30). Putting this new animism to work, however, is easier said than done. It requires taking topics usually discussed as beliefs (spirits, souls, animate beings) and putting them back into the social world in the form of actors. This disrupts a tightly bound theoretical paradigm that holds that only people are members of society and that only they have social agency.

In the modern scientific world the earth is no longer the center of the universe, and people no longer dominate the great chain of being, but archaeological social theory still revolves in an anthropocentric orbit. While insightful scholars recognize that artifacts and architecture shape or curtail human agency (for example, Schiffer and Miller 1999) and may see in those consequences a limited form of artifact agency (Gell 1998), ultimately there is no room, except in science fiction, for nonhuman social actors (but see Latour 1993, 1994, 2005). Our definitions of religion and nature have developed and canonized this fundamental assumption since the Enlightenment. Ironically it is those scholars interested in the study of animism and religion, such as Tylor (1871) and later ethnologists (for example, Horton 1993; Ingold 1988), who have addressed this contradiction most directly in their research.

Robin Horton (1993:31–32) brilliantly broke with anthropocentric social theory in the early 1960s, defining religion as "an extension of the field of people's social relationships beyond the confines of purely human society." In so doing, he rehabilitated and updated Tylor's definition of religion as the belief in spirits (Tylor 1871:383). Horton's goal, in part, was to expose the practices of religion often overlooked in debates that dichotomized religion and science (Horton 1993). Although a bold thinker, Horton recognized that following social relationships beyond society too far could be problematic. How times have changed (for example, Ingold 1988; Jones 2000; Serpell 1996)! Therefore, he suggested that "we should perhaps add the rider that this extension [of society's boundaries] must be one in which the human beings involved see themselves in a dependent position *vis-à-vis* their non human alters [nonhuman social actors]—a qualification necessary to exclude pets and other lesser social beings from the pantheon of gods" (Horton 1993:32).

Dogs and People

The sentiment of dependence expressed in Horton's caveat, however, excludes many spiritual forces of animals, plants, rocks, and so on, which, while interdependent with humans, are not always in a controlling position. Dogs are the oldest domesticate, and it should not surprise archaeologists that dogs' relationships with people often exemplify the very extension of society's boundaries that Horton advocated. For Hopi peoples of the American Southwest, Coyote is a witch's pet (Stephen 1929:9) who does his master's bidding, albeit sometimes also frustrating it. Worldwide, dogs and other animals are often social actors. It was not that long ago, for example, that European courts prosecuted and executed wild as well as domesticated animals for human crimes and natural disasters (Evans 1906). Rabid dogs that bit people were charged, tried, and executed for murder in seventeenth-century Europe (Evans 1906:176). Perhaps the dog has been with us so long that we take relationships with them for granted and leave them undertheorized. The colonial government of India learned this lesson the hard way in the Bombay Dog Riots of 1832 (Palsetia 2001). Authorities instituted an annual dog cull to reduce the stray and rabid population of dogs in the city, killing more than 63,000 dogs between 1822 and 1832. This incensed local dog owners, particularly the Zoroastrian Parsi population, which believed dogs were sacred because their souls stood on the Bridge of Judgment and accompanied righteous human souls to paradise. Dogs, like witches, are one of the most common nonhuman social actors cross-culturally (for example, Brownlow 2000:143; Keber 1991; Savishinsky 1974:464; Serpell 1995), and we should expect their lives to robustly shape traces of human practices in archaeological patterns (for example, Cole and Koerper 2002; Hill 2000; Onar et al. 2002; Tchernov and Valla 1997).

Religion and Anthropomorphism

Another way to look at Horton's caveat is to realize that a practice definition of society is incompatible with most definitions of religion and the anthropocentric foundations of social theory (Bell 1996:188). If we define society as a product of practice, we must be willing to follow the practices where they lead, even if they undermine what appear to be commonsense distinctions between people and objects, and definitions of society, nature, and religion.

When we extend agency to objects inhabited by spirits, then the boundary between people and things is called into question and cannot help impacting archaeological methods and theories. For example, within an historical particularist perspective, people and other animate forces (let's call them spirit people) would both be the creators of traits and cultures composed of clusters of traits. People and spirit people would also be diffusers, innovators, and immigrants.

But if we break down the barrier between things and people, we also run roughshod over the distinction between nature and society. As Gell (1998:29) eloquently notes in his synthesis of Tylor and other scholars of animism and magic, people often express the opinion that when using natural materials (wood, stone, earth) to construct idols, temples, and other animate artifacts, they report being guided by spiritual forces. These forces already inhabit or will inhabit the fetishes and temples under construction. As such, those interested in functionalist approaches to society, including cultural ecologists, should recognize that social structure includes relations with spirits and that many of those relationships are also relationships with the "natural" world.

Cushing, for example, highlighted such an intersection of worlds in his discussion of Zuni cornfield preparation. An important ritual technology involves the planting of stream-rolled clay balls (likely concretions) in the field to attract rainwater runoff to the crops. This power of attraction is considered analogous to power possessed by the kicking sticks Zunis used in cross-country races. The sticks drew runners to them and made them run faster (Cushing 1979:251–252). Following this logic, the clay balls planted in the fields are called the kicking sticks of the water they draw to them. In such a society it is clear that human and nonhuman agents (for example, clay balls, kicking sticks, water) create the spatial and temporal patterns that would be the focus of arguments about traits, social institutions, or ecosystems.

This example highlights the supposition that when we take religious practice seriously and give life to spiritual forces, then anthropocentric boundaries between people and things, beliefs and actions, and natural and supernatural realms lose their meaning. In short, a focus on religious practice undermines modern notions of religion, ritual, nature, and society. History and ethnographic informants, in their own fashion, have been demonstrating this to anthropologists for more than a century. The term "religion" rarely translates well. Counterintuitively, archaeologists interested in the study of religion and ritual should be happy to be rid of both concepts in preference for an expanded understanding of practice that focuses on the material relations between people and nonhuman agents in society. Often these practices are preserved and shaped by memories of past experiences.

Oral Tradition and Practice

We can elegantly complicate social theory by discussions of the role of objects in human communication (Schiffer and Miller 1999), embodiment, fractal personhood (Wagner 1991), and secondary agency (Gell 1998), but if at the end of the day few are willing to embrace nonhuman social agents, then we cannot assail the dichotomies between belief and action that render nonhuman agents and their object bodies material (Bell 1996). Method and theory are constantly drawn toward interpretations or explanations of the processes of human imagination and away from the materiality of human and nonhuman social relationships (Boast 1997; Olsen 2003). Nowhere is this more apparent than in the work of memory making that underlies oral traditions.

Because oral tradition is conceptualized as a thing of ideas—nothing more than spoken history—it is easy to dismiss as inaccurate. Mason (2000: 264) aptly illustrates this perspective, noting that "oral traditions are more often than not road blocks than bridges to archaeologists aspiring to know 'what happened in history.'" Despite notable efforts (for example, Echo-Hawk 2000; Pendergast and Meighan 1959), oral tradition continues to suffer a credibility problem for many archaeologists. It is time to evaluate the activities of oral tradition as a form of what Marx (1970:121) called sensuous practice.

Obviously from any anthropocentric perspective, scientific or otherwise, events described in oral narratives are surreal at best. However, if we treat oral traditions as practices within a nonanthropocentric social world, then they become something else—historical events themselves. As practices, the processes of oral traditioning contribute to the making of history, not simply its inaccurate recording. When oral traditions are practices, we can turn this problem on its head and recognize that oral tradition is a living, material thing similar to the practices of farming, feasting, or fighting. As a practice it becomes possible to consider the process of oral tradition as something occurring in the past rather than something that fails to reveal it. To explore the role of oral traditions and dogs, I begin with a description of the dog remains I have identified in the American Southwest.

DOGS, WITCHES, AND PUEBLO EMERGENCE TRADITIONS

Dog remains, and other faunal data, were not systematically recorded by Southwestern archaeologists until relatively recently. Not surprisingly, synthetic studies of prehistoric dogs in the Southwest have been rare (for example, Emslie 1978; Olsen 1972, 1976). The most comprehensive database of Pueblo dog deposits is embedded in Hill's (2000) larger study of animal interments among Hohokam, Mogollon, and Pueblo cultures. Prior to the heightened interest in contextual clues generated by the site formation process research in the 1970s and 1980s, site reports tended to concentrate on obvious animal remains, such as formal burials or other deposits, that struck excavators as purposeful or somehow out of place. They would note whole or partial skeletons, skulls, or select skull parts (for example, mandibles, maxilla) found in structures or features. The specificity of reporting, therefore, varied from relatively detailed descriptions of skulls in kiva ventilator tunnels to generic references to dog remains. Table 7.2 reflects this messy reality and includes a range of 10 descriptors: dog, dog skeleton, dog partial skeleton, dog remains, wolf skull, dog skull, dog partial skull, dog dentary, dog mandibles, and dog maxilla. There are a number of ways these data could be sorted. For example, these categories can be simplified into those relating exclusively to skulls, and those involving skeletons, partial or whole (Table 7.3). For the purposes of this paper I am most interested in the more general relationships that characterize all these deposits (Table 7.4).

In three cases, "contexts" were overlapping. Three sites possess dog burials that also occur as features within other structures. At Shabik'eschee, a village near Chaco Canyon, New Mexico, and Tse-ta'a, in Canyon de Chelly, Arizona, these burials occur in pit structures; and at the Artificial Leg Site, in southwest Colorado, a dog burial was recovered from a storage structure. In my summary of the contexts of dog deposits (Table 7.4), I categorized these cases as pit structure and surface structure deposits to highlight the importance of these places of deposition. They do not change the contextual frequencies dramatically but do highlight what I consider an important pattern. The vast majority of all reported dog remains, like those

TABLE 7-2
Pueblo Dog Remains (BM II–P V)

Remains	Site	Time	Pit Stratum	Kiva	Surface Stratum	Human Burial	Dog Burial	Midden	Other	Cases	Number of Dogs	Reference
Dog skeleton	White Dog Cave	BM II	0	0	0	1	0	0	0	1	2	Guernsey and Kidder (1921:15)
		BM II	0	0	0	1	0	0	0	1	2	
Dog skeleton	Cerro Colorado	BM III	1	0	0	0	0	0	0	1	4	Bullard (1962:40)
Dog skull	Prayer Rock Cave 1	BM III	0	0	0	0	1	0	0	1	1	Morris (1980:42)
Dog skeleton	Shabik'eschee	BM III	1	0	0	0	0	0	0	1	2	Roberts (1929:93)
Dog skeleton	Shabik'eschee	BM III	1	0	0	0	0	0	0	1	1	Roberts (1929:66)
Dog partial skeleton	Site 1644	BM III	1	0	0	0	0	0	0	1	1	Hayes and Lancaster (1975:8)
Dog dentary	Site 1676	BM III	1	0	0	0	1	0	0	1	1	Hayes and Lancaster (1975:16)
Dog skeleton	5mtumr 2347	BM III	5	0	0	0	1	0	0	6	10	Emslie (1978:169)
Dog	Artificial Leg Site	P I	0	0	0	0	1	0	0	1	1	Frisbie (1967:121–122)
Dog	Artificial Leg Site	P I	1	0	0	0	0	0	0	1	5	Frisbie (1967:121–122)
Dog skeleton	AZ:7:2103	P I	1	0	0	0	0	0	0	1	1	Olszewski et al. (1984:143)
Dog skeleton	AZ:7:2103	P I	1	0	0	0	0	0	0	1	5	Olszewski et al. (1984:143)
Dog skull	Governador 1	P I	0	0	0	0	1	0	0	1	3	Hall (1944:28)
Dog skull	Governador 1	P I	1	0	0	0	0	0	0	1	4	Hall (1944:28)
Dog mandible	Grass Mesa	P I	1	0	0	0	0	0	0	1	1	Morris (1988:887)
Dog maxilla	Grass Mesa	P I	1	0	0	0	0	0	0	1	1	Varien (1988:218)
Dog partial skeleton	Grass Mesa	P I	1	0	0	0	0	0	0	1	1	Dohm (1988:864)
Dog remains	Grass Mesa	P I	0	1	0	0	0	0	0	1	1	Lightfoot et al. (1988:598)
Dog skull	Grass Mesa	P I	1	0	0	0	0	0	0	1	3	Lightfoot et al. (1988:635)
Dog partial skeleton	IGN 7:23	P I	0	0	0	1	0	0	0	1	1	Carlson (1963:11)
Dog dentary	Site 1676 House 1	P I	0	1	0	0	0	0	0	1	5	Hayes and Lancaster (1975:62)
Dog dentary	Site 1676 House 1	P I	0	0	1	0	0	0	0	1	1	Hayes and Lancaster (1975:54)

Element	Site	Period									Total	Reference
Dog partial skeleton	Site 1676 House 1	P I	0	1	0	0	0	0	0	0	1	Hayes and Lancaster (1975:55)
Dog dentary	Site 1676 House 4	P I	1	0	0	0	0	0	0	1	1	Hayes and Lancaster (1975:45)
Dog skeleton	Site 1676 House 4	P I	0	0	1	0	0	0	0	1	4	Hayes and Lancaster (1975:37)
Dog skull	Site 1676 House 5	P I	1	0	0	0	0	0	0	1	1	Hayes and Lancaster (1975:46)
Dog dentary	Site 1676 House 6	P I	0	1	0	0	0	0	0	1	1	Hayes and Lancaster (1975:27)
Dog dentary	Site 1676 House 6	P I	0	1	0	0	0	0	0	1	1	Hayes and Lancaster (1975:29)
Dog skeleton	Site 1676 House 6	P I	1	0	0	0	0	0	0	1	1	Hayes and Lancaster (1975:29)
Dog dentary	Site 1676 House 7	P I	0	1	0	0	0	0	0	1	1	Hayes and Lancaster (1975:29)
Dog	Site 423-101	P I	1	0	0	0	0	0	0	1	1	Brown and Brown (1993)
Dog	Site 423-131	P I	1	0	0	0	0	0	0	1	3	Brown and Brown (1993)
Dog mandibles	White Water Dev U1P I	P I	0	0	0	0	1	0	1	1	1	Roberts (1939:176)
Dog partial skeleton	White Water Dev U1P I	P I	0	0	0	0	0	0	0	1	1	Roberts (1939:186)
Dog skeleton	White Water Dev U1P I	P I	0	0	1	0	1	0	0	1	1	Roberts (1939:Figure 44)
Dog skeleton	White Water Dev U2P I	P I	0	0	1	0	1	0	0	1	1	Roberts (1939:Figure 44)
		P I	12	2	7	3	4	0	1	29	49	
Dog partial skeleton	5mtumr 2347	P II	0	0	0	0	0	0	0	1	3	Emslie (1978:174)
Dog partial skeleton	5mtumr 2347	P II	0	0	0	0	0	0	0	1	1	Emslie (1978:174)
Dog partial skeleton	5mtumr 2347	P II	0	0	1	0	0	0	0	1	5	Emslie (1978:174)
Dog skull	5mtumr 2347	P II	1	1	0	0	0	0	0	1	2	Emslie (1978:169)
Dog skull	5mtumr 2347	P II	0	0	0	0	0	0	0	1	1	Emslie (1978:174)
Wolf skull	5mtumr 2347	P II	0	1	0	0	0	0	0	1	1	Emslie (1978:174)
Dog partial skeleton	5mtumr 2559	P II	1	0	0	0	0	0	0	1	1	Emslie (1978:175)
Dog skeleton	5mtumr 2559	P II	0	0	0	0	0	0	0	1	1	Emslie (1978:175)
Dog skeleton	5mtumr 2559	P II	0	0	0	0	0	0	0	1	1	Emslie (1978:175)
Dog skeleton	5mtumr 2559	P II	0	1	0	0	0	1	0	1	2	Emslie (1978:175)
Dog skull	5mtumr 2559	P II	1	0	0	0	0	0	0	1	1	Emslie (1978:175)
Dog skeleton	5mtumr 2559	P II	0	0	0	0	0	0	0	1	1	Emslie (1978:175)
Dog skeleton	AZ:D:11:1161	P II	1	0	0	0	0	0	0	0	1	Andersen (1978:119)
Dog skull	BC 51	P II	0	1	0	0	0	0	0	0	1	Kluckhohn et al. (1939:39)
Dog	LA 37595	P II	1	1	0	0	0	0	0	0	1	Mick-O'Hara (1994:185)
Dog	Pia Mesa Rd	P II	0	1	0	0	0	0	0	0	1	Zunie and Leonard (1990)
Dog	Pueblo del Arroyo	P II	0	1	0	0	0	0	0	0	2	Judd (1959:81)
Dog skull	Pueblo del Arroyo	P II	0	1	0	1	0	0	0	0	2	Judd (1959:74)
Dog skeleton	Sambrito Village	P II	0	0	0	1	0	0	0	0	14	Eddy (1966:248–249)

Continued

TABLE 7.2 (CONTINUED)
Pueblo Dog Remains (BM II–P V)

Remains	Site	Time	Pit Stratum	Kiva	Surface Stratum	Human Burial	Dog Burial	Midden	Other	Cases	Number of Dogs	Reference
Dog	Site 423-108	P II	1	0	0	0	0	0	0	1	1	Brown and Brown (1993)
Dog	Site 442-14	P II	0	1	0	0	0	0	0	1	4	Brown and Brown (1993)
Dog	Tseh So	P II	1	1	0	0	0	0	0	1	1	Hibben (1937:101)
Dog	Tse-ta'a	P II	1	0	2	0	0	0	0	1	2	Haag (1966:131)
Dog skull	5mtumr 2785	P III	6	13	2	0	0	0	1	23	50	Emslie (1978:175)
Dog skeleton	AZ:D:10:16	P III	1	0	1	0	0	0	0	1	2	Ambler (1994:463–464)
Dog dentary	Badger House 1453	P III	0	0	0	0	0	1	0	1	1	Hayes and Lancaster (1975:69–73)
Dog partial skeleton	Badger House 1453	P III	0	0	0	0	0	1	0	1	4	Hayes and Lancaster (1975:69–73)
Dog skeleton	Site 499 Mesa Verde	P III	0	0	0	0	1	0	0	1	1	Lister (1964:9)
Dog skeleton	Site 866 Mesa Verde	P III	0	1	1	0	1	0	0	6	10	Lister (1964:25)
Dog skull	Chavez Pass	P IV	0	0	0	1	0	0	0	1	1	Lucas (1897:544)
Dog skull	Homol'ovi II	P IV	0	1	0	0	0	0	0	1	1	Walker (1996)
Coyote skull	Homol'ovi II	P IV	0	1	0	0	0	0	0	1	1	Walker (1996)
Dog skeleton	Homol'ovi III	P IV	0	1	0	0	0	0	0	1	1	Adams (2001)
Dog skeleton	Homol'ovi III	P IV	0	4	0	1	0	0	0	5	5	Adams (2001)
Dog skeleton	Awatovi	P V	0	1	0	0	0	0	0	1	1	Smith (1972:70)
Dog skeleton	Gran Quivira	P V	0	2	0	0	0	0	0	2	2	Hayes (1981)
Total			24	22	10	5	7	2	2	72	128	

Presence and absence are denoted by 1 and 0, respectively, in all columns except Cases and Number of Dogs. Numbers in these columns are frequencies.

TABLE 7.3

Types of Dog Remains

Dog Remains	Number of Contexts	Number of Dogs Represented
Dog	11	22
Dog skeleton	24	51
Dog partial skeleton	9	14
Dog remains	1	1
Subtotal	45 (62.5%)	88 (68.8%)
Dog skull	14	23
Wolf skull	1	1
Dog partial skull	1	1
Dog dentary	8	12
Dog mandible	2	2
Dog maxilla	1	1
Subtotal	27 (37.5%)	40 (31.3%)
Total	72 (100.0%)	128 (100.0%)

of reputed witches (see Table 7.1), occur either in pithouses or kivas (Table 7.4). In earlier sites, pithouses predominate; in later sites, kivas do. This follows the historical trend of specialized ritual buildings (kivas) emerging from an earlier, less differentiated domestic and ritual place, the pithouse. This is a pattern common to the Southwest and Mesoamerica (see Walker and Lucero 2000). In both regions (see chapters by Lucero, Mills, and Joyce, this volume), oral traditions offer useful insights for exploring these patterns.

Emergence Traditions

Origin stories in the Pueblo world are histories of the world and its human and nonhuman agents (Parsons 1996 [1939]:210–266). Such histories are necessarily active and ongoing. They explain past actions and simultaneously provide contexts for future actions. In these histories, all things, people and nonpeople alike, are animated by agentic spiritual forces (Bunzel 1932:483). In that sense, all objects in the Pueblo world transcend the subject-object boundary. Despite variability within and between Pueblo groups, there are themes in their narratives that resist change, particularly the concept of emergence from a series of earlier underworlds. In Pueblo traditions humans and other beings, including dogs and witches, have lived in a succession of earlier worlds underneath this one. Many of their stories focus directly on the emergence process into

TABLE 7-4
Contexts of Dog Remains

Time (CE)	Pit Structure	Row %	Kiva	Row %	Surface Structure	Row %	Human Burial	Row %	Dog Burial	Row %	Midden	Row %	Other Feature	Row %	Total
BM II (<500)	0	0.0	0	0.0	0	0.0	1	0.0	0	0.0	0	0.0	0	0.0	1
BM III (500–700)	5	83.3	0	0.0	0	0.0	0	0.0	1	16.7	0	0.0	0	0.0	6
P I (700–900)	12	41.4	2	6.9	7	24.1	3	10.3	4	13.8	0	0.0	1	3.4	29
P II (900–1150)	6	26.1	13	56.5	2	8.7	0	0.0	1	4.3	0	0.0	1	4.3	23
P III (1150–1300)	1	16.7	1	16.7	1	16.7	1	0.0	1	16.7	2	33.3	0	0.0	6
P IV (1300–1540)	0	0.0	4	80.0	0	0.0	0	20.0	0	0.0	0	0.0	0	0.0	5
P V (>1540)	0	0.0	2	100.0	0	0.0	0	0.0	0	0.0	0	0.0	0	0.0	2
Total	24	33.3	22	30.6	10	13.9	5	6.9	7	9.7	2	2.8	2	2.8	72

this world and ascribe the origin of many attributes of their contemporary cultures (corn farming, death, afterlife, their current settlements, interactions with non-Indian peoples) to events taking place during and soon after that event. Today the underworld is still an active facet of the greater Pueblo world.

In Hopi creation stories, witches emerged with people from the underworld, bringing death with them. Kivas recreate the entry places of the emergence narratives. As animate beings in their own right, with names (for example, the Horn Kiva), they are central to ongoing activities and referencing past activities (see Walker 1999). Often the internal architecture of kivas, as well as that of earlier pithouses, includes features that reflect their status as points of communication and passage between the upper and lower worlds.

One such feature is a pit extending down from the floor of the kiva into the roof of the underworld. These pits are usually placed along the center axis of the structure in line with a hearth and a ventilation system. Southwestern archaeologists, based on Hopi ethnography, call these features *sipapus*, or literally, places of emergence. For Pueblo peoples, sipapus also include natural features such as deep canyons, lakes, caves, shrines, and other points of contact with the underworld. When we understand that oral traditions are not simply narratives, but as material as any other practice, then it's not hard to imagine that many recognizable and generally accepted patterns in the Pueblo archaeological record are indirect traces of past oral traditions. The orderly transformation from pithouses to kivas and the similarities in their features, for example, suggest that variable emergence traditions have been at play in the Pueblo Southwest for thousands of years. Given this tradition, it makes sense that the structure of deposits in those contexts would reflect the consequences of practices shaped by interactions between human and nonhuman actors (for example, dogs, witches, people), as well as memories of past interactions of such actors.

In one version of the Hopi creation story (Stephen 1929:8–9), a witch killed a chief's daughter and was about to be executed. The witch asked everyone to look down into the hole of emergence, or sipapu, to see that the soul of the daughter was alive and well in the world below. He said that she would reemerge in four days and live again with them. At this point, Coyote, who was a pet of the witch (Stephen 1929:9), tossed a rock over the hole, preventing forever the return of the dead (in human form) from the underworld. The people were angry and banished Coyote from their presence. Without Coyote, this story is told in Zuni Pueblo also (Parsons 1924:137–138).

In a Hopi-Tewa version of the creation story, it is Coyote who creates death. A young girl dies, and he explains death is necessary for people to value life. Without death the sun will not move through the sky. He dies himself to demonstrate this fact. The people peer down through the hole of emergence and see him there with the young girl, happily combing her hair. After this demonstration of where souls go at death, he returns to the world (Parsons 1994 [1926]:171–172).

More generally, Pueblo peoples ascribe sickness and environmental problems (floods, droughts, crop blights), as well as death, to witches. Coyotes are described as witches' pets in part because witches favor taking the form of coyotes in order to travel more stealthily at night. Other nocturnal hunters, such as wolves, owls, and nighthawks, are also popular forms, as are black animals (ravens, black dogs), which are difficult to see at night. At Taos Pueblo black dogs are suspected of being witches in disguise (Parsons 1940:163); at Hopi black dogs are also suspected, especially if they "bark or whine for no apparent reason or they dig up the ground around the house which is usually interpreted as a bad omen" (Malotki and Gary 2001:xx). Coyotes, like dogs, have a number of positive and negative social roles and appear in many oral traditions (Malotki 2001; Malotki and Gary 2001; Malotki and Lomatuway'ma 1984). The association between death and Coyote takes on a comic role in the majority of Hopi Coyote folktales (Luckert 1984; Malotki and Lomatuway'ma 1984). Again and again Coyote gets caught up in adventures in which he succumbs to a foolish death. Witches, coyotes, and dogs all have negative underworld associations that potentially link their deposition to sipapus represented by pithouses and kivas.

Relations between Spirits and People

Witches

In my earlier interpretation of witchcraft persecution (Walker 1998), I concentrated on identifying the ritual nature or structure of the deposits in question. That work was inspired by Wilshusen's (1986) seminal study of kiva abandonment practices and was part of growing interest in depositional approaches to religion among behavioral archaeologists (LaMotta and Schiffer 1999; Montgomery 1993; Schiffer 1987; Walker 1995, 1996), which paralleled emerging ritual and practice studies in Europe (for example, Hill 1995; Merrifield 1987, Pollard 1995; J. Thomas 1991). I developed a stratigraphic sequence model to demonstrate the purposeful closure of pithouses and kivas. I argued that burning, sealing of features (for example, ventilation tunnels, hearths, pits), and the inclusion of whole artifacts on their floors and in superimposed fill strata were evidence of structured or ritual deposition. Known witchcraft-persecution practices in the ethnohistoric and ethnographic Southwest seemed the best explanation for the deposition of human remains in these contexts. At the time it seemed reasonable that such a dangerous object as a witch would be disposed of in a ceremonial fashion. Beyond that general understanding of ceremonial context, I did not have a particular explanation of the logic in these places. Indeed, given the ritual structure of the deposits, I argued that they were fitting locales for the disposal of dangerous nonhuman social actors.

When placed within the narrative structure of Pueblo emergence traditions, a relatively specific interpretation becomes possible: witches were placed in these contexts to push them back through the hole of emergence into the world below (Walker 2005). Puebloans were applying the lessons of their history in their defense against witches. Many of these pithouses and kiva structures were burned, which may reflect an additional effort to purify or destroy them. Fire is a purifying punishment of witches in the afterlife. At Santo Domingo Pueblo, for example, they say that in the underworld, the Great Mother Iyatiku consumes evil ones in a fiery oven (White 1935).

For Pueblo peoples, the most potent and concentrated form of spiritual agency is found in water. Ancestors and spirit benefactors control rain and are often simply described as rain (Sekaquaptewa and Washburn 2004). This may explain a striking funerary pattern: while many surrounding cultures routinely practice more than one form of burial (for example, inhumation and cremation), the prehistoric and historic Pueblos overwhelmingly favored inhumation. Many Puebloan peoples fear that cremation will negatively affect the rainmaking power of the ancestors by releasing their water. Burning would therefore not only destroy the bodies of witches, but also neutralize their spirits. On the way to the underworld, Hopi souls come to a fork in the trail, at which point witches are forced down a path to a series of fiery pits, where they are purified and turned into other forms of life or, in the worst cases, destroyed altogether (Simmons 1942:122).

Of course, during the course of Pueblo prehistory, enacting the lessons of oral histories with respect to witches would vary in accordance with local historical contexts (Walker 2005). In some societies, like those associated with the Chaco World, witchcraft persecution may have assumed a form of political repression; in other, later prehistoric towns, witches may have been the focus of intervillage warfare and been held responsible for epidemic diseases. In the earliest pithouse villages, it is likely that shamans unsuccessful in their healing tasks were assumed to be covert witches and treated accordingly. Similarly, I think the long-term history of dog deposits reflects a varied process of the working and reworking of peoples' understandings and memories about their relationships with dogs and other spiritual actors. As I will argue, while some dogs would be social actors analogous to witches, others would have more positive relationships with people and spirits. Because both types of interactions involve relationships with the underworld, both could lead to similar depositional contexts in pithouses, kivas, caves, and other possible sipapus.

Dogs

Dogs are some of the more ambiguous members of Pueblo societies. They are companions, guardians, potential witches (Dumarest 1919:164), and, occasionally, meals (Stephen 1969 [1936]:266, 939). Their spiritual practice and agency overlaps that of witches and other social actors whose life histories involve passage through kivas, pithouses, and other sipapus. Their spirits were manifest in katsina masks and murals, their lives sacrificed to demonstrate proper behavior, and their souls sent as messengers and offerings to the ancestors (Smith 1952; Stephen 1969 [1936]:115–117, 555).

Such ambiguity, common worldwide, has been described in Jungian terms as an archetypical rendering of the conflicted ambivalence we have about ourselves (Serpell 1995:254). The common coyote folktales of western North America also tend to express such ambiguities and serve as a mirror for human conduct in Pueblo and other Native American cultures (Luckert 1984). Although dogs lack the sensational or exotic qualities of witches, and Pueblo ethnographers tended to neglect them, we can still glean hints of the importance of human/dog interactions that involve the underworld, witches, and domestication. Early Spanish conquistadors described dogs kept in underground pens at the Piro pueblos of New Mexico: "They breed many dogs, though not as fine or useful as those of Spain, keeping them in their pens underground" (Hammond and Rey 1928:292). The Hopi pueblo of Oraibi sits on a mesa top, and dogs are thought to have once lived in the ground beneath it.

> Descending a trail part of the way [down from the village] …there is an opening in the side of the mesa called *pokki* (dog house). Tradition says that a longtime ago the dogs lived in this opening but left it and moved to the village, where they have lived ever since. (Voth 1901:119)

This statement, in a very simplified form, is an emergence myth for dogs. Tellingly, this same Pokki grotto is also the assembly place for the impersonators of the Maasau katsina. Maasau is the most feared katsina.

He is the original owner of the Hopi lands and the lord of the underworld, and as such has power over life and death. Those who channel or manifest his spirit use a natural feature as their sipapu.

> The Massaw kachinas differ from all other kachinas in that they reside at Pokki, a shrine of their own, on the east side of Orayvi. There they live in a big hole in the cliff. There must be a wide ledge running along there which allows them to line up and practice their dance steps when they plan to make an appearance, for they are never seen rehearsing in a kiva. (Malotki and Lomatuway'ma 1987:228)

Maasau is also associated with fire and war. His "distinctive wail" is likened to that of a howling dog (Malotki and Lomatuway'ma 1987:33). In one version of the Hopi emergence story, it is Maasau who aids the first witch to kill a rain priest's daughter; when the witch's life is threatened, she points down into the sipapu, showing that the daughter still lives in the underworld (Cushing 1924:167). For the Hopis, there is a katsina for every important force in the universe, including the canines. The dog katsina, in particular, is accorded the honor of being the leader of all domestic animals.

The katsina deities arrive in Hopi from late December to early January and then leave the pueblo to return to their homes in the underworld in July, after the Niman (home going) ceremony. In an interesting example, Stephen (1969:115–117) described preparations being made on January 21, 1894, in all the kivas for the return of the katsinas. In the Horn Kiva they were making male (*pokkachina*) and female (*pokwuhti*) dog masks. The snouts were fashioned from carved gourds or cottonwood and then covered with dog skins. He said, "Many dogs have been killed this morning and their heads used to cover these maskette snouts." These dog katsinas danced with the clowns in the plaza the next day. His description begs the question: what happened to such masks (skulls) and other dogs' parts when their lives ended and their afterlives began?

The Niman ceremony celebrates the return of the katsinas to the underworld. One year, a dog was sacrificed by clowns during the ceremony. "About 3 pm, during the eighth act, one of the clowns lassoed a large white mastiff cur and another clown beat it to death, slowly, with a stone" (Stephen 1969:554–555). The killer then cut off the dog's head and opened the belly. Two other clowns pulled out the innards. They forced a third to eat some of the blood and then rubbed it on their faces. One wore the guts over his shoulder and chased the others around with the head. Each time he touched one of them, they pretended to die. He climbed up to a house roof followed by a Maasau katsina. The clown shook Maasau off the ladder four times, but on the fifth attempt the deity succeeded in reaching the roof. He took the dog's head from the clown and prepared it as an offering along with corn wafer (piki), corn mush, meat, prayer meal, and tobacco. He walked down from the mesa and deposited the materials in a crevice (Stephen 1969:554–555).

Fewkes (1990:303) described the same ritual but emphasized that the clown (a spirit person in its own right) wearing the dog's entrails was mimicking the god Maasau in a satirical fashion. Eventually the actual Massau katsina appeared and put a stop to this misbehavior. It is common for clowns to misbehave during Pueblo rituals and then be corrected by the katsina deities (in this case by Maasau himself). After correcting the clowns, he took the dog's head and reverently adorned it with corn wafers, corn mush, meat, prayer meal, and tobacco, and then walked down from the mesa and deposited its skull in a crevice. In this act he reminded the clowns and audience of proper behavior and transferred the soul of the dog to the underworld with honor. The use of the dog's head as an instrument of death and the act of climbing the ladder from the plaza below seem to link the emergence tradition, Massau's power over life, and the importance of dogs.

Eagles are also killed during the Niman ceremony. Their souls return home to the underworld with the katsinas, bringing messages to the dead. The feathers and wings, like those of the dogs' bodies, are used to make ceremonial tools (for example, masks, wands, prayer feathers), and their bodies are deposited in an eagle graveyard. Other raptorial birds have also been found in prehistoric subterranean structures such as kivas (for example, Walker 1996).

Ceremonies in other pueblos also integrate death, people, and dogs. The Tewa Pueblos of Santa Clara and Nambe celebrated a dog dance on the King's Day (January 6) and Easter Sunday. In the ritual at Santa Clara, a girl dances around a plaza with a nude, painted man on a leash (the dog) and collects food from the audience. At times she has to hold the dog back from biting the crowd. The Nambe ceremony was less comical: "The bowls of food people took out to the plaza for the dog were also intended for the dead (powaha) and were subsequently carried out to a field and thrown for the dead. The offerer was not to look back whatever noises he might hear, for the noises were made by the dead" (Parsons 1929:223). In the past a more elaborate version of this ritual, known as the Peace Dance, was performed on the Fourth of July in Picuris and Taos.

DISCUSSION AND CONCLUSIONS

Even though they also revolve around death and the underworld, Pueblo peoples' relations with dogs seem more ambiguous than the universally negative social relationships between people and witches. The particular attributes of these nonhuman actors build on their domesticated and natural behaviors. Coyotes and certain dogs, such as black dogs, were a favorite of night-traveling witches, perhaps because of the natural nocturnal camouflage of black dogs. More generally, however, dogs served in the capacity of nighttime guardians against people and witches. They also served as intermediaries between people and other domestic animals. This central role in human relations may have contributed to the perception of dog souls as messengers that, like eagles, could communicate between this world and the souls of the human dead in the underworld. At Hopi dogs die with the arrival and departure of the katsinas.

In the course of these social roles, skeletal remains are produced whose deposition in kivas makes sense. Kivas, pithouses, and rock crevices would have served as sipapus for dogs, as well as other human and nonhuman social actors. To ritually complete the transfer of the dogs' souls between this and the next world, their bodies would be placed at the threshold of the underworld. After all, dogs originally emerged from beneath the ground in oral traditions. Certainly this would be reinforced by the fact that the dens of wild dogs and coyotes are often dug into the ground. Their associations with the dead, their communicative roles, and their nocturnal habits all link the sounds of dogs with the sounds of the night, the underworld, and ancestors in the case of the Tewas, or the god of death in the case of the Hopis. Ultimately, in their guardian role the spirits of dogs, as revealed by the contextual and stratigraphic clues of pithouse and kiva deposits, may have kept witches and other unwanted social actors from returning through the hole of emergence. As such, although located in contexts like those of witches, they may have been honored rather than feared.

In conclusion, it is clear that expanding our understanding of society to include nonhuman social actors is useful for interpreting archaeological patterns. Inferences about the practice of such actors are facilitated by examining the traces they leave behind in the practices of human agents. The memory work of oral traditions provides important clues for conceptualizing the possible narrative ordering of those traces. In the Pueblo Southwest, emergence or creation traditions illuminate deposits involving people, witches, dogs, and subterranean buildings.

8

Dogs, Pythons, Pots, and Beads

The Dynamics of Shrines and Sacrificial Practices in Banda, Ghana, 1400–1900 CE

Ann B. Stahl

Just over a decade ago, Pierre de Maret (1994:183) opened a review of archaeological evidence on African religion with the observation, "It seems that most archaeologists are afraid of religion....Somewhere in the archaeologist's subconscious, the religious dimension is associated with failure." Though the last decade has seen greater attention to issues of religion, symbolism, and ritual in African archaeology (for example, Childs and Dewey 1996; Huffman 1996; Insoll 2003, 2004; Lewis-Williams and Pearce 2004; Schmidt 1997), the shelf space devoted to archaeological studies of African religions is dwarfed by that in anthropology, history, or art history. For some, this reflects the limits of archaeological sources, the greater material visibility of the mundane compared to the supernatural (Posnansky 1972:30). But more foundationally, our inattention has been conditioned by a view of ritual and religion as components of an ideological or superstructural realm, a residue of beliefs or systems of thought that tell us little about what people did (Insoll 2004:1, 47). Reminiscent of Hawkes's (1954: 161–162) "ladder of inference," we envision ourselves on securer methodological and theoretical ground when we address questions of economy, trade, or settlement (Bradley 2005:193–196). Our view of them as safe domains builds on what Catherine Bell (1992:6) describes as "an initial bifurcation of thought and action" that runs deep in Western intellectual traditions, combined with a presumed universal Durkheimian distinction between sacred and profane realms (Goody 1961:147–149). These bifurcations inform our tendency to equate the study of ritual with questions of meaning and symbolism, considered distinct from domains dominated by function and utility (Bell 1992:69–74; Bradley 2005:28–36, 193–196; Brück 1999:317; Goody 1961:145; Schmidt 1997; Walker 1998:249).

The supposition that life can be parsed into discrete domains has methodological and evidential implications (Bell 1992; Brück 1999; Insoll 2004). We seek traces of ritual in special depositional contexts (for example, burials, monuments, or special-purpose structures; Pollard, this volume) and plumb what we conceive as the symbolic dimension of material traces for insight into belief and meaning systems (for example, de Maret 1994). "Ordinary refuse," on the other hand, seems more likely to provide insight into mundane, especially economic activities (compare Brück 1999; Hill 1995; Moore 1982). Yet ethnographers of Africa have long argued against analytically separating religion and ritual from the domain of daily life (Evans-Pritchard 1937; Goody 1970:216; Goody 1961, 1962: 37–40; Tait 1961:21), and recent technological studies in Africa and elsewhere underscore the extent to which production is ritualized and belief systems materialized in metals, ceramics, and other media (Ackerman et al. 1999; David and Kramer 2001:328–347; Frank 1998:101; Herbert 1993; Lechtmann 1984; McNaughton 1988; Schmidt 1997; van der Merwe and Avery 1987). Even here, however, a tendency to see ritual as a site where culture and meaning are powerfully condensed and through which structures of knowledge are reproduced subtly reinscribes a dichotomy between thought and action (Bell 1992:31, 75–80). Overcoming this requires what Bell (1992) envisions as a shift from a study of ritual as an analytical object to a focus on ritualization as strategic practice. This shift has methodological and evidential implications. Whereas a focus on ritual directs attention to special-purpose contexts, features, or "special paradigmatic acts" (Bell 1992:7), ritualization directs attention to the ways in which ritual activity is simultaneously embedded in and distinguished from the flow of daily social activity, as well as the effects of those practices on social life—in other words, how ritualization works and what is accomplished through it (Bell 1992:89). As underscored by other contributors to this volume, ritualization is bound up in memory work, in that practice is a site through which past and present coexist (Argenti and Röschenthaler 2006), with implications for how we approach continuity and change. Thus we must consider ritualization in relation to a wider array of depositional contexts than the burials, monuments, or shrines emphasized in archaeological studies of ritual (Bradley 2005; Brück 1999; Hill 1995), and approach meaning, culture, and memory as emergent rather than inscribed in a distillable symbolic dimension of artifacts or contexts.

To view meaning and culture as emergent reframes questions surrounding continuity and change, and challenges us to consider the forms and practices of memory in cultural transmission (Connerton 1989; Rowlands 1993). Archaeologists of Africa and the African diaspora tend to view religion and ritual as sites of conservative, traditional practice and therefore continuity (DeCorse 1992; de Maret 1994). In diasporic contexts, evidence of African ritual and religion is seen as a form of resistance through which African descendants maintain(ed) traditions in the face of overwhelming oppression (for example, Ruppel et al. 2003; Wilkie 1997), or more recently as part of a complex "memoryscape of slavery" (Argenti and Röschenthaler 2006:36). Underscoring continuity potentially diverts attention from the *dynamics* of ritualization, how ritual is recast or recontextualized (J. Thomas 1991) in relation to changing circumstances. An extensive literature in African history and anthropology underscores shrines, divination, and sacrificial practices as key sites through which political economic dislocations of the last several centuries (slave trade, colonial rule, modernization) were and continue to be negotiated (Argenti 2006; Baum 1999; Comaroff and Comaroff 1993; Goody 1957; Kuba and Lentz 2002; Lentz 2000; McCaskie 1981; Mendonsa 1982; Parish 1999, 2000; Parker 2004; Röschenthaler 2006; Shaw 1997, 2002; Ward 1956). Traces of these negotiations may be discerned in the palimpsest character of ritual practice operating as a form of practical, embodied memory (Shaw 2002:5–10). This dynamism is not surprising, since the domain of knowledge and practice that we call religion is a primary site through which people cope with evil and uncertainty, struggle to ensure the well-being of self, family, and community (van Beek 1994), and through which power operates (Argenti 2006; Baum 1999; McCaskie 1981:139–140; Mendonsa 1982: 10–12, 202–208; see Bravmann [1974], Parker [2004], and Röschenthaler [2006] on intercultural flows of ritual products and knowledge). But an emphasis on the dynamics of ritualization should not be construed as synonymous with a focus on change. Continuities do not occur by default; they too are worked at and emerge through practice, just as do the discontinuities that we read as evidence of change (Joyce, this volume; Rowlands 1993:144; Shaw 2002:9–10).

A focus on ritualization and its entailments as memory belies another bifurcation that implicitly conditions many studies of cultural dynamics: that between culture and history. As Dirks (1996) has argued, the anthropological privileging of culture over history has analytical and narrative consequences. We seek to discern structures or objects that we subsequently put in motion (culture, then history; cosmology, then ritual; meaning, then practice; statics, then dynamics). An emphasis on practice does not, in and of itself, overcome these bifurcations (Bell 1992:75–80).[1] But as underscored throughout this volume, the object we call culture emerges through embodied action in the world and a materiality that defies our privileging of ideas over action, custom over process (Moore 1993:3), and encourages a consideration of memory as process.

In this study I focus on the dynamics of ritualization in the Banda area of Ghana in relation to political-economic dislocations associated with the Atlantic trade and colonial rule. My goal is to explore analytical strategies that put into practice the conceptual reframings outlined above and elsewhere in this volume (for example, Joyce; Mills and Walker). With few exceptions (Ogundiran 2002), the burgeoning archaeological literature on global entanglements in African societies has been curiously silent on issues of ritual and religion. Taking my own work as an example, we have felt more comfortable exploring continuities and discontinuities in realms that archaeologists do not fear: the "hard surfaces" of production, consumption, settlement, and exchange (Cruz 2003; Stahl 1999, 2001b, 2002; Stahl and Cruz 1998; Stahl and Stahl 2004). Yet if we take seriously the propositions outlined above, we need to consider anew the possibilities for investigating the dynamics of ritualization through archaeological sources. After a brief summary of the Banda case study, I explore a strategy for investigating ritualization that builds on Kopytoff's (1986) notion of object biographies (see also Gosden and Marshall 1999).[2] By following object classes and their co-occurrence through varied depositional contexts, this approach works to cast object biographies in relation to depositional practices as a platform for exploring their social effects (Walker 1998; Walker and Lucero 2000).

GLOBAL ENTANGLEMENTS IN BANDA, GHANA

The Banda area of west central Ghana lies immediately south of the Black Volta River along the southern margins of the wooded savanna (Figure 8.1). The region occupied a strategic position in interregional trade from at least the thirteenth century CE, when a series of entrepôts emerged along the northern margins of the forest (Arhin 1970, 1979). Here, forest products such as gold and kola were transferred to caravans whose pack animals were susceptible to forest zoonoses. Commodities from centers on the Niger River and ultimately the Sahara and beyond passed through these entrepôts. The sixteenth and seventeenth centuries wit-

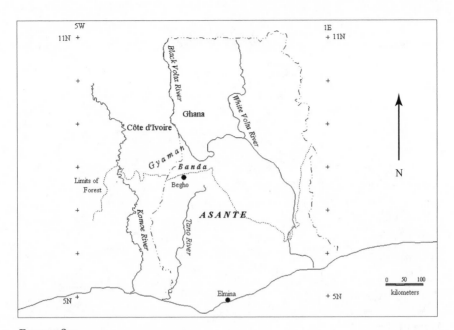

FIGURE 8.1
The Banda area, Ghana.

nessed a southward shift in interregional exchange as Atlantic connections were forged with diverse European groups (DeCorse 2001). In the eighteenth century, the powerful forest state of Asante embarked on expansionist military campaigns directed in part at capturing control of the northern trade (Wilks 1975). This ushered in a period of Asante hegemony over the area today encompassed by the nation-state of Ghana. Political economic dislocation characterized the late nineteenth century as the British sought to extend their influence into Asante's hinterland and later established direct colonial control over the Gold Coast Colony. Although Banda entered into a treaty agreement with the British in 1896, they remained a distant colonial presence until the 1920s, when they asserted their administrative presence (Stahl 2001b:82–106).

Drawing on archaeological, oral-historical, and documentary sources, the Banda Research Project has focused on how daily life in the Banda area was shaped by these global entanglements (Stahl 2001b:107–214). Extensive archaeological investigations at two village sites (Makala Kataa and Kuulo Kataa; Figure 8.2) have been augmented by small test excavations in a regional testing program (Stahl 2007). Makala Kataa (Figure 8.3) is a multicomponent site abandoned in the 1920s, when British officials

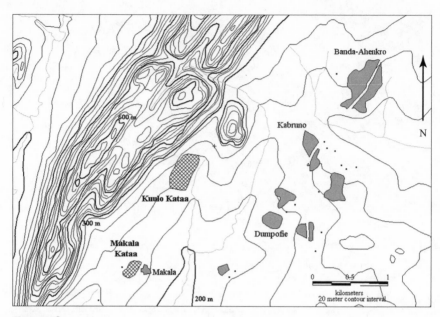

FIGURE 8.2
Makala Kataa and Kuulo Kataa.

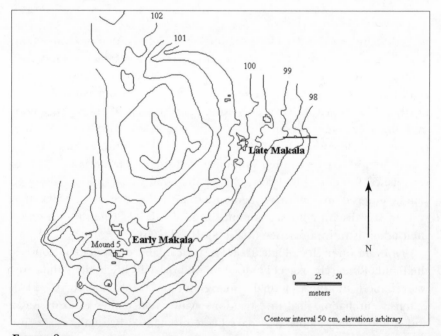

FIGURE 8.3
Makala Kataa.

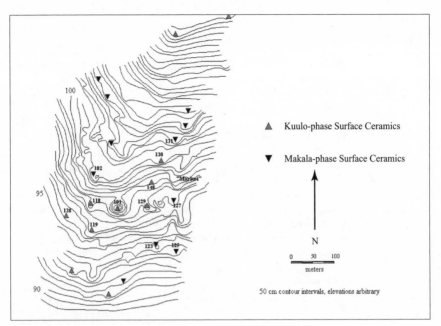

FIGURE 8.4

Kuulo Kataa, showing mound numbers and affiliations based on surface-collected ceramics.

promoted rebuilding of villages laid out on a grid system with greater seg-regation between living areas and refuse, burials, and latrines (Stahl 2001b:103–105). "Late Makala" refers to the village that had been occupied for roughly 25 years before it was abandoned under pressure from colonial officials. An earlier settlement ("Early Makala") was occupied in the period of Asante hegemony, from the final decades of the eighteenth century until about 1820. Archaeological evidence is consistent with rapid site abandon-ment, as suggested by oral accounts that Banda villagers fled the area under pressure of attack by a neighboring polity (Gyaman; Ameyaw 1965). Based on the assumption that usable goods are typically removed when a site is abandoned (Cameron and Tomka 1993), configurations of whole pots (some stacked), hearthstones, and grinding stones suggest that resi-dents either abandoned the site rapidly and/or moved some distance away (compare Brück 1999:330 for critiques of utilitarian assumptions in aban-donment literature; also Walker 1998:259–264). Other early nineteenth-century sites demonstrate a similar pattern.

The multicomponent site of Kuulo Kataa (Figure 8.4) evidenced a Makala Phase 2 occupation (equivalent to Early Makala) and an earlier, ceram-ically distinct Kuulo-phase occupation radiocarbon dated to ca. 1400–1650 CE

TABLE 8.1

Working Chronology for Banda-area Sites

Date	Event	Archaeological Site	Archaeological Phase
1925	Increased presence of British colonial officials.	Late Makala abandoned.	Makala Phase 1
1896	British troops deployed against Samori.	Late Makala established.	Makala Phase 1
1818–1819	Asante war with Gyaman; Banda villagers fled north of Volta River.	Early Makala abandoned.	Makala Phase 2
1773–1774	Asante invaded Banda; Banda incorporated into Asante state.	Early Makala occupied after (and possibly before) Asante invasion.	Makala Phase 2
1722–1723	Begho "sacked" by Asante; shift from trans-Saharan trade to Atlantic trade.		—
From ca. 1600	Atlantic influences felt in Banda area (tobacco pipes, maize).	Kuulo Kataa.	Kuulo phase
From ca. 1400 CE	Height of Begho's influence; exchange between Volta Basin and Niger River with links to trans-Saharan trade.	Kuulo Kataa.	Kuulo phase

calibrated (Table 8.1). The Kuulo-phase occupation of Kuulo Kataa thus spans the period when the Banda area was enmeshed in the Niger River trade but was simultaneously being drawn into Atlantic networks. Villagers produced crafts (ceramic, metal, and ivory) and participated in the regional network centered on Begho, a large town on Banda's southern margin known to Arab chroniclers as an entrepôt where northern commodities (copper alloys, salt) were exchanged for gold and other forest products (Bravmann and Mathewson 1970; Posnansky 1979, 1987).

Archaeological investigations have documented changes in the character of settlement, production (both subsistence and craft), exchange, and consumption across the range of occupations at Kuulo and Makala Kataa. New crops were embraced and new objects desired (Stahl 1999, 2001b, 2002; Stahl and Cruz 1998). Confronted simultaneously with novel opportunities and constraints, ethnicity was refigured, labor practices altered, and the character of chieftaincy transformed (Stahl 1991, 2001a). Our work to date has centered on the "accessible" dimension of these transformations, and as such my accounts have been largely silent on ritual practice as a component of Banda people's negotiation of them. Yet if we take inspiration from the ethnographic and historical literatures on ritual practice in Africa, several insights are warranted: ritualization is bound up in responses to stressful conditions; ritual practice both reproduces and transforms social and political relations; it is intimately linked to technological processes; and it is simultaneously pervasive and punctuating—it envelops daily life at the same time as it sets particular moments apart. Through their materiality (Joyce, this volume), ritual practices have the power to transform mind, body, and surroundings (Lentz 2000; Mather 2003; see Gillespie, Pauketat, this volume), and to shape social memory (Argenti and Röschenthaler 2006; Connerton 1989; Shaw 2002:1–23). How then can we approach a study of ritualization in relation to the global entanglements that conditioned the daily lives of Banda peoples? What evidential sources and analytical strategies help us to discern the dynamics of ritualization through this turbulent period, when Banda's social fields were being reconfigured through global entanglements?

SOURCES OF EVIDENCE

Ethnographic information provides a potentially rich source of analogical insight when used comparatively (Stahl 2001b:19–40, 2004; Wylie 1985). Shrines (compare Insoll 2004:104–105 on definitional issues) are integral to the negotiation of well-being in the Banda area today (Table 8.2). Though Christianity and Islam have found converts among the Nafanas, who numerically dominate the Banda area, the majority of Nafanas are "animists" who practice ancestor veneration. Like many West African peoples (for example, Baum 1999:37–42; Rattray 1923:139–144), the Nafanas believe in an almighty God (Nyiɛpɔɔ) who cannot be approached directly; however, three categories of intermediary spirits or deities are accessible: the ancestors (*kuulo*); *nyiɛ* (small gods), associated with nuclear families; and the spirits associated with *sɛɛn* (often glossed as "fetishes"). These spirits are not tied to a specific location; however, collections of objects or locations provide a focus for the offerings that attract them or in which they may temporarily reside. Ancestors of each *katoo* ("house"/matrilineal grouping) are associated with a room where the wooden stools of former family heads are stored (Bravmann 1972:160, 162, Figure 9.1; see also Rattray 1923:95–100).[3] Ancestors are routinely appealed to through libations and periodic offerings of prepared food in specific ritualized contexts (New Yam festival; girls' nubility rites; Stahl 2001b:51–60). Though libations may be poured anywhere, and elderly people often place small quantities

TABLE 8.2

Select Shrines from the Banda Area

Shrine Name/Type	Attributes	Sacrifices/Offerings
Ancestral shrines; family stool room	Protects katoo ("house"/lineage); focus of purification rites in cases of moral violation; embodied by ancestral stools.	Routine: libations; prepared plant foods offered to ancestral stools; moral violations require animal sacrifice (goat, sheep).
Nyiɛ; located on house wall	Protects husband, wife, and children.	Periodic offerings of hens.
Land shrine; tree in bush	Maintains productivity of land; associated with specialist priest (*trafun*; formerly *kahole wura* [see Goody 1964:193–194; Stahl 2001b:58]).	No vegetal foods; periodic offerings of fowl (chicken, not guinea fowl), goat, or cows.
Tano; Jaalɔɔ Stream	Linked to chieftaincy; political legitimacy (Rattray 1923:172–202; Warren and Brempong 1974).	Annual sacrifices offered at New Yam festival; offered yams, eggs at Jaalɔɔ; chicken, sheep, and cow sacrificed at palace; cannot be approached by those who eat goat meat.
Taplapɔɔ; small lake in western hills	Protects entire Banda area.	Paramount chief sacrifices a sheep or cow annually; individual supplicants offer sheep or cow.
Jafun; base of tree on outskirts of town	Protects the town; originated from Senyon; specialist priest (*Jafun bɔɔnyiifun*).	Yualie (sorghum harvest) festival; annual offerings of beer and porridge, chicken, and goat; taboo violations require sacrifices of goats.
Danlui	Led Nafanas in times of war; protects Sie Kwabena Manje house from evil; heals disease.	Annual sacrifice of a goat; periodic animal sacrifices when Danlui identifies misfortune.
Jakari; shrine bundle kept in shrine room	Protects the town; punishes witchcraft and adultery by women.	Annual sacrifice of a cow or goat, a sheep, and three cocks; violators offer drink, chickens, goat, and cash.
Sie Kwadjo	Protects supplicants from witchcraft and evil; shrine cluster in abandoned dwelling.	Periodic offerings of chickens.
Tie	Ensures prosperity in farming and business.	Annual sacrifice of three-year-old cock; offered a hen by a man on the death of his wife; former focus of an annual festival in which paramount chief sacrificed cocks, a sheep, and a dog.

This list represents shrines mentioned in the course of Banda Research Project family history interviews. It is not based on systematic investigation of shrines in the Banda area and should not be taken as a comprehensive list.

of food on the ground for the ancestors prior to eating, food is more typically offered to the stools on formal ceremonial occasions (also Rattray 1923:137, Figures 34, 35).

Nyiɛ, associated with the well-being of a husband, wife, and their children, are established during the celebration of marriage rites (*bijam*). On the first day of Nafana wedding rites, the groom provides a hen, which is killed by his best friend and used to establish a shrine on an outside wall of the groom's room. This becomes the focal point of periodic offerings by the husband to ensure the health and well-being of his wife and subsequently his children. By contrast, sɛɛn are not associated with specific families. Sɛɛn are established in a variety of ways. Some are ancient and associated with the land. Their associated spirits are appealed to at specific locales, often the base of a large tree or near a sacred body of water, with offerings intended to ensure the well-being of the community (also Insoll 2006:225–226; Kuba and Lentz 2002:392–395; Lentz 2000; Mather 2003). Other sɛɛn are acquired by individuals, sometimes by traveling to powerful shrine sites or through an association with individuals (often travelers) who possess knowledge of powerful spirits (Parish 1999; Parker 2004:394, 420). They comprise bundles of natural and cultural objects (animal teeth, bone, beads, metal artifacts) secreted within a ceramic vessel drawn from the repertoire of mundane pottery (Cruz 2003:247, 265, 284) that is placed on an earthen support or sometimes rests on exhausted metal head pans or mortars situated on verandas or in corners of enclosed rooms (Cruz 2003:Figures 7.32, 7.33; also Insoll 2006:228; Rattray 1923:145–150). They may continue to be active after the surrounding rooms have collapsed. Notably these shrines comprise mundane objects that have been recontextualized (J. Thomas 1991) through ritualization.

Despite their diversity, contemporary shrines share several features: many demand sacrifice of specific domestic animals—today, chickens, goats, sheep, or cattle. Domestic animals are seldom killed solely for food, but rather as sacrifices or as part of divination practices (also Fortes and Fortes 1936: 248; Goody 1962:106, 153–155, 211, 368; Insoll 2006:230; MacDonald 1995; Parish 1999:431, 443; Mendonsa 1982:133; Rattray 1923:186–187, 192; Tait 1961:21, 29). Though animals are sacrificed and their blood disgorged near to or on shrines, their meat is consumed elsewhere (for example, Goody 1962:119; Mendonsa 1982:127; Rattray 1923:51, 59, 61, 97–98, 130, 169); we should not, therefore expect bony residues of sacrifices to be concentrated near shrines, particularly those body parts that are socially valued (also Klenck 1995:65; but compare Brown 2005; Insoll 2006:Figure 8). Today, protocols guide the distribution of body parts, particularly hind limbs, which are the prerogative of specific elders or chiefs (also Fortes and Fortes 1936:249; Goody 1962:114, 166, 172–182; Maier 1983:58; Mendonsa 1982:126–127). Butchery and consumption of sacrificed animals occurs away from shrines, with body parts dispersed across and sometimes between sites. After consumption, bony residues are deposited in a variety of contexts, often alongside everyday refuse, rather than in spatially segregated structured deposits. Importantly, these flows of body parts do not simply map social relations. Rather, they both *generate* and *disrupt* relations, as tellingly captured in accounts of the origins of the long-standing Banda chieftaincy dispute. In the late 1970s a subject chief in line to inherit from the aging Banda paramount, Kofi Dwuru II (Bravmann 1972:Figure 9.4), began to usurp the right to the hind quarters of hunted animals (Stahl 2001b:74). Though the dispute's origins are more complex (Bravmann 1972:166; Stahl 2001b:72–76), narrative encapsulates them in the strategic practices associated with the biographies of sacrificed animals. In similar fashion, narratives surrounding the 1996 destoolment of the incumbent paramount chief centered on his unwillingness to offer specific sacrifices (Stahl 2001b:xv). Thus, consumption of animal sacrifices is intimately bound up in the creation and maintenance of political power.

Though much ritual activity is shrine based and therefore locationally circumscribed, shrines are not confined to settlements and may be widely distributed on the landscape (Insoll 2006; Kuba and Lentz 2002; Lentz 2000; Mather 2003; Tait 1961:200–201). These "off-site" shrines and their associated practices will remain invisible in standard site-based archaeological investigations. Regional site surveys may help to identify some such locales; however, the perishable nature of many offerings (blood, eggs, vegetal foods) and their spatially restricted character mean that locating shrines through survey will likely be a needle-in-the-haystack exercise (compare Brown 2005 on Maya hunting shrines). Yet even shrines associated with settlements and durable object classes may be difficult to identify archaeologically. Objects that comprise shrines are typically drawn from the range of items used in daily contexts (also Brück 1999; Insoll 2006:228; Hill 1995:95–101; Walker 1998; Walker and Lucero 2000:133). Associations may help to distinguish objects that have been recontextualized through ritualization. For example, several late eighteenth- and early nineteenth-century Makala Phase 2 contexts (at Makala Kataa, Kuulo Kataa, and site Banda 40) yielded ceramic vessels associated with configurations of objects suggestive of shrines. Upper levels of Mound 131 at Kuulo Kataa yielded portions of two ceramic vessels resting on a gravel floor associated with a concentration of locally produced iron objects (a hoe blade, two rings, four bracelets, a rod, a disc, and several indeterminate pieces), five imported blue hexagonal beads, an imported gunflint/strike-a-light, and 27 python vertebrae, many of which were burned. These objects fall within the range of artifacts recovered from across the site, some used in everyday contexts. Yet their concentration and configuration lend credence to the inference that they were brought together through ritualization.

Rich as the data on ethnographic shrines may be, they provide an illusory thickness and obscure our understanding of dynamics if merely projected onto earlier contexts. Archaeological sources suggest that shrine configurations changed over time, an insight initially based on another excavated context. A fifteenth- to mid-seventeenth-century Kuulo-phase context at Kuulo Kataa (Mound 119) yielded a tight cluster of six dog mandibles associated with a fist-sized angular piece of milky quartz (Stahl 2001b:Plate 8). Adjacent excavation levels yielded seven more canid mandibles, representing a minimum of seven dogs. Our Banda workmen interpreted this as a dog shrine, though dogs are neither routinely sacrificed nor eaten in the area today (for research in other areas, see Apentiik 1997; Fortes and Fortes 1936:249; Goody 1962:59, 113–114, 152, 212, 370; Linseele 2002; Rattray 1923:60–61). Though such formal loci can inform on the dynamics of shrines through time, a feature-oriented archaeology of shrines is a hit-or-miss proposition. However, if we lift our gaze to consider not just the features but more broadly the *depositional practices* associated with shrines, we broaden our analytical strategy and thus potentially enhance our understanding of ritualization as dynamic practice.

ANALYTICAL STRATEGIES

Kopytoff's (1986) notion of object biographies provides a useful entry point into the dynamics of ritualization (see also Ogundiran 2002; Walker 1998; Walker and Lucero 2000). As indicated above, the biography of a sacrificed animal does not end with its death; the animal is butchered, its parts often dispersed, its meat consumed, and its remains deposited, often in generalized refuse deposits. This biography suggests an analytical strategy: *follow the bones* (also Brown 2005). A place to begin is by following the animals whose bones we know were incorporated into formal shrine contexts (here, dogs and pythons). Another potentially productive strategy is to follow other objects found in shrine configurations to explore strategies of ritualization—for immediate purposes here, pots and beads (see Ogundiran 2002 for a provocative analysis of cowries and beads). Of course we are not following the biography of an individual bead or sacrificed animal. We recover these as traces in specific archaeological contexts; but by

Table 8.3

Canid Remains from Makala-phase and Kuulo-phase Contexts at Makala and Kuulo Kataas[a]

Context	NISP[b]	MNI[c]	Volume (m³)[d]	NISP /m³	MNI/m³	Total NISP[e]	% Canid[f]
Late Makala (Makala Phase 1)	11	2	90.0	0.12	0.02	3,028	0.4
Early Makala (Makala Phase 2)	9	2	132.0	0.07	0.02	2,441	0.4
Kuulo Kataa (Makala phase)	19	5'	9.3	2.04	0.54	1,802	1.1
Kuulo Kataa (Kuulo phase)	574	36	159.0	3.60	0.23	27,778	2.1

a. Included are specimens identified as *Canis familiaris*, *Canis* cf. *familiaris*, *Canis*, *Canis* cf., Canidae, and Canidae cf. Canidae include domestic dogs (*Canis familiaris*), jackals (*Canis adustus*), and foxes. A working assumption in this paper is that canid specimens likely derive from domestic dog.
b. Number of identified specimens.
c. Minimum number of individuals. This represents a conservative estimate based on the number of sided elements grouped by mound context.
d. Volume of excavated deposit by context.
e. NISP of all faunal specimens from the site.
f. Percentage of canid NISP in relation to all faunal specimens from the same context.

considering the range of contexts in which these objects are found, we gain insight into varied moments in the biographies of an object class and to the pathways through which they become recontextualized as components of shrines. In the case of sacrificed animals, I am concerned to trace their pathways *out* from shrines. By following what happens to sacrificed animals as they are butchered and dispersed, we gain insight into how the flow of body parts through a settlement potentially created, maintained, or perhaps disrupted social relationships.

FOLLOWING DOGS AND SNAKES

Canid specimens[4] were recovered in small quantities from Early and Late Makala (number of individual specimens [NISP] = 9 and 11, or .07 and .12 per cubic meter, respectively), comprising less than half a percent of the total faunal assemblage, with an MNI (minimum number of individuals) of two for each occupation (Table 8.3). This is consistent with expectations based on contemporary practice. Small, rail-thin animals typical of the pariah dogs of West Africa (Linseele 2002:318) are common in Banda villages today. They are used in hunting, sometimes treated as pets,

TABLE 8.4

Canid Remains from Kuulo Kataa by Mound

Mound	NISP	MNI	Volume (m³)	NISP /m³	MNI/m³	Total NISP	% Canid
Kuulo-phase contexts:							
101	55	4	8.1	6.8	0.49	5,407	1.0
102 (L24 and below)	4	1	1.4	2.9	0.70	635	0.5
118 nonpit	269	7	38.7	7.0	0.18	7,897	3.4
118 pit	41	3	1.8	22.8	1.70	902	4.5
119	65	9	10.9	6.0	0.83	1,657	3.9
129	6	1	6.2	1.0	0.16	1,235	0.5
130	45	2	34.3	1.3	0.06	4,341	1.0
131 (L5 and below)	2	1	1.8	1.1	0.55	330	0.6
138	6	1	17.6	0.3	0.06	361	1.7
148 nonpit	55	4	35.2	1.6	0.11	3,705	1.5
148 pit	20	2	1.9	10.5	1.10	867	2.3
Market	6	1	1.6	3.8	0.63	441	1.4
Total	574	36	159.5	3.6	0.23	27,778	2.1
Makala-phase contexts:							
123	7	1	1.2	5.80	0.83	247	2.8
102 L1–L23	2	1	3.6	0.55	0.28	639	0.3
125	2	1	1.8	1.10	0.56	90	2.2
127	7	1	3.6	2.10	0.30	756	0.9
131 L1–L4	1	1	0.9	1.10	1.10	70	1.4
Total	19	5	11.1	1.70	0.45	1,802	1.1

but more often tolerated as scroungers. Banda peoples typically do not eat dogs today, nor, with the exception of the Tie shrine (see Table 8.2), are they sacrificed. Though 4 of the 20 canid specimens from late eighteenth- and nineteenth-century contexts at Makala Kataa showed signs of burning, none evidenced butchery, and we have assumed that they are the remains of dogs that lived and died on the site.

A different pattern was observed at Kuulo Kataa, where canids were recovered in substantial quantities, particularly in fifteenth- through mid-seventeenth-century Kuulo-phase contexts (NISP = 574, or 3.6 per cubic meter; MNI = 36; Table 8.3). Though they comprised only 2.1 percent of the total NISP, canid specimens were ubiquitous and invariably disarticulated. Every mound at Kuulo Kataa, whether Kuulo phase or Makala phase in affiliation, yielded canid specimens, and in several mounds they accounted for more than 2 percent of the total NISP (Table 8.4). Though

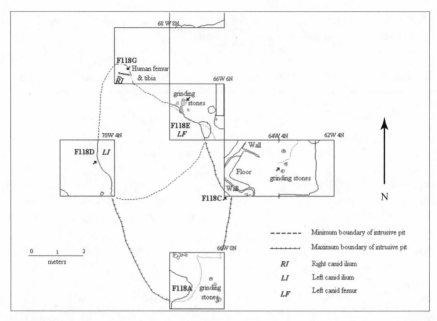

FIGURE 8.5

Mound 118, Kuulo Kataa, showing intrusive pits (F118A, F118C, F118D, F118E, and F118G) and associated features 100–120 cm below datum.

neither butchery (just over 2 percent of canid NISP) nor burning (slightly less than 3 percent) were common, the number (MNI = 36 and 5 in Kuulo- and Makala-phase contexts, respectively) and ubiquity of canids suggested they were treated differently from those of Makala Kataa. The cluster of dog mandibles in Mound 119 (above) suggested that the biographies of at least some canids at Kuulo Kataa were bound up in ritualization through sacrifice. If so, was consumption of these animals bound up in the forging of social relations (of deference and power)? A potential analytical pathway is opened when we consider the distribution of canid body parts in relation to depositional context.

Two subrectangular mounds (Mounds 118 and 148; Figure 8.4) yielded a substantial number of canid specimens (MNI 10 and 6, respectively; Table 8.4). Both mounds evidenced complex depositional histories. Lower levels were characterized by architectural features (floors, walls) as well as object clusters and features suggestive of living surfaces (grinding stones, hearths) or technological activities (possible forge in Mound 148; Figures 8.5 and 8.6). Upper levels accumulated when these occupational surfaces were no longer maintained and the structural features collapsed. They

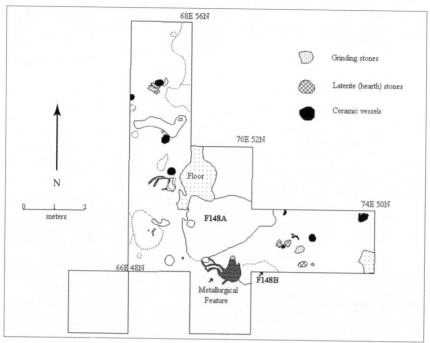

FIGURE 8.6

Mound 148, Kuulo Kataa, showing intrusive pits (F148A, 148B) and associated features, 100–120 cm below datum.

comprised refuse-rich deposits (Needham and Spence 1997:80) with high densities of broken pottery, iron slag, and animal bone. Subsequently, several large pits were excavated into both mounds. These intrusive pits were filled with refuse-rich deposits. Ceramics in pit fill were indistinguishable from those in other mound contexts; all were Kuulo phase in affiliation.

Though limitations of space preclude a detailed recounting of contextual associations, Tables 8.5 and 8.6 show the distribution of canid elements by excavation unit and level in relation to floors and other features in Mounds 148 and 118 (*excluding* the intrusive pit features). Mounds 148 and 118 yielded a substantial number of canid specimens (NISP = 55 and 269, respectively) that derived primarily from refuse-rich upper levels. Upper levels in both mounds were dominated by head and lower limb elements (85 and 93 percent of NISP in Mounds 148 and 118, respectively), with proportionally fewer upper limb and body elements (15 and 7 percent of NISP, respectively). This pattern is consistent with density-mediated survivorship (Lyman 1994:234–258);[5] however, the pattern is less marked in intrusive pit

TABLE 8.5
Camid Remains in Mound 118 (Exclusive of Pit) at Kuulo Kataa

Unit	66W 0N	64W 4N	62W 4N	70W 4N	66W 6N	68W 8N	66W 10N	66W 12N	62W 12N	66W 14N	66W 16N
Level 1	–	–	–	–	L1	B1	–	–	–	–	–
Level 2	B1, L3	H1, T2	–	L5	H2, T5, B1, L2	–	H5, T3, B2, L1	H5, T3, B1, L1	–	T1	–
Level 3	H2, L3	H3, T4, B1, L2	H1, T1, L2	L6	H1, T1, B1, L5	T1, L1	H2, T3, L2	H6, T2, L7	H1, T5, B1, L2	T3	–
Level 4	H1, T8, B1, L7	–	–	H6, L4	H2, T1, B1, L5	L1	–	H1, B1	–	H3, T3, L3	G H1, T1, B1
Level 5	–	H2	**Floor** L1	H1, T1, B1, L3	H1, T1, L6	H1, T2, L3	T1, B2, L6	T1, B1	H1	H1, T2, L3	G T1, B1, L3
Level 6	L2	**Floor**	L1	H1, T1, L3	T1, L4	T2, L1	–	T1	–	H1, T5, L1	H1
Level 7	–	–	**Floor**	**Floor** H1, L2	**Floor** H1, L1	L4	–	H1	–	L1	L2
Level 8	**Floor**	–	–	**Floor**	L1	–	–	L1	–	–	L3
Level 9	**Floor**	**Floor** T2	–	–	–	L2	L1	–	–	–	–

Stratigraphic distribution by 10-cm excavation level within 2m² excavation units. Number (NISP) of head (H), teeth (T), body (B), and lower limb (L) elements. Large grinding stones are indicated by **G**. Bolded units are those with intrusive pit deposits. Body elements included vertebrae through upper limbs (femur and humerus). Lower limbs included radius, ulna, tibia, fibula, and foot elements.

TABLE 8.6

Canid Remains in Mound 148 (Exclusive of Pit) at Kuulo Kataa

Unit	66E 48N	68E 50N	68E 52N	68E 54N	68E 56N	70E 48N	70E 50N	70E 52N	72E 50N	74E 50N
Level 1	–	–	–	–	–	–	L1	–	–	–
Level 2	–	B1, L2	–	–	–	–	–	–	L1	–
Level 3	L3	L1	T1, L4	–	–	L1	H2	–	–	H1, B1, L1
Level 4	H1, L1	B2, L2	H1, T1, L1	–	–	–	T1, L4	H1, L1	B1	–
Level 5	B1, L3	T1, B1, L1	–	–	–	–	L1	H1, L1	–	**Floor**
Level 6	H1	B1, L1	–	–	–	–	–	–	H L1	–
Level 7	**BI** T1	–	–	**G**	**G**	**Forge**	**Forge**	–	**H**	–
Level 8	T1	–	**Floor**	**Floor**	–	–	**Forge**	**Floor**	**H** L1	**BA**
Level 9	–	L1	**Floor**	–	–	–	–	–	–	–

Stratigraphic distribution by 10-cm excavation level within 2-m^2 excavation units. Number (NISP) of head (H), teeth (T), body (B), and lower limb (L) elements. Body elements included vertebrae through upper limbs (femur and humerus). Lower limbs included radius, ulna, tibia, fibula, and foot elements. Burials are indicated by **BI** (infant) and **BA** (adult), large grindstones by **G**, and hearths by **H**. Bolded units are those with intrusive pit deposits.

TABLE 8.7

Stratigraphic Distribution of Canid Remains in Intrusive Pits, Mounds 118 and 148, Kuulo Kataa

Mound 118 Pit: Unit Feature	66W 0N F118A	64W 4N F118C	70W 4N F118D	66W 6N F118E	68W 8N F118G
Level 4	–	L3	–	–	–
Level 5	H3	–	–	–	–
Level 6	H1	–	H1	B1, L1	–
Level 7	H1	–	–	H1, B1, L2	–
Level 8	–	–	L1	–	–
Level 9	–	–	–	T1, L3	–
Level 10	–	–	H1, T1	T2, B2, L4	–
Level 11	–	–	–	H2	–
Level 12	–	–	B1	T1, B1, L2	–
Level 13	–	–	–	B1, L1	B1

Mound 148 Pits: Unit Feature	68E 50N F148A	70E 50N F148A	70E 52N F148A	72E 50N F148B
Level 4	–	–	–	B1, L1
Level 5	–	–	–	–
Level 6	–	B3, L2	–	B1
Level 7	–	H1, B1, L1	H1, B1	–
Level 8	T1	–	–	–
Level 9	–	L1	L1	H1, T1, B1
Level 10	–	L1	–	–

Body parts indicated as in Tables 8.5 and 8.6.

features, suggesting that factors other than density-mediated survivorship contributed to the distribution of canid specimens, as well. Intrusive pit deposits in Mound 118 yielded a higher proportion of canid body and upper limb elements (20 percent body and upper limb, 80 percent head and lower limb; NISP = 41) than generalized refuse from the same mound (Table 8.7). Though the sample of canids from Mound 148 pit contexts is small (NISP = 19), a similar pattern prevailed (42 percent body and upper limb, 58 percent head and lower limb). Thus it seems likely that differential depositional practices contributed to this patterning, with upper limb and body elements more likely to be recovered from intrusive pits than from generalized refuse.

The distributional patterns described above inform on the biography of sacrificed animals. Canid remains were virtually all disarticulated, with heads and lower limbs (including tibiae, fibulae, and ulnae) separated from upper limbs (femora and humeri) and body elements. Whereas head and lower limbs were more likely to be discarded in generalized refuse deposits, upper limbs and body elements were more likely to enter a particular kind of refuse deposit—pits excavated into formerly occupied house mounds. Yet there was a notable absence of canid upper hind limb elements relative to other taxa (including comparably sized bovids) and to canid lower limbs. Only four canid femora (three proximal ends, one distal end) were identified in the faunal assemblage from Kuulo Kataa. Fragmentation might account for their apparent absence; however, upper hind limbs of canids may be rare in excavated contexts because they were being systematically removed. In other words, the biography of upper hind limbs may have differed from that of other canid body parts, their flow and consumption perhaps bound up in the ritualized production of social relations. A closer look at the small sample of canid femora and their associations substantiates this possibility.

Two of the four recovered canid femora at Kuulo Kataa were recovered from Mound 118. One derived from a level associated with a cluster of broken grinding stones (Level 4, Unit 66W 16N). The other was recovered from the basal levels of Feature 118E, part of a large intrusive pit in Mound 118, portions of which appeared in three excavation units (F118D, F118E, and F118G; see Figure 8.5). Canid remains establish a connection between these intrusive pit deposits. A shaft fragment of a right ilium displaying four cut marks on its medial surface was recovered from the lowest levels of F118G (L13). A left ilium blade fragment from the lowest levels (L12) of F118D displayed a chop mark on the medial surface of the ilium shaft. Because they were fragmented, precisely comparable measurements could not be taken (von den Driesch 1976); however, the smallest height of the shaft of the ilium (right pelvis sh = 14.23 mm; left sh = 14.43 mm) and the smallest circumference of the shaft of the ilium (right pelvis sc = 7.36 mm; left = 8.09 mm) suggest that these two elements derive from a single animal. This is corroborated by the position of butchery marks (opposite one another on the left and right medial surfaces of the ilium shaft), indicating that the ilium shaft was severed on both sides in an effort to detach the hind limbs from the vertebral column. The recovery of a left femur fragment (of a size consistent with that of the ilium fragments) from L12 of F118E suggests that these three elements derived from a single canid. Excavation of the F118G pit from which the right canid ilium was recovered stopped at L13 when disarticulated human remains (a femur and tibia) were encountered.[6] During the course of excavation, we understood this refuse-rich pit as yet another form of midden deposit; however, a follow-the-bones strategy forces us to consider anew the depositional practices that brought upper limb and pelvic elements (otherwise rare in the assemblage) of a single canid into association with disarticulated human limbs, and the social effects of those practices.

In sum, the biographies of canid body parts in Kuulo-phase contexts varied. Some mandibles were incorporated into formalized shrine loci. Some teeth were drilled, likely for use as ornaments. Low-utility elements were deposited as part of generalized refuse, while body and upper limb elements more often occurred in pits, in one case in association with disarticulated human remains. A paucity of upper hind limbs is only partly accounted for by density-mediated survivorship, and their flows were likely bound up in ritualized production of social relations. By contrast, the paucity of canid specimens at Makala Kataa suggests that dog sacrifice dropped from the repertoire of practices (see Table 8.3) and therefore ceased to be socially consequential (J. Thomas 1991:100). That this shift was uneven, however, is suggested by the continued presence of canid specimens in late eighteenth- and nineteenth-century Makala-phase contexts at Kuulo Kataa. This underscores the variegated nature of ritualized practice in both time *and* space, and cautions against homogenizing practices within the spatiotemporal units that frame our analyses. I return to the implications for social memory below.

Turning more briefly to pythons, the formalized Makala-phase shrine locus at Kuulo Kataa (Mound 131, above) suggests that the biography of (some) constrictors was ritualized. The concentration of constrictor remains was unique to this context; however, small numbers of disarticulated constrictor vertebrae were recovered from Makala-phase contexts at other sites, as well (Table 8.8). Five Boidae vertebrae from Early Makala derived from a single house mound (Mound 5; Stahl 2001b:169–172). One occurred in refuse-rich upper layers of the mound, while two others (Size Classes 3 and 4) derived from adjacent levels of a single excavation unit (4E 2S) associated with grinding stones and several potsherd clusters, beneath which was a floor associated with four shell beads. A ceramic vessel from an adjacent unit (4E 0S, L10) yielded the fifth constrictor vertebra. Constrictor vertebrae were also recovered from Kuulo-phase contexts at Kuulo Kataa (NISP = 16; Table 8.8). Space limitations preclude a detailed exploration of their contextual associations, but in one instance a constrictor vertebra (Mound 118, 66W6N, L6) was associated with floor deposits, fragmented grinding stones, and an iron bracelet. A cluster of broken grinding stones and several pieces of glassy slag beneath this context were

TABLE 8.8

Constrictor Remains from Banda-area Sites

Site	Mound	Python cf. *sebae* (NISP)	Boidae (NISP)	MNI
Kuulo Kataa	101	–	1	1
	118	–	1	1
	129	3	–	1
	130	4	–	2
	131	*30*	–	*1*
	148	6	–	2
B-123	–	4	–	2
Banda 40	4	4	–	1
Banda 41	–	4	–	2
Early Makala	*5*	–	*5*	*2*
B-112	–	*1*	–	*1*
Banda 12	–	–	*1*	*1*

Italicized contexts are Makala phase; nonitalicized contexts are Kuulo phase.

identified as a possible shrine by several of our local workmen. This is one among a number of contexts in which broken grinding stones that we initially interpreted as discarded tools may provide insight into the dynamics of shrines and sacrificial practices (also Insoll 2006:Figures 3 and 4). A strategy of following constrictor bones leads to a potentially recurrent association with grinding stones, unsettling our initial working assumption that they were simply discarded kitchen equipment.

POTS AND BEADS

Contemporary practice provides a platform for considering the dynamics of pots and beads as shrine components. As outlined above, ceramics drawn from the repertoire of everyday pottery enclose shrine bundles today (Cruz 2003:247, 265, 284). As such, the biographies of at least some ceramic vessels include a ritualized phase. Bead biographies may be similarly complex. Caton (1997) documented the importance of beads in ritualized practice and adornment. Female elders curate collections of sacred beads used in various rites of passage. These assemblages comprise heterogenous imported glass beads similar to those occasionally recovered from late eighteenth- and early nineteenth-century Makala Phase 2 contexts (for example, Early Makala; Caton 1997; Stahl 2002:839) and consistent with the range of beads imported in large quantities to West Africa during the height of the Atlantic slave trade (for example, Ogundiran

2002). Beads acquired through international exchange were thus recontextualized in the interim as focal objects in the ritual practices that produce Nafana women (Stahl 2002). How do these contemporary practices compare with the biographies of pots and beads in archaeological contexts? The association of shrines with ceramic vessels that characterizes contemporary practice is borne out in Makala-phase contexts. The clearest example comes from the Mound 131 (Kuulo Kataa) shrine described above; however, flotation of interior contents of whole pots has yielded varying combinations of beads, bones from a variety of animals (including snakes), and a few human incisors (Table 8.9). A whole vessel from site Banda 40, a nineteenth-century Makala Phase 2 occupation sampled through regional testing, yielded a particularly rich array of objects, including snake, bird, fish, and mammal bone, along with several blue beads. The interior contents of this vessel seem "special" (Brück 1999:328–330) and are therefore consistent with an interpretation that this context was ritualized, perhaps functioning as a shrine. Yet an examination of Table 8.9 suggests that sorting "shrine pots" from "everyday pots" is not a straightforward process. A number of virtually intact pots were recovered from Mound 5 at Early Makala in what appeared to be primary (in the sense of Schiffer 1972:161) kitchen contexts, as suggested by the presence of hearths, large grinding stones, and an array of storage, cooking, and serving vessels (Stahl 2001b:169–171, Figure 6.6, Plate 10). Most pots yielded no interior contents through flotation; however, a number yielded beads, animal bones, and occasionally pottery sherds. How do we interpret this array? Were pots that contained beads ritualized, whereas vessels containing fragmented animal bones were associated with mundane practice (for example, meal preparation)?

The perspectives outlined at the outset of this chapter and elsewhere in this volume suggest that an effort to sort distinct ritual and nonritual domains diverts our attention from ritualization as a process embedded in daily life. Instead of endeavoring to sort among specific shrine and nonshrine pots in the Mound 5 assemblage, we might focus instead on how configurations of pots, beads, and bones inform on the embedding of ritualized practices in the ongoing activities of food preparation and other daily activities. Assuming that beads did not enter pots postdepositionally, their secreting in pots, and the associations of those pots with contexts of daily social reproduction, provide insight into the practices through which Early Makala inhabitants altered the biographies of trade beads, recontextualizing them through ritualization in ways that are not evident in earlier Kuulo-phase contexts.

TABLE 8.9

Interior Contents of Makala-phase Vessels Recovered through Flotation

Unit	Level	Pot No.	Form	Beads	Fauna	Other
Makala Kataa, Mound 5:						
8W 4S	4–5	8	–	1 wire wound, 1 drawn glass	–	6 sherds (3 rims, 1 base, 2 body)
4W 2S	5	14	Bowl	–	1 deciduous tooth, size 3 bovid.	–
4W 2S	5	15	Jar	–	8 unidentifiable bone fragments.	–
4W 4S	5	2	–	–	5 Mammalia (2 long bone, size 1; 3 unidentified); and 1 axis, Rodentia.	–
4W 4S	4	1	Jar	1 drawn glass	1 scapula, size 2.5, bovid; 1 long bone, size 3.5, Mammalia; 1 partial incisor (human?).	–
4W 4S	5	4	Jar rim	–	4 mandibles, Mustelidae; 4 long bone, size .5, Mammalia.	–
4W 4S	6	5	–	1 wire-wound barrel	–	–
4W 4S	7	7	Jar	–	12 Osteichthyes; 1 supraoccipital Siluriformes.	Carbonized sorghum
0W 2S	5	–	Bowl base	1 seed bead	–	–
0W 2S	5	Rim D	–	1 shell bead	–	–
0W 4S	5	12	–	–	1 spine, Osteichthyes.	–
0W 4S	5	13	Bowl	–	1 long bone, Mammalia.	–
2E 2S	4–5	A	Base	–	1 shell, Achatina.	–
4E 2S	10	B	Jar	–	1 vertebra, Boidae.	–
Banda 40, Mound 1:						
–	5	2	Jar	3 drawn blue-glass beads (2 tubular, 1 barrel)	1 vertebra, Crotalid snake? (*Elaphus*?); 1 adult human incisor (lower right); 1 femoral shaft, Aves; 12 vertebrae, medium-size fish; 1 spine, fish; 1 branchiostegal; 2 rib, small mammal; 1 epiphysis, 16 long-bone fragments, Mammalia.	5 sherds (3 rims, 2 body); 1 fired clay/daub

Turning briefly to Kuulo-phase contexts, it is notable that, although fewer intact vessels were recovered, none yielded interior contents through flotation. Though sampling issues confound our ability to make definitive claims, available evidence suggests that the secreting of shrine bundles in pots practiced today and evidenced in nineteenth-century contexts was *not* practiced in earlier centuries. Shrines may well have taken a different form, for example, the cluster of canid mandibles and milky quartz, or the clusters of broken grinding stones, sometimes associated with metallurgical slag and intriguingly in some instances with constrictor vertebrae. When combined with the insight that canid sacrifice dropped from the repertoire of at least some nineteenth-century Makala Phase 2 peoples, it suggests a dynamism surrounding shrines and sacrificial practices that can only be discerned through close attention to depositional practices and their contexts.

FINAL THOUGHTS

The analytical strategies pursued here may help us overcome the fear of failure described by de Maret (1994). They resonate with published studies (Brown 2005; Dietler 1998; Ogundiran 2002; Walker 1998; Walker and Lucero 2000; among others) that pursue a biographical or life history approach to objects and the depositional practices through which they enter archaeological contexts. These strategies are not without ambiguity; we cannot assume that the biographies of all dogs, pythons, pots, or beads were ritualized. The picture that emerges from this preliminary analysis is, like much African social history, messy and incomplete, resistant to generalization (McCaskie 1981:145). But by considering ritualization as a potential component of object biographies and using constellations of objects and their contexts as guides, we can glean, if only in phantom form, how the social consequence of various objects was redefined through practices of ritualization (J. Thomas 1991:100; also Dietler 1998). Following objects through their varied associations draws attention to unexpected configurations (for example, the association of broken grinding stones with potentially ritualized animal remains) that provide a platform for considering how Banda peoples negotiated global entanglements through dynamic strategies of ritualization. It encourages us to consider ritualization beyond formal loci such as shrines and to reconsider those depositional contexts that, during excavation, we assumed to be "simply" refuse (Hill 1995; see also Moore 1982).

Applied more broadly, across sites and regions, this analytical strategy can help us to discern the materiality (Joyce, this volume) of what Parker

(2004:420) terms the "dynamics of trans-regional ritual innovation." By constructing genealogies of practice through a comparative analysis of material remains through time and space, archaeological investigations can provide a platform for considering the dynamics of ritualization in relation to the broader political economic developments that conditioned daily lives, and for discerning the operations of practical memory. As an example, the differential persistence of canid sacrifice in late eighteenth- and nineteenth-century contexts (present at Kuulo Kataa, absent at Makala Kataa) suggests a variegated landscape of ritual practice. Foregrounded in relation to the political economic uncertainties of the nineteenth century (Stahl 2001b:148–165), these patterns suggest differential social memories, the practices in one community bearing traces of earlier propitiatory practices (canid sacrifice) that are abandoned (forgotten? suppressed?) in another. Further, we see evidence that continuity exists alongside innovation (for example, nineteenth-century Kuulo Kataa, where canid sacrifice is practiced alongside the use of new ceramic shrine forms). This underscores the palimpsest quality of ritual practice; performance draws from repertoires of past practice, renewing and often reforging the past in the present through the operations of social memory. But the strategy also allows us to appreciate instances of discontinuity when ritualization takes on new forms, reminding us that social memory encompasses forgetting as well as remembering (Mills, this volume). Either way, the approaches outlined in this and other chapters of the present volume help us to appreciate the dynamics of ritualization, and by extension to apprehend the emergent quality of the analytical object we call culture.

Acknowledgments

Research has been conducted under license from the Ghana Museum and Monuments Board with funds from the British Academy (1986), the Wenner Gren Foundation for Anthropological Research (1989, G5133), the National Geographic Society (1990, Grant 4313-90), and the National Science Foundation (1994–1997, Grant SBR-9410726; 2000–2003, SBR-9911690). I am particularly indebted to Banda chiefs and elders, whose support was crucial; the men and women of Banda; and graduate students who have worked on the Banda Research Project over the years. Restrictions of space preclude a full listing. Faunal remains from the 1990 season at Makala Kataa were identified by Andrew Black. All other remains were analyzed by Peter Stahl using comparative collections of the Archaeological Analytical Research Facility at Binghamton University and the American Museum of Natural History in

ANN B. STAHL

New York, whose staff has been gracious in providing access to collections. I am exceptionally grateful to Peter Stahl for the time and energy invested in this enterprise and for his patient advice, which has shaped my interpretation of the faunal assemblages. Thanks to Clayton Tinsley for providing a copy of Linseele (2002). And finally, special thanks to Barbara Mills and Bill Walker for organizing the most productive and congenial intellectual exchange in which I have been privileged to participate.

Notes

1. See, for example, Hill (1995), who, despite his nuanced study of depositional practices and a concern to overcome dichotomies between ritual/nonritual and sacred/profane, reproduces the tendency to place culture/structure before history/practice in the final analysis (Hill 1995:111–112). In similar fashion, despite his emphasis on ritualization as action, Bradley (2005:34) places ideas before action: "By following the development of rituals in this way, it should be possible to identify a few of the ideas that they were meant to express."

2. Though limits of space preclude an extended discussion, a focus on object biographies need not imply the meaning-centered approach outlined by Gosden and Marshall (1999). I have outlined my concerns about meaning as an analytical focus elsewhere (Stahl 2002; see also Pollard, this volume).

3. R. S. Rattray was a government anthropologist who published prolifically on Asante religion and lifeways. Though his monographs remain primary sources, they must be read with a critical eye, particularly in view of the emphasis he placed on specific "greybeard" informants (see McCaskie 1983; von Laue 1976).

4. Canid remains in this analysis include specimens identified as *Canis familiaris*, *Canis* cf. *familiaris*, *Canis*, *Canis* cf., Canidae, and Canidae cf. Although the Canidae family includes domestic dogs (*Canis familiaris*), jackals (*Canis adustus*), and foxes, a working assumption of this paper is that the canid specimens are primarily from domestic dog.

5. Limitations of space preclude a detailed discussion of taphonomic concerns, which will be taken up more fully in a separate publication. Preliminary tests using recently published density figures for canids (Novecosky and Popkin 2005) suggest that a statistically significant relationship between body part and survivorship (calculated as grams per cubic centimeter of scan sites ÷ percent of survivorship of scan sites) exists in the Mound 148 assemblage ($r_s = 0.426$, p = 0.00 for canid specimens in Mound 148 pits; $r_s = 0.501$, p = 0.00 for Mound 148 canid specimens from nonpit contexts).

6. It is standard practice on the Banda Research Project to cease excavations of deposits in which human remains are encountered. The remains are covered after minimal exposure, and elders are brought to the site to pour libations (Stahl 2001b:110, 112).

9

Memorializing Place among
Classic Maya Commoners

Lisa J. Lucero

The southern lowland Mayas lived in a tropical setting where agriculture was rainfall dependent (Figure 9.1). The rainy and dry seasons, each about six months long, determined religious and agricultural cycles because seasonal rainfall vagaries required continual supplications to supernatural entities. We know this from royal iconographic and hieroglyphic records. However, all Mayas made supplications to supernatural forces, a fact Maya archaeologists are beginning to reveal. Mayas prayed and proffered offerings to ancestors, rain and maize gods, and other deities important in daily life at agricultural fields, near water sources, in public plazas, in caves, and in the home, as found today among traditional Mayas (for example, Vogt 1970, 1998). But it is in the home where the remnants of ceremonial life are most apparent, as was the case in prehispanic times.

Through ceremonial practices they conducted in the home, Classic Maya commoners (ca. 250–850 CE) created their place in the community, society, and history. Maya ceremonies revolved around life, death, and renewal, and were conducted by all Mayas, from royals to commoners. These domestic dedication, ancestor veneration, and termination rites leave telling material evidence. In fact, the depositional histories of Maya structures reflect the continuous flow of ceremonial behaviors that in the end comprise much of the structure itself (for example, Walker and

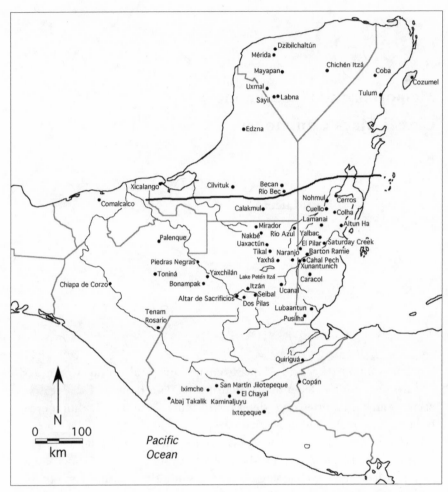

FIGURE 9.1

The Maya area.

Lucero 2000). Thus, the chronology of residential construction is a history of the families who lived within its walls; it is a history that fellow Mayas recognized and could read because everyone in Maya society used the same means to record their family stories and their place in society. Through a discussion of residential ceremonial deposits at the minor center of Saturday Creek, Belize, I will explore how Classic Maya commoners established place though caching or destroying objects and interring the dead.

Worldwide, people establish social and sacred places through ceremonial practices that include the sacrifice of socially significant items or social things (Appadurai 1986; Kopytoff 1986; for example, Halperin 1994) and the interring of specific members of the community. The act of secreting away or destroying inalienable items transfers their social powers and transforms a location or a structure to a sacred or significant place (Chapman 2000a; Rowlands 1993). Interring the dead serves a similar purpose. Ancestor veneration, a worldwide phenomenon, is reflected in the burial of specific family members in the domestic sphere and/or the deposition of parts of the bodies of ancestors (for example, Geller 2004; McAnany 1995). The placement of corporeal remains thus takes on cultural significance to the living, and their ancestral history often embodies claims in the physical world (for example, land rights).

CEREMONIAL PRACTICES

Ritual or ceremonial practices pervade all aspects of society and life (Leach 1966). It is thus ironic that scholars tend to conflate them with religious beliefs; they typically focus on the religious aspects of ceremonies rather than the ceremonial aspects of religion. Ceremonial practices are distinct from beliefs or ideologies in that they can be observed, whereas thought processes cannot. As a matter of fact, rites do not require participants to believe the same things to promote group feeling and solidarity (Kertzer 1988; Rappaport 1999:119–120; Robertson Smith 1956 [1894]:16–17). The important thing is to "make it look right" (Lee 2000:5). For example, Daniel B. Lee (2000), through his study of the Weaverland Conference Old World Mennonites of New York and Pennsylvania, demonstrates that they did not share common beliefs while participating in group rites because the action of rites transcends "the personal beliefs of individuals" (Lee 2000:1). For example, when asked about the significance of the "kiss of peace," each person responded differently: "Our ancestors brought the kiss with him or her from Germany and Switzerland. We want to hold on to those traditions"; or, "The kiss was established by the early leaders of the church"; or, "It's from the Bible. The disciples did it"; or, "I don't know why we do it" (Lee 2000:4–5). Individual beliefs and feelings are irrelevant and are overridden by rules of engagement.

Ceremonies have multiple meanings (Cohen 1974:29, 36; Durkheim 1995 [1912]:390). While archaeologists cannot elucidate their multiple meanings or the beliefs surrounding them, we can reveal their material manifestations and significance, especially since they are conservative, whereas beliefs are not. Repetitive behaviors, ceremonial or otherwise, result in specific sequences of deposits in the archaeological record that reflect these actions (for example, Bradley 1990:10–14; Walker 1998, 2002). Consequently, strata, in addition to reflecting chronology, signify sequences of (ceremonial) practices because "all acts of ancient worship have a material embodiment, which is not left to the choice of the worshipers but is limited by fixed roles" (Robertson Smith 1956 [1894]:84). We thus need to rid ourselves of the utilitarian/nonutilitarian dichotomy (Walker 1998, 2002) because we cannot assume the social value of items based on our functional classificatory schemes (Meskell 2004:41). By doing so, we can evaluate each piece of the past as imbued with social significance. A step in this direction, as several scholars have shown, is by taking into account the context of artifacts (for example, Meskell 2004:6; Richards and Thomas 1984; Walker 1998, 2002; Walker and Lucero 2000) as well as their arrangement (Pollard 2001, this volume) and association with other items (Douglas and Isherwood 1996 [1979]:49).

PRACTICE MAKES PLACE

The lack of inscribed objects or written documents about commoner Maya life requires us to use alternative means to illuminate more mundane ceremonial deposits and their significance. Assessing context and depositional histories is critical toward this end (Richards and Thomas 1984; Walker 1998). The types of goods sacrificed have not changed for centuries, though their quality, quantity, and diversity distinguish commoner, elite, and royal offerings (Lucero 2003, 2006; for example, Garber et al. 1998). All Mayas offered the same kinds of items (for example, vessels, stone objects, shell), though commoner offerings were made with less "expensive" materials from less exotic places (for instance, more freshwater and land shell versus marine shell; see, for example, Garber et al. 1998; Lucero 2003, 2006). However, what we might describe as utilitarian, that is, widely available and inexpensive items, likely had immeasurable value to a person, family, or community (compare Weiner 1992).

I mention similarities and differences among commoner, elite, and royal deposits because of what they indicate in general about ceremonial practices. If emerging elites, and later rulers, replicated and expanded traditional domestic practices to promote political agendas, as I have argued elsewhere (Lucero 2003, 2006), then we should be able to apply some of what we have learned about the significance of royal ceremonies and offerings to ones performed by commoners. For example, Joyce (2000a, 2003b), based on inscribed items from noble and royal tombs, clearly demonstrates the importance of heirloom objects, since some were deposited 100 years after their inscribed date. The hieroglyphic record also is replete with information about dedication and other ceremonies, illuminating them in ways that would not be possible without the written word (see, for example, Houston and Stuart 1996; Schele and Freidel 1990; Schele and Miller 1986; among others). Thus, if many royal practices are domestic ones writ large, perhaps it is possible to translate a similar significance for commoner practices. Ensoulment, the memorialization of ancestors and place, and deanimation thus take on greater importance as explanations for commoner practices.

In the ethnographic present, Mayas perform dedication ceremonies to animate new houses and other objects. The former include the caching of objects under house floors (for example, Vogt 1993). They conduct ancestor veneration rites to honor and thank ancestors, which involve keeping an ancestor's remains close to home and making offerings (for example, Vogt 1970). Some Maya groups call children and grandchildren *kexol*, or "replacements" (Schele and Miller 1986:266), signifying the continued connection of the living and the dead. Grave goods tell us much about the person and those who were left behind. For example, among the Zinacantecos of Chiapas, Vogt (1998:28) found that grave goods "are said to possess the soul of their owner." Part of the renewal ceremony consists of terminating the old, for the New Year, for example, or after the death of a family member, when life must begin anew. And since all objects have animate qualities, Mayas also perform termination ceremonies to deactivate or deanimate houses or objects (for example, Tozzer 1941:151), thus releasing their soul before renewal. Rites involve breaking objects, partially destroying houses, and burning incense (Mock 1998).

In the archaeological record, dedication caches are found beneath floors and typically consist of burned or unburned whole objects such as jade items, obsidian, ground stone, eccentrics, and ceramic vessels (some lip-to-lip) (Becker 1992; Coe 1959:77–78, 1965; for example, Chase and Chase 1998; Garber 1989:98; Guderjan 2004; Mock 1998). Mayas buried their dead, typically with grave goods, in the floors of houses, shrines, palaces, or temples (for example, Gillespie 2000; McAnany 1995:535). Commoners buried their dead in their homes, the wealthy built shrines to their ancestors (usually the eastern structure of their residential compound), and royals buried their own in temples. Termination deposits, found on floor surfaces, typically consist of broken and burned items (for example, ceramic vessels; Coe 1965; Garber 1986, 1989; for example, Rice 1999).

MEMORY IN THE MAKING

The sacrifice of material objects, simple or ornate, was part of the process of the production of memory (Rowlands 1993). This is particularly true of new items sacrificed and taken out of circulation forever. Throughout the Maya area, the material act of "making" embodied memory production, the end signified by the removal of objects from the living world that were burned, destroyed, or cached. Objects made expressly for ceremonial deposition were never animated and thus did not have to be terminated or killed. Goods people used in life, in contrast, had to be killed before deposition because of the forces they personified. In the former case, objects had no history; in the latter, they did. By terminating an item, the Mayas ended its history as an object for use in life and initiated its life history or afterlife history (see Walker, this volume) as a dedicatory (typically whole), termination (broken), or grave offering (whole or broken).

Mayas performed these rites for over a millennium. It is unlikely, however, that beliefs about social identity and meaning remained untouched in light of changing sociopolitical conditions, including the emergence and demise of semidivine kings, increasing numbers of people in any given area, and increased interregional interaction. In turn, conducting the "same" ceremonial practices through time only emphasized tradition in the face of change. People put all they had, both alive/animated and dead/terminated, back into their homes. Having fellow community members witness the material concentration of ceremonial acts served to socially emphasize and recognize the home, but not at the expense of the community. Participants publicly acknowledged these acts of creating memory (see Chesson 2001; Joyce 2001) and expected the same when it was their turn to bury the dead, terminate the old, and dedicate the new.

Tying together Maya ceremonial practices is death. Upon the death of certain individuals, family members had to start life anew, which meant conducting termination ceremonies for both the deceased (funerary practices) and the house (razed before rebuilding). The recently deceased, by their burial in the home, became ancestors and defined material place as social space (along with grave goods). Funerary practices reflect the fact that people were not interring the dead so much as creating an ancestor who would remain involved in the lives of the living (for example, Meskell 2001; Nielsen, this volume). Once such practices had been performed, the family was ready to begin living again, which was materialized in the building of a new home on top of the former home. They built it and dedicated it, literally over the recently created ancestor. Memory and place were thus created in the ceremonial cycle of dedication, ancestor veneration, and termination practices, commemorating both the living and the dead. Family and friends witnessed and participated in ceremonies and in doing so publicly notarized the family's claims to land, status, identity, and/or other entitlements (Becker 1992; Gillespie 2001, 2002; McAnany 1998). Funerary rites in particular brought people together because of the need to acknowledge the loss of a community member. This collective rite was critical in the Maya lowlands, since most farmland and concomitant farmsteads were dispersed, and people needed ways to maintain family and community ties.

I will illustrate how ceremonial practices created a material record of memory production at the minor river center of Saturday Creek, Belize. While I focus on one site, it is important to note that the ceremonial histories described are similar to those at other Maya centers, small and large, and highlight how a large portion of all Maya construction depositional histories—commoner, elite, and royal—actually are the result of dedication, ancestor veneration, and termination practices.

SATURDAY CREEK

Saturday Creek is along the Belize River on an extensive floodplain in central Belize on the eastern periphery of the southern Maya lowlands (see Figure 9.1). The Valley of Peace Archaeology (VOPA) project, which I directed under the aegis of the Institute of Archaeology, National Institute of Culture and History, Belize, mapped 79 structures within a .81-km^2 area bounded by roads (Lucero et al. 2004). Many mounds are shorter and more spread out than formerly because most of the site has been extensively plowed. Mayas lived at Saturday Creek from at least 900 BCE to 1500 CE (Conlon and Ehret 2002) in dispersed farmsteads consisting of solitary mounds and mound groups, or *plazuelas* (Figure 9.2). A ball court, temples up to about 10 m tall, and elite compounds comprise the site core.

Saturday Creek's former inhabitants included commoner farmers, part-time specialists (for example, potters), and elite or wealthy farmers. Surface collections and excavated materials indicate their relative wealth, not to mention long-distance contacts (for example, Pachuca obsidian from central Mexico, polished hematite items, jade, and marine shell; Lucero 1997, 2002). Saturday Creek also illustrates a community where inequality was based on wealth differences rather than political power per se (Lucero 2006). Inhabitants were not beholden to rulers, since there were none, and did not have to bother with tribute payments, rely on water or agricultural systems, build royal palaces, and expend energy on monumental public iconography; nor did they have a need for, or access to, inscriptions. Interestingly, their being surrounded by fertile alluvium and year-round water basically kept them free from political machinations. Wealthy members of the community, however, sponsored feasts and rites, organized the construction of the ball court and temples via community

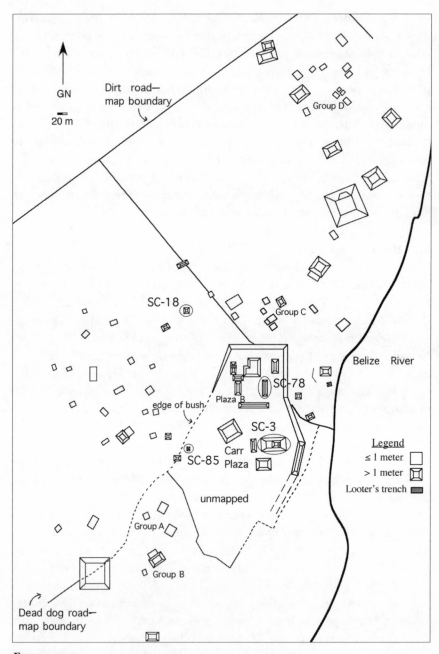

FIGURE 9.2

Saturday Creek, showing excavated structures.

and/or compensated labor, and fulfilled other patronal duties. The nearest major site is Yalbac, a medium-size center 18 km to the northwest, and Saturday Creek's occupants may have had some kind of relationship with its residents, not necessarily political.

In 2001 we excavated two solitary mounds or commoner residences (SC-18 and SC-85), an eastern structure of an elite compound (SC-78), and a temple ball court (SC-3; Lucero 2002). We used the Harris Matrix method of recording natural strata to highlight depositional sequences (Harris 1989).

One commoner residence (SC-18) on prime alluvium has at least six construction phases consisting of thin plaster floors, cobble ballasts, and single- or double-course foundation walls for wattle-and-daub structures (Lucero and Brown 2002). Another commoner house (SC-85), found on more clayey soils, also has six major construction phases consisting of a series of thin plaster floors with less substantial ballasts, a cobble surface, earthen surfaces, and foundation walls (1–3 courses; Lucero et al. 2002b). Residents were less wealthy than their counterparts at SC-18, likely a result of their having lived surrounded by less productive soils. The Mayas lived at both residences from at least ca. 400 through 1150 CE.

The elite structure at Saturday Creek consists of a stepped platform with several relatively substantial domestic and specialized structures. Some structures have thick plaster floors, ballasts, and standing walls with cut-stone blocks, while others are of wattle and daub (Lucero et al. 2002a). The Mayas lived there from at least 600 BCE to 1500 CE. The noticeably lower density of artifacts compared to those at SC-18 and SC-85 indicates that fewer people lived here than at commoner houses and that some structures had specific functions (for example, kitchen, storeroom, work area, shrine, sweat bath). The temple sits on top of a platform, which comprises the eastern half of a ball court (Jeakle 2002; Jeakle et al. 2002). The excavation trench revealed several major construction phases, including steep, tiered walls and a platform with several construction phases and plastered steps. Excavated material dates from at least ca. 300 BC to 1500 CE.

Most of the deposits date to the Late Classic period (ca. 550–850 CE), when population was at its peak. Brief descriptions of elite deposits will highlight similarities with and differences between them and commoner deposits (for a more detailed discussion of ceremonial deposits, see Lucero 2006:86–102).

All four structures yielded dedication caches. Commoner offerings include notched and unnotched obsidian blades, mano and metate fragments, polished stone, bone needles, shaped bone, drilled marine shell

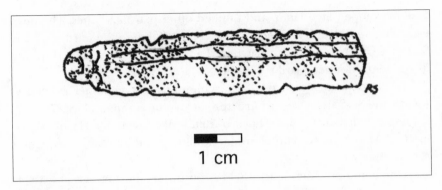

FIGURE 9.3

A notched obsidian blade. Drawing by Rachel Saurman.

and bone, chert cores, spindle whorls, a celt, a bark beater, marine shell, burned and unburned faunal remains, figurine fragments, ceramic disks, a few ceramic sherd concentrations, and a few small jade and hematite inlay or mosaic pieces (Lucero and Brown 2002; Lucero et al. 2002b; Figure 9.3). A ceramic concentration at SC-85, consisting only of layered body sherds, may include pieces of heirloom vessels, since their dates range from 300 BCE to 600 CE. Elite structures (SC-78, SC-3) yielded the same dedicatory items as commoner houses did, with the addition of more diverse and expensive goods, including speleothems from caves, coral, monkey finger bones, mica, vase sherds, and more jade items (Jeakle et al. 2002; Lucero et al. 2002a).

Eight Late Classic burials were recovered from the two commoner houses, four with grave goods (Piehl 2002; Sanchez and Chamberlain 2002), some of which I describe here. The three burials at one of the commoner houses (SC-18) all have grave goods, including an adult, likely female (Burial 7, ca. 20–30 years) interred sometime between ca. 700 and 750 CE with a bowl over her knees, an olla, and freshwater shell disk beads (Figure 9.4). A seated adult, perhaps male (Burial 11, unknown age), was interred slightly later (ca. 750 CE), facing south with an inverted dish over his skull. When the Mayas buried this individual, they had to dig through the woman's remains. As a result, her entire upper torso and skull were removed. Her long bones were placed in front of the seated adult, perhaps reiterating their family ties. We do not know what happened to the rest of her remains. Later, between ca. 800 and 900 CE, the Mayas buried another seated individual (Burial 2) slightly south of the earlier ones—a young adult (14–20 years, unknown sex) facing south with a large inverted dish over his/her skull, an olla near the right knee, a hammerstone next to the

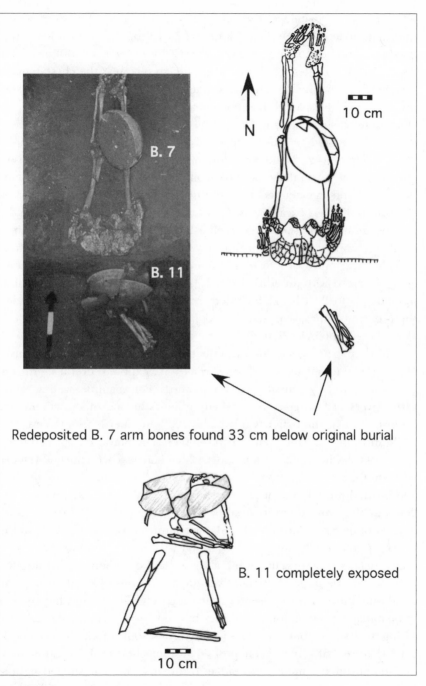

Redeposited B. 7 arm bones found 33 cm below original burial

B. 11 completely exposed

10 cm

FIGURE 9.4
Burials 7 and 11, SC-18.

olla, an inverted plate over the left knee, and marine shell disk beads near the right ankle. The sole Late Classic burial (Burial 8) with obvious grave goods at the other commoner dwelling (SC-85), likely of an adult male (ca. 24–30 years), includes a dish near his skull; an olla near the chest; a mano fragment; marine shell; two heavily eroded, untempered, poorly fired vessels over the upper legs; a polished bone near the mandible; and other artifacts (for example, sherds dating from 300 BCE to 600 CE). The burials without grave goods include a bundle burial of an adolescent (Burial 3, ca. 10–12 years, sex unknown); an extended and prone adult female with filed incisors (Burial 1); an extended and prone child (Burial 4, ca. 4–6 years, sex unknown); and an extended, supine adult female (Burial 9, ca. 30–34 years).

Due to limited excavations at Saturday Creek elite structures, we did not locate any burials. However, elite burials from a comparable minor river center about 25 km from Saturday Creek, Barton Ramie, demonstrate that they are more ornate than commoner burials. For example, grave goods interred with an adult (Burial 3) at BR-260 (40 x 30 m, with four mounds up to 2 m high) included three vessels, three obsidian blades, three carved bones, a jaguar-shaped jade pendant, and a polished celt (Willey et al. 1965:267–270, 557).

All four structures yielded termination deposits, which largely consist of smashed and burned vessels on surfaces. We exposed several sherd concentrations, mostly consisting of body sherds. For example, we recovered three layers of burned and smashed ceramics at one of the commoner houses (SC-18), the majority of which were body sherds (96 percent, n = 209), and some of which date to 400–600 CE. The Mayas had placed them on top of a textile or mat of some sort, which had also been burned (Figure 9.5). In a later termination event at the same house, the Mayas smashed and burned three layers of ceramics, mostly body sherds (97 percent, n = 266). In the same deposit we also found a complete but broken bowl, burned bone, and marine shells. Mayas conducted similar practices at the other commoner dwelling (SC-85) when they broke and burned several items such as ceramics, including a large, flat body sherd containing the long bones of a large mammal, likely deer. They also placed an undecorated miniature jar on a burned surface at ca. 600–700 CE. In what appears to be a major termination event, they burned and smashed ceramics consisting of 10 sherd concentrations with few rims, some of which were poorly fired (Figure 9.6). They also deposited a Colha-chert tool, a ceramic bird- or fish-figurine fragment, an obsidian blade, marine shell, shaped serpentine, and a metate fragment. Some of the sherds dated to ca. 250 CE and could represent heirloom objects.

FIGURE 9.5

Termination deposit, SC-18. The stain of a burned mat or textile is visible in the lower photograph.

The major difference between commoner and elite termination deposits is the kind of vessels smashed. At the solitary mounds, Mayas smashed plain or monochrome-slipped bowls, jars, and plates, and only a few polychrome vessels. The elite structure and temple also yielded more diverse items than

FIGURE 9.6

Examples of termination deposits, SC-85. The lower photograph shows a deposit from an earlier level, east of the deposit in the upper photograph. Also, included is a photograph of a figurine fragment of a bird or fish.

the commoner deposits, including drum vases, polychrome vessels, molded ceramic pieces, drilled and carved marine shell, powdered marl, burned plaster fragments, and human bone. For example, the Mayas at the elite structure (SC-78) burned an entire structure of wattle and daub sometime during the ninth century CE. One wall collapsed on a deposit of several burned and smashed decorated vessels (100 percent body sherds); a human ulna placed on top of a large and burned rimless plate; an incised, drilled marine shell pendant; and a drilled shell. At the foot of the temple (SC-3), the Mayas inverted a rimless and burned Platon Punctate plate on a burned surface (Jeakle 2002:56–57). This ceramic type was not found anywhere else at Saturday Creek (Conlon and Ehret 2002); Gifford et al. (1976:257) note that it was only found in burial contexts at Barton Ramie. In most cases, however, smashed-sherd concentrations at all structures largely consist of body sherds with few or no rims.

DISCUSSION

Commoner dedication practices at Saturday Creek included the caching of the same types of goods throughout the entire occupancy of the houses we excavated, over 600 years (ca. 400–1150 CE). Mayas conducted small-scale ceremonies for family and members of the community. Ceremonial events increase in scale at the elite building and the temple platform (for example, monkey finger bones and mica). For example, evidence from the ball court alley (faunal remains, decorated serving vessels) indicates feasting, likely sponsored by elites for all community members (Jeakle 2002; Jeakle et al. 2002). Evidence also suggests that all Mayas offered heirloom vessels, albeit broken ones. No matter whether they were purposely or accidentally broken, their significance lies in the role they played in maintaining "social continuity" in house and family identity (Gillespie 2001).

Commoner funerary practices at Saturday Creek did not change in over 600 years, indicating the importance of the cyclical re-creation of space and memory (McAnany 1995:161; for example, Geller 2004: 316–322).[1] The number of burials does not reflect all the people who lived in the home for all those centuries. Thus, it appears that only select people were buried in houses—that is, those selected to become ancestors. In general, males are more common at small residences in the Maya area (Sanchez and Piehl 2002; for example, Haviland 1997; McAnany et al. 1999).[2] The burials without grave goods are children and females, which may indicate a different ancestral status—a question that needs further addressing. Several burials are seated, which may indicate high status within the family or community (McAnany 1998; Sanchez and Piehl 2002). Inverted vessels on a burned surface or over decedents' heads may indicate another way of deanimating ceramics and the deceased. While the burial patterns at Saturday Creek at first appear simple, they actually involve complex behaviors. For example, when residents at one of the commoner houses (SC-18) buried an adult between ca. 400 and 600 CE (Burial 5, sex unknown), they first dug a pit in which they burned and broke pottery and placed chert flakes (Lucero and Brown 2002). They then placed a deer antler in the center of the pit, followed by fill and the deceased person. More fill was added, followed by the burning and smashing of more vessels. Afterward, they placed mano and metate fragments and more ceramics near the body, then more dirt. Finally, they burned more items and placed vessels just south of the skull and burned the entire deposit again. Clearly, the creation of ancestors involved much ceremonial time and effort.

Termination practices also show little or no change over the centuries among Saturday Creek's commoners. Smashed and burned items, particularly plain and decorated ceramics, are common. In addition, the inclusion of older vessels as termination offerings suggests the sacrifice of heirlooms as ceremonial trash once they broke or were broken (for example, Walker 1995). Deposits often consist of three layers of burned and smashed, largely rimless vessels. The number three is one of the most significant numbers in Maya cosmology, perhaps reflecting the three major layers of the universe—the heavens, earth, and underworld (Sharer 1994:523; for example, Garber et al. 1998; compare Guderjan 2004). And based on a preliminary analysis of ceramic types and forms used in this layering practice, it appears that the Mayas often used Uaxactún unslipped jars for the top and/or bottom layers of 7 of the 18 ceramic sherd concentrations (unfortunately, not all the necessary information was recorded in 2001), as well as relatively rare ceramic types such as Vaca Falls Red jars, which are typically only manufactured as bowls and dishes (see Gifford et al. 1976:235, 275).

It is clear that fragmented or incomplete objects were significant and differed from complete, whole, or broken items. Depositing ceramics with few or no rims may have been a way to kill vessels in dedication and termination rites. Even if we had excavated associated middens, which we did not, and found the missing rims, we still need to explain why some vessels were broken and their pieces separated—whereupon some sherds/pieces became part of the structures' life history—while others did not. Perhaps Mayas threw rims in trash piles or used them for fill; whether or not they did, one would expect them to have discarded the entire vessel. The point to keep in mind is that they separated out pieces of broken items, some for deposition in special deposits (sacred), and others elsewhere (profane). The separation of pieces from the same object is the critical fact.

What did they do with the rims, and what do the differences in their final resting places signify? Does each sherd represent the social significance of the entire vessel? If so, why use body rather than rim sherds? It is interesting to evaluate such deposits in light of Chapman's (2000a) research on Mesolithic and Neolithic Balkan artifact assemblages. He proposes that the life history of items typically continues long after they were purposely or accidentally broken and suggests that objects, as part of the enchainment process (creating relationships between people through objects), are purposefully broken, exchanged, and then, eventually, ceremoniously deposited "throughout the settlement and beyond" (Chapman 2000a:23).

Some *chultun* (chambers dug into the soft bedrock and used for dry storage) deposits include jar necks and rims without bodies (for example, Yax Caan, Belize), as do some cave deposits (Cameron Griffith, personal communication 2003). Alternatively, at Actun Tunichil Muknal, a large cave in western Belize, Moyes (2001:75) found that 39 percent of the sherds (278 out of 718) could not be refitted and suggests that "they were brought in as offerings in and of themselves." Caves, chultuns, and other openings in the earth are considered portals to the underworld, a place through which the dead must pass before emerging as ancestors (Schele and Freidel 1990). Thus, in certain situations and ceremonies fragmented objects were just as significant as the whole. Perhaps each family or community member received a piece of an item owned by a recently deceased relative or important individual (and soon-to-be ancestor). And the keeping and/or depositing of fragments signified their place in an individual's or family's life (history) and memory. However, the fact that ceramic fragments are more noticeable in dedication and termination deposits than in burials may suggest collective rather than individual ownership (see Mills 2004), further indicating their role in the establishment of place and family versus the commemoration of a person. In other words, the Mayas likely buried entire objects with the deceased, perhaps objects they owned, but used family objects in dedication and termination rites, whereby only parts were deposited and the remaining parceled out to family and community members who shared in the significance of particular items. What determined which objects' fragments were to have social and sacred power is a question for future study.

CONCLUDING REMARKS

Mayas performed traditional rites for over a millennium throughout the Maya area, and they conducted them for family and members of the community to acknowledge a family's loss—and a new beginning. People interred the dead to create ancestors who remained involved in the lives of the living. Building and destroying houses thus relate to the life history of ancestors. The death of particular family members often represented the need for a new house, which meant the old one had to be destroyed and terminated after funerary rites, and a new one built and dedicated over the remains of the recently deceased. These behaviors are inextricably linked events that comprised a vital component of the construction process. One cannot separate such practices and construction events—they are one and the same. Memory and place were thus created in the ceremonial cycle of dedication, ancestor veneration, and termination practices. And the fact that the majority of structures throughout the southern Maya lowlands were continuously occupied for centuries suggests that they became, quoting Chapman (2000a:4), "a key element in the maintenance of cultural memory."

Without written words with which to document their histories, commoners relied on mnemonic devices, especially since oral stories about individuals rarely go beyond a few generations (for example, Meskell 2001, 2004:62–63). Domestic ceremonial practices, by their materiality, solidify residents' membership in the household, family, and society. Mayas conducted ceremonies that involved offerings to make permanent and materialize the feelings, meanings, and intent of the rites. Depositional histories thus reflect not only ceremonial behavior, but also the lived lives of occupants. They reflect that houses were not just homes, but charged places embodying the living and the dead (compare Joyce 2001).

In conclusion, offerings established a sense of place through memorializing structures as homes through dedication, ancestor veneration, termination, and other practices. The depositional sequence of a structure thus embodies histories of the people who lived and died within its walls just as much as it chronicles building, razing, and rebuilding.

Acknowledgments

I gratefully acknowledge the National Science Foundation for funding for the 2001 season at Saturday Creek (BCS #0004410) and the Institute of Archaeology, National Institute of Culture and History, Government of Belize, for their permission and support. I also want to thank Barbara Mills and Bill Walker for inviting me to participate in the SAR seminar and this volume, as well as Sandra Andrade for conducting the preliminary analysis on the sherd concentrations.

Notes

1. Evidence from other sites throughout the Maya lowlands demonstrates that these practices extend nearly a millennium before those found at Saturday Creek (for example, Cuello, Barton Ramie). I have no doubt that we would have found Preclassic burials with further excavations.

2. McAnany et al. (1999:132) note, however, that "smaller, thinner bones [of subadults and females] often deteriorate much more quickly, and thus their skeletons many be particularly fragmentary, especially if stored and moved for secondary interment."

10

The Materiality of Ancestors

Chullpas *and Social Memory in the Late Prehispanic History of the South Andes*

Axel E. Nielsen

What might have been and what has been
Point to one end, which is always present.

—*T. S. Eliot,* Four Quartets, *1943*

During the first half of the second millennium CE, South Andean peoples experienced a series of dramatic political transformations that included the formation of highly integrated multicommunity polities and two waves of conquest, first by the Inkas, and then by the Spaniards. In this paper I will consider the role played by ancestor veneration in these changes, putting emphasis on how certain forms of material culture—specifically, *chullpa*-towers—contributed to inventing, remembering, contesting, and forgetting a past in which present social relations were always contained. This exploration will focus on archaeological data from the North Lipez region, in the southern Bolivian altiplano. First I will discuss some ideas regarding collective memory, social reproduction, and materiality to put into focus the theoretical background of this investigation.

MEMORY AND MATERIALITY

Collective memory is a shared understanding of the way things were in the past and how the present came into being. As many authors have pointed out, it is not a simple reflection of the past, but a social construct through which the past is brought to bear on the present. Like collective visions of the future or ritual-productive calendars, social memory references human action in time, in the same way that cultural models of place and landscape operate in relation to space. People don't live in empty or neutral time/space coordinates but are immersed in these shared understandings of the world, which shape the experiential base (or doxa) upon which habitus is built.[1] From this point of view, collective memory is best conceived as a historical dimension of culture (Abercrombie 1998), a nexus between past experience and current disposition.

Social memory tends to reproduce social order, because power relations are immanent to the patterns of action and interaction that it helps to replicate (Connerton 1989; compare Bourdieu 1977:78; Giddens 1976:110–113). Typically, this ideological function is also performed by creating the perception that current conditions are the inevitable outcome of history, thus effecting "the misrecognition of the arbitrariness on which they are based" (Bourdieu 1977:164), turning contingency into necessity. In the words of T. S. Eliot, "If all time is eternally present, all time is unredeemable."

If dominant social memories help to sustain hegemonic structures, it follows that alternative accounts of the past can undermine them. More generally, the interdependency of memory, practice, and power leads to the expectation that significant political changes will always involve transformations of collective representations of the past, which can range from a more or less subtle resignification of existing views and memory-laden objects, to the complete erasure of the past and its practical referents, followed by the invention of a new tradition.

Knowing what social memory does, however, does not explicate how it is reproduced in practice. How is a "collective" memory (therefore a collectivity itself) created and transmitted across generations through individual action? Social memory is conveyed through language, bodily practice, and material culture, an analytical distinction that obviously cannot be taken too far. Since practice is always "three substances in one" (act, material/body, and mind), the reproduction of memory always involves the concerted and reinforcing operation of all three aspects of social reality. This fact is best exemplified by commemorative ceremonies, in which narratives, bodily movements, and objects are performatively intertwined (Connerton 1989).[2]

In this paper, however, I am particularly interested in the specific roles of materiality in memory transmission. The notion of materiality, understood as the material dimension of practice (culturally and historically situated social action), highlights the process through which materials (artifacts, monuments, landforms, and so on) and human agents, objects, and subjects are reciprocally constituted (Miller 2005). The question about the materiality of memory, then, can be rephrased as: how do materials contribute to turn the past into a shaping force of current practice?

The most common answer to this question is based on the textual model of material culture that has been the hallmark of contextual and structural archaeologies. Through symbolic codes, objects invoke representations of the past that inform people's action (Hodder 1992; Tilley 1993). Others have focused on the direct, physical interaction between the material world and bodily practice (body *hexis*, in the sense of Bourdieu 1990:66–79). This approach highlights the ways in which the built environment and artifacts in general—crafted by previous practice—facilitate or induce, almost "ergonomically," certain perceptions and actions, while preventing or discouraging others (Moore 1996; Nielsen 1995).

The more recent literature on materiality has pointed out other ways in which materials bridge the gap between past and present, which could be termed "consubstantiality" and "object animation." Everything changes, constantly. Material attributes, however, can change at a slower pace than people, ideas, and actions, creating the essentialist illusion that objects defeat time, that they remain the same. Perhaps, as Heraclitus put it, we never bathe twice in the same river, but it seems we do. Consequently, objects that are thought to have participated in significant events or belonged to important persons or deities (for example, heirlooms, historical buildings) are experienced as consubstantial with those facts and beings: they were there and share their identity and some of their essential qualities (Lillios 1999; Weiner 1992). Unlike narratives and performances that recall history through symbolic codes and enactments, objects carry history in their very fabric, allowing a direct reengagement with the past (Rowlands 1993:144).

The ability of materials to turn the past into present force is particularly important in the case of objects that are practically understood as endowed with agency. Whether this quality applies to some extent to the entire material world or only to a few special objects and how object animation compares to human (true?) agency are still matters of debate (for example, Boast 1997; Gell 1998; Gosden 2005; Latour 1993; Meskell 2004; Olsen 2003; Walker 1999). Most scholars seem to agree, however, on the fact that in all cultures, some objects are experienced as having intentions, awareness, and the power to influence people's lives. Whether these abilities dwell in the objects themselves or are bestowed upon them by other invisible forces (including people's minds), object animation allows entities from the (mythic or historic) past—gods, ancestors, or ghosts—to continue participating in current social practice. By the same logic, the disappearance of ancient objects or the killing of "artifact beings" can effect an irreversible social amnesia. This is why the purposeful destruction or removal from public experience of memory-charged artifacts and features, especially "animated" ones, is central to politically orchestrated acts of forgetting.

I do not believe we should reject any of these formulations. They highlight different but conjoining ways in which materials weave themselves into social practice, and, in so doing, they ground our existence in time. We should not assume a universal relationship between memory and objects. As social historians, our challenge is to understand through thick, contextual analysis how these various aspects of materiality concurred in specific cases.

ANDEAN ANCESTORS

Ancestor Worship as Recalling Practice

Ancestor cults are religious practices that allow the continued participation of deceased individuals in the affairs of the living. These practices are frequently tied to the negotiation of strategic resources (for example, land, rank) among the living as part of a practical logic that explains social difference through descent and kinship. This is not to say that ancestor veneration always supports hierarchy or that it should be treated as the hallmark of a particular type of social structure; indeed, these cults are present in societies with very different degrees and forms of inequality. Rather, we should think of them as just a common way in which the past is brought to bear on the present, an institutional framework that places the memory of the dead at the center of power negotiations, keeping in mind that the results of these negotiations are diverse and historically contingent.

The cornerstones of ancestor cults are a series of practices meant to perpetuate the agency of the dead (usually of only some of them) so they can continue interacting with the living. In this way, ancestor cults not only contribute to naturalizing the arbitrariness of power relations by conceiving them as a consequence of a social order (more or less asymmetrical) that existed in the past, but turn that order into a present fact by incorporating those mythical agents and their relationships into current experience.

In order to do this, ancestor veneration involves distinctive ways of remembering, mostly based on inscribed forms of memory (in the sense of Rowlands 1993). These typically include (1) material referents of the dead, that is, durable objects endowed with ancestral agency; (2) their meaningful incorporation into the stream of community life; and (3) strategies for establishing hierarchical relationships among these representations or contesting them.

Ancestorship and Society in the Andes

Many authors have stressed the importance that ancestor cults had among Andean peoples at the time of the European invasion (for example, Duviols 1979; Kaulicke 2001; Saignes 1993; Salomon 1995; Zuidema 1989). Ancestorship was central to the constitution of *ayllus*, the basic units of economic and political organization found throughout the area at the time. Ayllus were corporate groups that held land in common and conceived of themselves as descendants of a (sometimes purely mythical) ancestor who, as the original founder of the community and conqueror of the territory, was the ultimate owner of all the resources. In their smallest expression, these units comprised a few hundred households (minor ayllus), which were inclusively integrated into more encompassing organizational levels (major ayllus, moieties, ethnic groups) to form segmentary hierarchies in which each building block maintained its identity together with some control over basic resources and local decisions (Izko 1992; Platt 1987).

The positions of authority at different levels of these organizations were occupied only by the members of certain lineages within the ayllus, and only some of them (often referred to as *collana ayllu*) provided the *mallkus* that led the moieties and ruled over the entire ethnic group (*capac mallku*). Political office, in turn, entailed a differential appropriation of collective resources, especially corvée labor. To meet their redistributive obligations and responsibilities as officers in the cult of the *wak'as*, or deities (ancestors included), the mallkus administered and usufructed the *mit'a*, or labor tax, owed by every adult member of the community.[3] These privileges were also justified in terms of ancestorship and descent, since they were reserved to those individuals and lineages that were considered genealogically closer to the founder of the community and cornerstone of political authority. Moreover, the ancestors themselves were hierarchically arranged in a genealogy that recognized as ultimate forebearers celestial deities such as the Sun and the Stars (Cobo 1990 [1653]). Transposed to their descendants, these mythical asymmetries introduced further inequalities among the ayllus that were the building blocks of segmentary formations.

The role played by ancestor worship in the reproduction of social identity and hierarchy explains the great emphasis that, according to the sixteenth-century Spanish witnesses, the Inka nobility and subordinated provincial elites placed on the transmission of ancestral memory. It also implies that challenges to the established economic and political order must have involved ways of contesting these dominant forms of social memory. To assess this possibility in specific cases (one of my goals in the second part of this paper), we need to consider the ways in which representations of the past were created and sustained.

According to historical sources the transmission of ancestral memory in the Andes engaged multiple media and practices (Kaulicke 2001). Oral accounts of the life and achievements of dead Inkas, ethnic lords, and other important dead individuals, for example, were recited at funerals and various celebrations of the ritual calendar that in this way assumed an explicitly commemorative dimension. These narratives, as well as dynastic recounts and creation myths, were accompanied by songs or music and were often the responsibility of specialists who recalled them with the aid of knotted strings known as *quipus* and other mnemonic devices, for example, textiles with codified geometric designs (*tocapus*) or painted wooden objects. Performative recalling involved processions to the sepulchers, shrines, and other significant places associated with the ancestor, pilgrimage, ritual battles (*t'inku*), dances, and sacrifices.

Most importantly, however, these cults always involved carefully curated material referents of the ancestors themselves. These included not only the mummy or some of the bones of the dead person (*malqui*), but also the sepulcher (frequently a visible structure that granted access to the dead body when needed), bundles containing hair and fingernail clippings, masks, figurines, stone monoliths, distinctive architectural styles, special textiles, curiously shaped rocks, or unmodified landforms such as mountains or caves. The same ancestors could have several material referents of the same kind (for example, more than one sepulcher) or of a different one (for example, the mummy, a sepulcher, and several idols), so they could be simultaneously present in many places and contexts.

The infusion of ancestral powers into a variety of objects, features, and places was critical for transposing their memory to different contexts and allowed them to engage with social practice in new ways. Unlike the corpses, nonperishable objects could transcend time, giving permanence to the prototypical order they embodied. Materials could be scaled up to acquire monumental proportions or scaled down to be carried with a person or image at all times, endowing them with ancestral qualities. As artifacts, they were able to serve various functions, transforming multiple activities into acts of remembering. Ancestral embodiments allowed people to see, touch, and interact directly with their forebearers.

As an example of this physical interaction, consider Guamán Poma de Ayala's description of the "feast of the dead" (Figure 10.1), which is just

 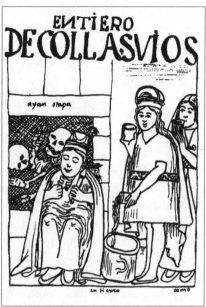

FIGURE 10.1

Left: *The feast of the dead.* Right: *Burials in Collasuyu (Guamán Poma de Ayala 1980 [1615]:230 and 268, respectively).*

one of many testimonies left by the Europeans who witnessed the participation of ancestor mummies and idols not only during funerals, but in all kinds of public events, from the crowning of a new inka to the celebration of the harvest:

> In this month [November] they take the deceased out of their vaults which they call *pucullo* and they give them food and drink and they dress them with their rich clothes and put feathers on the head and sing and dance with them. And they put them on litters and take them from house to house and along the streets and on the plaza and then they put them back into their *pucullos*, giving them their food and wares, made of silver and gold for the principal and of clay for the poor. And they give them their rams [llamas] and clothes and bury it [*sic*] with them and they spend very much in this feast. (Guamán Poma de Ayala 1980 [1615]: 231, my translation)

This account, like others, emphasizes the importance of sharing special foods and beverages (for example, meat, maize beer [*chicha*], coca leaves) with the ancestors, a practice that may have contributed significantly to the sensory and emotional engagement that effectively turned the mythical past into present experience. It also points out some of the ways in which the hierarchical relationships among ancestors were recalled and negotiated during these rituals, in this case through the different materials used in the wares offered to them. We know from other documents that these rank differences involved also the quality, color, and shape of the mummies' clothes, their spatial arrangement in the public area, the number of servants that attended them, and the material, size, and elaboration of their sepulchers and images, to mention just a few.

Impressed by the magnificence of public commemorations, the Spaniards did not pay so much attention to other forms of ancestral recalling that may have been more integrated to domestic contexts and daily life. These less spectacular but probably more pervasive and enduring forms of memory transmission await archaeological investigation. Except for some general comments on the ways in which the dead were worshiped in different parts of the Inka Empire (for example, Cobo 1990 [1653]:39–43; Guamán Poma de Ayala 1980 [1615]:262–272), historical sources cannot give us a sense of the variability in ancestor cults across the Andes or how these practices came into being. This last issue is particularly important, since archaeology has already proven that in this area the involvement of the dead in the affairs of the living predates the Inkas by millennia.

One of the earliest examples of ancestor veneration in the Andes is the elaborate tradition of mummification and periodic removal of dead bodies from their tombs that characterized the preceramic Chinchorro tradition (ca. 6000–500 BCE) of northern Chile (Rivera 1995). Related practices have been documented for other Archaic peoples, like those occupying Inca Cueva 4 (northwestern Argentina)[4] by 3200 BCE, who buried a young female accompanied by naturally mummified parts of several human bodies (including three heads) that had been wrapped in specially designed bags, ready for transport (Aschero 2000:56). The removal and ritual manipulation of selected parts of the human body, especially heads, continued throughout the Andes during late preceramic and Formative times (for example, Hastorf 2003; Yacobaccio 2000). During the Formative period of northwestern Argentina (ca. 1000 BCE–900 CE), for example, ancestors were represented in new material forms, including funerary stone masks; "mask-like" motifs in rock art; monoliths; and "supplicants," portable stone sculptures probably depicting a flexed human body (García Azcárate 1996; Pérez 2000).

The great antiquity and spatial distribution of ancestor veneration in the Andes leads to the conclusion that these cults were present in multiple

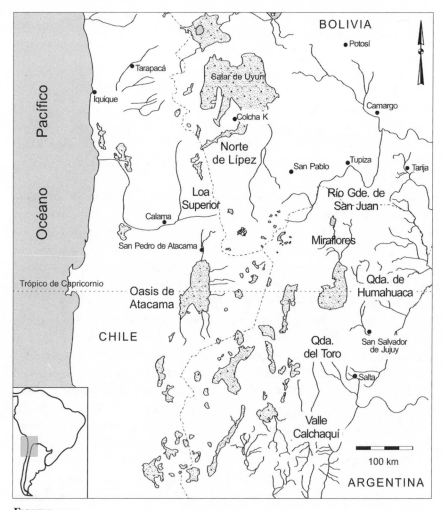

FIGURE 10.2

The South Andes, showing North Lípez and other regions.

kinds of societies and participated in different social processes. This invites archaeology to undertake a historical analysis of this phenomenon, establishing differences of activity and context; identifying origins, genealogies, and discontinuities of practice; looking at the contingent relationship between ancestorship and power; and demonstrating how ancestors and their living descendants shaped each other under changing conditions. In the following section, I would like to address some of these issues through the analysis of archaeological traces of ancestor veneration in the southern Bolivian highlands, a region also known as Lipez (Figure 10.2).

CONTESTED ANCESTORSHIP IN THE SOUTHERN BOLIVIAN ALTIPLANO

Archaeological Background

As I just mentioned, forms of ancestor worship are already present in the South Andes (highlands of southwestern Bolivia, northern Chile, and northwestern Argentina) during Archaic and Formative times. It is during the Regional Developments period (RDP, ca. 900–1400 CE), however, when these practices become ubiquitous and seem to have acquired new social significance.

The early phase of this period (900–1250 CE) is a time of dramatic reorganization marked by the gradual disintegration of macrorregional structures related to the Tiwanaku formation. These structures include long-distance trade networks and widely shared ritual practices reminiscent of Tiwanaku religion, two phenomena that probably also involved a web of political alliances among autonomous and loosely integrated communities or small, multicommunity polities. The fragmentation of these structures coincides with a long-term cycle of drought, which may have been partially responsible for the collapse of Tiwanaku itself (Binford et al. 1997), and increasing levels of intergroup violence, two possibly related phenomena that peak during the late phase (1250–1400 CE). The RDP is also marked by the constitution of different material culture traditions in most regions, a phenomenon that justifies the name given to the period. These traditions include distinctive ceramic styles, textiles, house forms, settlement layouts, and burial practices.

Another characteristic of the period is a sustained tendency toward population aggregation, which is slow during the early phase and very rapid during the late one (Nielsen 2001, 2002). By 1400 CE large, conglomerate settlements can be found throughout the area, with maximum community sizes that range between 600 and 3,000 people, depending on the overall productivity of each region. This change is probably part of a process of "segmentary fusion" (Platt 1987:95) that also entailed progressive political integration among communities, as indicated by the development of settlement hierarchies. These involve not only contrasts of size and internal complexity among settlements, but also the differential distribution of public areas or "plazas" that become a well-defined component of site structures by 1250 CE (Nielsen 2006). This is also the time when, under different forms, the dead become omnipresent among the living.

Archaeological indicators of ancestor worship are not particularly visible during the early phase of the RDP. During the thirteenth century, however, highly visible and enduring representations of ancestors appear throughout the South Andes. These "monuments" include the chullpa-towers of the Poopo and Uyuni Basins (Bolivia) and highlands of northern Chile; the stone monoliths (*wankas*) of the Puna basins of Yavi, Pozuelos, and Miraflores (Argentina); the "above-ground graves" found in certain sites of Quebrada de Humahuaca and Quebrada del Toro; and (perhaps) the mounds with inset funerary cists of Calchaquí Valley, in Argentina (Nielsen 2001).

The best known of these are the chullpas built throughout the Bolivian altiplano after the collapse of Tiwanaku. According to the Aymara dictionary of Bertonio (1984 [1612]:II:92) the word *chullpa* meant "burial or container in which they place their dead." These tower-shaped structures, which vary in size, shape (cylindrical, prismatic, hyperboloid), fabric (stone or mud), finish (cut stone, plastered, painted), and location (near towns, in the fields, isolated) caught the attention of the sixteenth- and seventeenth-century chroniclers, who were amazed to see that the Indians put more care into the construction and maintenance of these sepulchers than into their own houses (for example, Cieza de León 1995 [1553]:Chapters 62–63; Guamán Poma de Ayala1980 [1615]:262–272). Later travelers and, more recently, archaeologists have repeatedly described these structures, venturing new interpretations of their use and meaning, as exemplified by the widely cited hypotheses that they served as elite burials (Hyslop 1977) or Isbell's (1997) recent argument that, by securing access to the bodies of malquis, chullpas and "open sepulchers" in general should be taken as correlates of ancestor veneration and related ayllu social organization.

I basically agree with Isbell's argument regarding the relationship between chullpas, ancestor veneration, and corporate ayllu organization but have to question his (and most authors') functional interpretation of the chullpa architectural form as only mortuary and equivalent to "the open sepulcher." Based on archaeological data from Lipez, I will argue that these towers were subject to multiple uses, burial being just one of them. This combination of multiple uses in a single form was fundamental for incorporating collective memory into daily experience and is important to grasp pre-Inka notions of ancestorship in the region. More generally, I would like to stress that the ways in which artifacts combine form and function in a single substance are crucial to understanding the way in which materiality incorporates the past into the present, shaping social practice in unique ways.

Towers as Ancestors

To develop my argument, I will first consider separately the form, spatial context, and use of these structures. The chullpas of Lipez are towers with thick (.6–1 m), double-faced walls made of carefully fitted stones laid with mortar, corbeled roofs made of stone slabs occasionally reinforced with wooden beams, and (in most cases) stone-paved floors. They vary in color (white, beige, gray, black, red) depending on the rocks used (always locally available): volcanic ash, basalt, or andesite. Initially they were only built in circular or elliptic plans (cylindrical or tronco-pyramidal), but beginning around 1400 CE they were also made in square or rectangular plans, usually with round corners. The maximum sizes we have recorded are 3 m high and 3 m in diameter (cylindrical) or 3.5 m on their longest side (rectangular). They always have one square opening measuring around .4 x .4 m, just enough to allow the passage of a human body. This feature can be placed at ground level or as much as 1.7 m above the ground surface; when the opening is high, immediately below it there is a step or small platform on the outside and a precarious stairway made of one or several slabs sticking out of the inside wall to facilitate climbing in and out of the structure. Other features occasionally present (perhaps with chronological implications yet to be established) are a cornice, two stones protruding near the upper corners of the opening, and a wall reinforcement similar to a ring at the bottom. Typically, they are freestanding single structures, but there are a few examples of two or even three abutting towers. I will use the term *chullpa-tower* to refer to this architectural form (Figure 10.3).

In Lipez, as in other regions, chullpa-towers appear in multiple contexts: (1) in great numbers clustered along one side of settlements; (2) surrounding fortresses (*pukaras*); (3) on one side of public areas within settlements or plazas; (4) in domestic areas, as a single structure next to the dwelling; (5) forming one small group near settlements, or (6) dispersed, occupying high, visible points near them; (7) isolated or in groups away from any settlement, usually in association with farmland, marshy areas with good pastures, or water springs; (8) inside rock shelters near areas with good potential for farming; and (9) among the ruins of earlier sites already abandoned at the time, either surrounding them or built on top of the ruined buildings. Some of these locations may be restricted to certain periods; for example, (2) and (3) probably belong exclusively to the late RDP, while (4) seems to occur only after European contact. The others, however, seem to coexist from the thirteenth century on.

As indicated, most chullpa-towers are in open areas, but sometimes they are also found inside caves and natural overhangs. More commonly, however, what is found in rock shelters are other structures that are formally different from the towers (walled caves, rooms built against the back wall of the shelter, semisubterranean vaults) but share with them a number

FIGURE 10.3

Chullpa-tower from the site of Cruz Vinto (North Lípez).

of traits, for example, equally sized and placed square openings, and similar masonry style. This gives towers and these other features a very similar aspect, especially when compared with the architecture used in other structures, for example, dwellings and defensive walls.

Turning to their use, surface and excavated evidence indicates that chullpa-towers (and probably some of the other, formally related structures as well) participated in many activities, at least including burial and storage. Refuse in front of the openings of some of them suggests also their use as altars (compare Aldunate and Castro 1981), while the extraordinary visibility of others points to their potential role as landmarks. Indeed, the possibility of the same structures being used in different ways, simultaneously or sequentially, cannot be ruled out.

Based on the assumption that "chullpas are sepulchers," some authors have tried to define "diagnostic traits" that could be used to differentiate them from silos—for example, the position of the opening and the shape or location of the structure. Our data indicate, however, that the same combinations of form and location are associated with more than one use. We have documented human remains in towers with their openings at ground level (Talapaca) or high above it (Illipica), forming clusters or "cemeteries" near settlements (San Juan de Chuycha), surrounding abandoned sites (Itapilla Kancha), or inside caves (Chillchi Wayko, Llaqta Khaka); but we have also recorded towers with the same formal traits (sometimes in the same sites) used for storage.

The premise that sepulchers and silos *are* different things, however, underlies most discussions of chullpa-towers in the literature. Following the lead of early Spanish sources, the term *chullpa* is employed when the authors think that the towers were used as burials, whereas *silo* or the Quechua word *collca* is applied when the inference is that they served for storage, even if the structures look alike and are found in a similar context. When the evidence contradicts this form-equals-function assumption, it is common to report "a sepulcher that was never used" or "a silo used for burial."

These attempts to separate functional types of towers and other chullpa-like structures (implicitly linked to the assumption that these were different things for their creators) reflect a common tendency to essentialize our own cultural taxonomies (compare Meskell 2004) and only obscure what I believe is most important about chullpas—that they link multiple activities and activity settings to one, highly emblematic architectural form.[5] The multifunctionality of the chullpa-tower wove different practices, actors, and contexts of social interaction into a single field structured around the ancestor. Through these structures, ancestors became omnipresent not only on the landscape, but also in the stream of activity through which it was experienced (the "taskscape," in the sense of Ingold 1993), transposing notions of ancestorship well beyond mortuary ritual. Tasks that otherwise could hardly be related to the dead or considered "cultic," such as farming, tending the herd, storing, going back home, traveling to a neighboring village, or repelling attacks, became empirical referents of ancestral memory, turning daily life into remembrance. Rather than equating chullpa-towers with sepulchers, then, we should look at them as monumental embodiments of the ancestor itself, capable of doing what ancestors do, that is, guard the fields and herds, and promote their fertility; protect the harvest; bring prosperity to their descendants and provide them with food, water, and other (stored) goods; represent the group before outsiders; defend the community and its territory; fight their enemies; inspire political decisions; attend the pledge of the community gathered at the plaza; and so on.[6]

The Politics of Ancestorship

The presence of chullpa-towers in plazas, recorded in at least three large conglomerates of the region (Laqaya, Churupata, and Cruz Vinto)

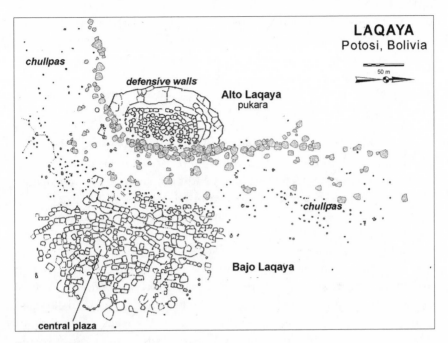

FIGURE 10.4

Plan of Laqaya.

and dated to the late RDP, is of particular interest because it points to the regular participation of these structures in public gatherings and other practices directly related to community politics. I will consider as an example the central plaza of Laqaya, one of the largest RDP settlements known in the region, where we have focused our research.

Laqaya comprises three well-differentiated areas (Figure 10.4). To the west, on top of a butte, a fortress, or pukara (Alto Laqaya), is protected on its vulnerable west side by two defensive walls. At the bottom of the butte there is a concentration of more than 300 chullpa-towers (mostly circular, but also rectangular). Immediately to the east of this area, on the plain, a residential conglomerate (Bajo Laqaya) formed by over 200 single-room dwellings was built with dry stone masonry.

Toward the center of Bajo Laqaya, a 300-m^2 open area or plaza is enclosed by a low wall. In some parts this wall has a bench attached on the inside. At the center a rock-lined pit is filled with rocks. On the east flank of the plaza there are three rectangular chullpa-towers measuring on the outside, from south to north, 4.8 x 4.0 m (Chullpa 1), 4.1 x 3.4 m (Chullpa 2), and 3.6 x 3.0 m (Chullpa 3). We ignore the original height of the structures because this part of the site was severely affected by the extraction of rocks for road construction a couple of decades ago, but if we consider the proportions that towers usually have (taller than wide), they must have been at least 3 to 4 m high, an estimation that is ratified by local people, who remember that they were "taller than a modern house." We know by looking at the bottom part of the walls that are still preserved that their openings were high above the ground.

We excavated Chullpa 2 completely and tested the other two without finding human remains. In Chullpa 2 we recovered reconstructible vessels and remains of wool bags filled with quinoa (*Chenopodium quinoa*), suggesting its use for storage. The textiles and their content were burned, as well as the wooden beams that had supported the roof of the structure sitting directly on top of the stone pavement. Above this level the tower was filled with trash and wall fall.

As long as we accept that chullpa-towers embodied ancestors, the monumental proportions of these structures indicate that ancestors played an important role in all public gatherings, regardless of whether they were explicitly devoted to the dead. Indeed, the presence of quinoa (the main crop grown in the region and probably the basis of subsistence at the time) in one of them establishes a practical connection between ancestorship and agriculture (for example, fertility, abundance), something that was pointed out by the Spaniards, who repeatedly observed in other parts of the Andes the participation of the dead (mummies or other representations) in public celebrations related to the agricultural calendar. Certainly this does not exclude the possibility (also noted repeatedly in written sources) that the actual bodies of the dead could also be brought to the plaza in certain opportunities.

As noted before, ethnohistorical data indicate that (at least in the sixteenth-century Andean highlands), ancestors were considered mythical founders of corporate groups or ayllus; and segmentary polities were formed by the union of such groups in progressively inclusive organizational levels without having ayllus lose their identity and relative control over local decisions and production (Nielsen 2006). Given these facts, the presence of *three* towers in the plaza of Laqaya and other contemporary sites (for example, Churupata) becomes significant, because they could reveal a ternary segmentary structure for the community or polity. By placing their own ancestors in the plaza, each ayllu was recalling its origins and rights to resources within the larger political formation. These kinds of ternary structures have also been documented in Spanish accounts, as illustrated by the following passage, referring to the province of Collaguas:

[T]hey appointed for each ayllo a cacique [chief], and there were three ayllos, called Collona, Pasana, Cayao; each ayllo of these had three hundred Indians and a principal whom they obeyed, and these three principals obeyed a principal cacique, who was the chief of all. (Ulloa Mogollón 1885 [1585]:45, my translation)

The Qollana-Payan-Kayaw (as they are most commonly spelled) classi-fication, found in other Andean polities, involved a ranking of social units. In Aymara, *Qollana* meant "excellent, the best thing" (Bertonio 1984 [1612]:II:50) and was applied to the main ayllu, which provided the lead-ers for different levels of the segmentary structure (for example, Platt 1987:73). The size differences among the towers, then, could convey a hier-archy among the ayllus that formed the community, probably expressed also in oral narratives, ritual performances, and other actions articulated around these structures in the course of public events.

On the opposite (west) side of the plaza there is an irregular structure (whose function we ignore at this point) and three subrectangular build-ings (8 x 5 m; 10 x 6 m; 10 x 6 m) that had gabled roofs. The excavation of one of these buildings revealed traces of the thatch roof that had been sup-ported with two wooden posts, and a hearth protected by an air deflector next to the doorway. Associated with the floor we found abundant refuse, mainly camelid bones and bowl fragments, mostly decorated in the dis-tinctive regional ceramic style of this period, known as Mallku. This room, and probably the other two flanking it, replicate the shape and structure of the houses at the site, whose internal organization is extremely patterned, except they are twice the size. This building had also been burned and later filled with trash.

The archaeological evidence just described associates public gather-ings with feasting, highlighting the importance of commensalism in the political formations that crystallized at the beginning of the late RDP. The wide distribution of Mallku ceramics, not only in domestic contexts but also in this public area, suggests that it operated in a corporate style, con-tributing to the reproduction of a collective identity through the simple acts of eating and drinking. If our interpretation of the three chullpa-towers as reflecting a tripartite organization is correct, the presence of three similar buildings in front of them could imply that the preparation and distribution of food and beverage for feasting was organized on the basis of a similar structure.

FIGURE 10.5

Artist's reconstruction of the plaza of Bajo Laqaya in the fourteenth century. Note the three chullpa-towers on the right. Drawing by Monica I. Nielsen.

In the course of these celebrations, the ancestors drank and ate with their living relatives. This involved a particular ritual technology (burning, pouring, burying) through which the dead "took" food, chicha, and other offerings. We suspect that the stone-lined pit and large rocks at the center of the plaza could have been involved in these practices (Figure 10.5), perhaps analogous to those witnessed by Pedro Pizarro in 1533 at the central plaza of Cuzco:

> [F]or the dead they made fires before them.... [T]hey burned here everything which they had placed before the dead in order that he might eat of the things which they eat, and here in this fire they consumed it. Likewise before these dead people they had certain large pitchers, which they call verquis, made of gold, silver or pottery, each according to his wish, and into [these ves-

sels] they poured the chicha which they gave to the dead man with much display.... When verquis were filled, they emptied them into a round stone in the middle of the plaza, and which they held to be an idol, and it was made around a small opening by which it [the chicha] drained itself off. (Pizarro 1921 [1571]:251–252)

By engaging the ancestors in the consumption of food and drink, these feasts not only reproduced a sense of community among the living, but also blurred the frontiers between life and death, between the present and the prototypical characters and events being commemorated. In the altered states of consciousness induced by alcohol—probably enhanced by mixing it with hallucinogenic substances—those who participated in these banquets were able to communicate directly with the dead, incorporating collective representations into their bodily experience (Saignes 1993).

The symmetrical design of the plaza, the absence of internal restrictions of visibility or access, and the relative homogeneity in the quality of the plaza architecture (which is true of the entire site) suggest that no significant or fixed differences were established among those who participated in these celebrations, beyond perhaps those derived from ayllu affiliation, as argued before.[7] This offers a point of contrast between Lipez and other places in the Andes, where public architecture—sometimes also involving representations of ancestors—is explicitly designed to produce inequalities among individuals and groups (compare Moore 1996; Nielsen 1995). This variability underscores the contingent relationship that exists between ancestor veneration and power, while pointing out some of the ways in which this relationship is negotiated in practice and, specifically, in materiality.

Radiocarbon data indicate that this public area was built in the mid-thirteenth century. The structures around the plaza and the perimeter wall were erected on top of an earlier occupation, meaning that the construction of the public space involved the remodeling of an existing settlement. The emblematic Mallku ceramics are not present in these earlier deposits. The plaza was abandoned around 1400 CE, an event that was apparently accompanied by the (purposeful?) destruction of the surrounding buildings by fire. The trash fills found in the excavated structures indicate that other parts of the settlement continued to be inhabited after the public area was abandoned. This late occupation was probably on the northern edge of Bajo Laqaya, where we have documented domestic structures dating to the seventeenth century.

The (archaeologically) simultaneous beginning of chullpa-tower construction, remodeling of settlements to accommodate plazas presided over by ancestral representations, and the adoption of the emblematic Mallku ceramics attest to the "invention of a tradition" (in the sense of Hobsbawm and Ranger 1983). We know that analogous changes were taking place at approximately the same time in some other regions of the South Andes, in a context of intensified conflict and rapid population aggregation.

In Quebrada de Humahuaca, for example, new and distinctive ceramic styles were adopted around 1250 CE, and at least one of the main settlements of the valley (Los Amarillos) was remodeled to build a well-defined public space that included material representations of ancestors in the form of *three* "above-ground graves" and was a stage for feasts (Nielsen 2006). If similar processes are documented in other regions at this time (and there are some indications that already point in this direction), we could further conclude that the processes of political integration that started during the early RDP culminated in the thirteenth century with the invention of a tradition that, reworking ancient concepts regarding the continued relationship between the dead and the living, featured ancestors as mythical founders of a socioterritorial order and corporate identities. In this view, rights over land and other resources, identity contrasts, and political hierarchies were conceived as an extension of that prototypical order, made present through ritualized oral recounts, commemorative feasts, and particularly, through the daily interaction with ancestral beings.

Redefining Ancestorship in the Age of Empire

Our view of the Inka Empire (Tawantinsuyu) has been mostly shaped by written documents. Certainly, ethnohistory has made a significant contribution to Andean archaeology by calling attention to the unique institutions and practices that may have produced the archaeological record, but too often it has prevented archaeologists from interpreting material remains in their own terms, limiting their ability to make an original contribution to our knowledge of the past. Only during the last few years, archaeologists have begun to systematically excavate Inka sites in the South Andes. This work has already challenged many previously unquestioned truths, such as the notion that the Inkas introduced little change in the economic and political structure of the peoples they conquered and—what is more important for this paper—that they respected local *wak'as* (deities) and cults.

What was the Inkas' attitude toward local ancestor veneration, which had been so important for the constitution of RDP South Andean polities?

The violent destruction of Laqaya's plaza at about the time this region was incorporated to Tawantinsuyu offers an archaeologically eloquent answer to this question. But the case of Laqaya is not unique. In Quebrada de Humahuaca, the "above-ground graves" of Los Amarillos were demolished at about the same time, and their content, including the three bodies and their wealthy mortuary offerings, were meticulously destroyed and burned. The whole artificial platform on which these monuments had been erected was burned and then used to build domestic structures. The ruins of the old sepulchers were covered with a midden that included a high frequency of Inka pottery, revealing the close connection between those living on top of the old plaza and the empire (Nielsen and Walker 1999).

In the Upper Loa region of northern Chile, the Inkas dismantled several of the chullpa-towers erected during the late RDP on the east side of Turi—one of the largest conglomerates of the Atacama Desert at this time —to build on top of them a plaza (*aucaipata*) with a magnificent *kallanka* on one side. Unlike the chullpas and the rest of the architecture at the site, which was made of black basalt, the kallanka, one of the most emblematic forms of Inka public architecture, was entirely built in white adobe (Aldunate 1993).

I suspect that further archaeological research in the public areas of important South Andean RDP settlements will expose more examples of this historically undocumented but systematic "forgetting campaign" implemented by the Inkas during their expansion. Within the cultural logic that structured the ayllus, the memory of the ancestors was the foundation of their political autonomy and their territorial rights. The institution of new power relations and forms of resource appropriation by the empire required a dramatic reformulation of these collective representations. The selective destruction of politically significant ancestor monuments or the abduction of ancestral images to become hostages of the empire in Cuzco (Rowe 1946) was one side of this transformation. The other was the creation of a new past, one in which the Inkas, as direct descendants of the Sun, occupied the top of a mythical hierarchy of ancestorship and therefore became the ultimate holders of political authority and owners of the land. It is worth noting that, unlike the Europeans later, the Inkas transformed power relations and associated memory without challenging the principles on which they were based. As in earlier history, the political and economic order imposed by the Inkas was at least partially based on genealogical representations and analogous forms of remembering.

The destruction of the public area of Laqaya correlates with the abandonment of the fortress of Alto Laqaya (and perhaps all RDP fortresses in the region) and most of the lower settlement. The local seat of political power probably moved to Chuquilla Kucho, a site only 3 km to the west that is mentioned in early historical accounts as a "principal town" (Lozano Machuca 1992 [1581]:31). Although the site has been heavily disturbed by later occupation (the modern town of Santiago K), the abundance of Inka pottery on the surface and the presence of wealthy Inka burials reveal the political importance of this settlement in the Tawantinsuyu era. Chullpa-towers still preserved on the outskirts of town, in visible locations around it, and on top of the ruins of an old early RDP site nearby (Itapilla Kancha) demonstrate that towers continued being important forms of transmitting the memory of local ancestors.

The new position that the Inkas adopted in cosmological hierarchies was also inscribed on the local landscape, for example, through the construction of shrines devoted to the solar cult on the summit of the most important mountains throughout the empire. Mountain spirits were worshiped by South Andean peoples as higher-order ancestors, as mediators between the community forefathers (malquis) and further-removed celestial deities. Still today in the southern altiplano, they are called mallkus (chiefs, leaders) or *achachilas* (grandparents) and are ritually invoked through animal sacrifices (*wilanchas*) to provide fertility in the form of water or herd reproduction. By erecting state shrines on top of the mountains, they literally placed mountain spirits and their subordinate ancestors and living descendants under the authority of the Inkas and their forefather, the Sun. In the case of Lipez, we know that one of these Inka shrines is on the mountain right above Chuquilla Kucho (Cerro Caral Inka), and we have indications of the existence of others on the main peaks that dominate the local horizon, like Cerro Chiguana and Cerro Llipi, the mountain that may have given its name to the entire region.

Epilogue: Struggling to Remember

The Spaniards undertook a still more radical transformation of Andean social memory. They imposed completely new principles of power legitimacy based on biblical mythology and European medieval notions of history. They not only attacked specific malquis or wak'as, as the Inkas had done before, they questioned the very logic of ancestorship as a valid principle for the creation of economic rights and political hierarchy. Toward the end of the sixteenth century, this effort became systematic when Spanish authorities began a large-scale operation to exterminate Andean religious practices. This campaign, known as the "extirpation of idolatries," involved recording the cults, destroying the associated material culture, confiscating the economic resources that supported them, and punishing the worshippers. Given the importance of ancestor veneration in pre-columbian times, it is not surprising that the representations of the dead, especially mummies and ancestor images, became an important focus of this prosecution. In 1574 Viceroy Toledo, for example, explicitly ordered local officers to destroy the burials in towers and vaults in their districts, placing the mixed bones of the deceased in large pits (Gisbert 1994:437).

Deeply inscribed on the landscape, fragments of ancestral memory survived in spite of repression and indoctrination. Chullpa-towers, as embodiments of ancestors, played an important role in keeping this past alive and meaningfully integrated into daily experience long after the bones and the mummies had disappeared. One of these structures, excavated near Laqaya (in Itapilla Kancha), for example, contained a malachite ornament and European beads made of blue glass. Whether these objects were left behind when the human body was removed or had been deposited there as offerings to the tower/ancestor itself, this kind of evidence (documented in other regions as well) demonstrates that in Lipez, the towers continued articulating commemorative practices during the Spanish Colonial period.

Centuries of cultural domination, however, finally alienated Andeans from their own history. Until recent times—and still today in many areas—rural peoples rarely recognized themselves in the materiality of their past. A short time ago in northwestern Argentina, for example, most peasants vaguely attributed the archaeological remains around them to a pagan race (*gentiles*) that was destroyed by the Flood "before their [the peasants'] own time."

In Lipez, people today use the term *chullpa* to refer to an ancient people that lived in darkness before the first sunrise. They were cold and ate everything raw, human flesh included. When the sun came out, the chullpas crawled into caves and their oven-shaped houses (towers)[8] trying to protect themselves from the painful brightness, where they dried up (turned into *charki* ["jerky"]) and can be found today with their clothes, dishes, and other belongings. The towers, which still can be seen everywhere in this region, are called *pirwas* (*silo* in Quechua, the language they speak today), a name that points to their similarity with structures that today are used only for storage. Like the sun-dried bodies of the chullpas, pirwas are imbued with an extraordinary and dangerous force that can do harm to the living but can also be used to heal. People fear and revere them.

Although dissociated from the representations and actions through which their builders once gave them historical meaning, the towers continue carrying in their materiality some of the ancestral powers they had

FIGURE 10.6

Members of the communities of Santiago K and Santiago Chuvica dancing in the central plaza of the ruins of Laqaya to celebrate the declaration of the site as a Bolivian national monument. The shadowy structures in the background are chullpa-towers.

in the past (Figure 10.6). I believe these powers will be crucial for the difficult task of reconstituting a collective memory that indigenous peoples throughout the Andes are facing today.

Acknowledgments

Research in Lipez was conducted through an agreement between the Viceministerio de Cultura (Bolivia) and Proyecto Arqueológico Altiplano Sur. I am particularly grateful to the community of Santiago K for their support and hospitality.

Notes

1. The importance of memory in the constitution of habitus is implicit in the very definition of this construct as "a system of lasting, transposable dispositions which, *integrating past experiences*, functions at every moment as a matrix of perceptions, appreciations, and actions and makes possible the achievement of infinitely diversified tasks" (Bourdieu 1977:82–83, my emphasis; compare Giddens 1979:64).

2. Here again, the close connection with habitus highlights the relevance of

Bourdieu's (for example, 1977:87–158) work on objectification and embodiment to understanding the reproduction of collective memory.

3. Indeed, the Inka Empire (Tawantinsuyu) was built (at least initially) on the basis of the same principles. The imperial administration (controlled by one segment, the Inka ethnic group and the royal ayllus or *panacas* within them) represented just the most inclusive level in a pyramid that encompassed multiple ethnic groups and confederations with their own segmentary organizations.

4. "South Andes" refers to the southernmost portion (south of Parallel 19) of the more commonly used categories of "South Central Andes" or "Andes Meridionales," excluding the Titicaca Basin and major eastern valleys, such as Cochabamba. In this way, I want to concentrate on the most arid portion of the Andes, with common economic and demographic characteristics that differ in their scale from those found in the Central Andes, including the northernmost part of the Bolivian highlands.

5. This interpretation introduces a possible variation to Sillar's (1996:282) provocative argument that the storage technology of Inka *qollqas* was a historical derivation of earlier burial in chullpas. Since their birth during the RDP, chullpas may have been involved in the multiple practices that belonged to the ancestors' semantic domain.

6. In support of this interpretation, we can recall the case of the chullpas of the Lauca River and the Pacajes area to the north, which are made of adobe and decorated with polychrome designs that replicate Inka textiles (*uncus*), as if the towers were "wearing" tunics (Gisbert 1994; Pärssinen 1993). In Lipez we have only seen examples of "decoration" in Colonial-period structures built inside caves, for example, one with malachite inlays (Llacta Khaka), another with pictographs (Qhatinsho), both around the opening.

7. A similar impression is given by the striking regularity of the domestic architecture and house layout at the site.

8. This story shows an interesting parallel with Guamán Poma de Ayala's (1980 [1615]:45) mythical account of the "second age of the Indians" (Uari Runa), who "built little houses that look like ovens which they call *pucullo*." The same word and/or icon is later used to represent the tower-shaped sepulchers of peoples in different provinces of the empire (Guamán Poma de Ayala 1980 [1615]:262–271).

11

Memory Work and Material Practices

Lynn Meskell

This collection brings together an impressive array of themes that goes well beyond the single-issue type of analysis to which we are accustomed in archaeology, the singling out of seemingly unitary topics whether landscape, agency, or gender, for example. While this volume may have begun as a type of rethinking of depositional practice, we have instead been presented with a global set of papers that embraces contemporary thinking about memory and forgetting; the role of practice and the place of monumentality; philosophies of materiality, object agency, and circulation; problems of taxonomy; the merging of subject-object dualities; the tacit power of revelation and secrecy; and so on.

ABOUT REMEMBERING

Let me try to tease apart some of these themes, despite the fact that the authors have done an impressive job at interweaving them together so cogently. The first is the inseparable relationship between memory and forgetting; indeed, the whole idea of history is enmeshed in choosing which of those practices to privilege. After several decades of public and scholarly investigation into the uses and abuses of memory, we have ostensibly reached memory fatigue (Huyssen 2003:2–3). Despite this saturation, a simple moving on from memory potentially risks forfeiting lessons from the past and forecloses our imagining alternative futures. Modernity's expansion of imagined futures and reconstructed pasts, specifically in extending the horizons of time and space beyond the local, the national, and even the international, reflects significant shifts in our ways of thinking and living temporality itself. In recent decades we have witnessed the proliferation of sites of memory, material memorials in the form of objects and museums, courts of memory and forgetting such as the Chilean and South African Truth and Reconciliation Commissions, human rights activism, and even memory work in the form of trauma tourism (Meskell 2006). Ultimately these examples reflect a crisis in the representation of history more generally, which means that memory itself has necessarily become a topic of sustained interrogation.

Given that archaeology is a historical discipline, it may strike many as odd that we have not come to the question of memory practices at an earlier moment (Van Dyke and Alcock 2003). What the papers do not advocate, however, is that there is a singular or unilaterally sanctioned memory or set of remembered events out there to be retrieved subsequently by individuals. Perhaps due to the residues of positivist thinking in our discipline, some scholars have envisaged that this work on memory, or more particularly collective memory, is tightly scripted around notions of replication or reiteration of a particular reality. Older sociological accounts posited relatively stable formations of social and group memories, yet they failed to apprehend the dynamism of contemporary media, technology, and lived time we experience today (Huyssen 2003:17) and undoubtedly frame past societies in a limited modality. Instead, the papers here speak more to the processes of making memories or facilitating them in a constant dialogic process rather then one of pure recall, since even this potential is shot through with explicitly individual experience. As the famous French example makes clear, there was not one French Revolution but rather thousands, each constructed by the individuals who lived through those events and constructed them uniquely in their own minds. This is not to say that real events do not take place or that they lack cohesive facticity—such denials would be irresponsible and unethical—but rather that researchers have to allow for the possibility of subjective inflection through the processes of recall and reconstitution.

For decades historians and philosophers have referred to this as counter-memory (Davis and Starn 1989; Foucault 1977), underlining the challenges and alternatives sustained by so-called official versions of history. Like the constitution of memory, forgetting might also constitute a long-term strategy. Hobbes (1991) once claimed that forgetting was the basis of a just state and that amnesia was the cornerstone of the social contract. While for Nietzsche, creative forgetting was nothing more than selective memory (Huyssen 2003:6). Forgetting is an unavoidable strategy, since no individual or community can afford to retain everything. Taking Mills's (this volume) example of Chacoan great houses, certain strategies of forgetting might also reveal how culturally inalienable objects might have been taken out of circulation in a process she terms ritual retirement. Recent work in anthropology on the centrality of forgetting ironically came at the moment when archaeologists were just discovering the place of memory (see Meskell 2004). The two are clearly inseparable, and both are in dialogue with materiality and specific material objects. Western concepts of memory are inflected with the Aristotelian principle that memory is a physical imprinting. According to this classic view, material substitutes are thus necessary to compensate for the fragility of the human memory (Forty 1999:2). An alternative position imputes that collective memory does not necessarily dwell in ephemeral monuments, no matter how seemingly didactic their functions. And more significantly, embodied acts and ritual may be more successful in iterating memory than simply the forging of objects. And of course, memory and commemorative acts are also those that instantiate identity, another theme that implicitly runs through the papers in this volume.

So how do we accommodate the impossibility of memory? A dialectic position advocating that both physical manifestation and iterative performance are required for the instantiation of memory is surely preferable. Nielsen posits a triadic relationship based on practice, materiality, and representation, arguing that the "reproduction of memory always involves the concerted and reinforcing operation of all three aspects of social reality." In light of this archaeologists should not assume a universal relationship between memory and the object. And this is complicated by the acknowledgment that in many cultural settings objects do not inhabit their object taxonomies. Materiality is intimately linked to doing and making, the sensuous process of human interactions with things, and in that sense is about the productive relationship between material and immaterial domains (Meskell 2004). Here Pollard is correct in underscoring the performative dimension of object deposition, which links back to the reworked notions of memory involving a social, practice-based element that is supramonumental. Pollard is offering here an understanding of materiality that extends beyond the typical, static, material culture approach.

Several papers look at the mortuary lifeworld and the object choices made in regard to issues of disappearance and longevity. Interestingly, this is a topic that British ethnographers seem to have recently embarked upon. Hallam and Hockey (2001:3) call for a "contextual and comparative analysis, which reveals historical and cultural specificity as well as the ways in which memory and death are caught up in processes of personal transformation and social change. Memory practices and experiences shift over time as perceptions of the past are reworked in the context of the present and in anticipation of the future." Lucero provides a cogent example for the ancient Maya and the array of evocative materials cached for purposes of dedication. Yet she tracks the social contours of wealth and status by articulating the commonalities and differences of specific material deposits. This analysis reminds us of the place of heirlooms, objects with particular valences that offer material bridges in terms of social continuity both of house and familial identities. Rosemary Joyce and Susan Gillespie (2000) have brought this particular view of materiality to the fore and eloquently link memory, materiality, circulation, and temporality within a detailed contextual analysis. As Lucero demonstrates, these practices are long lived, although the embodied and experiential meanings attached to them undoubtedly shifted through time and were highly subjective, even though there would have been collective resonances. What does it mean to have one's ancestors literally underfoot, to build them within the very fabric of the dwelling, to embody the generations in the material structures of daily life? From Lucero's perspective, memory, continuity, lineage, and place are continually made and remade in the ceremonial cycle of ancestor veneration and termination practices, of centering the living and the dead at particular moments.

As archaeologists in the business of sustaining and excavating memory, the question of whether there is such a thing as memory, in any reified sense, may be destabilizing. Memory cannot exist in a thinglike state since it is always subjective and spatiotemporally situated. Yet several papers foreground ancestors, both people and things, and such contexts provide windows onto ancient moments where memory forging and fabrication were at play. Nielsen provides a provocative account of Andean ancestors, whether mummified individuals or even stone architecture, that can be called upon to labor in the service of the past. Gillespie's account of the Olmec and their particular crafting of cultural biography is an attempt to transcend the limits of any individual's specific history. And history is very much at issue in this paper. Gillespie returns to the classic dilemma of what constitutes history versus myth. She seems to be articulating a moment where a new history is made, and a mythical history relegated to times past. Pierre Nora (1989) sees memory and history as now inhabiting fundamental oppositions, the former being in permanent evolution open to the dialectic of remembering and forgetting, while the latter is a reconstruction, always problematic and incomplete. Memory ties us to an eternal present, while history is a representation of the past.

As the last few years of memory research in archaeology have demonstrated, we cannot be satisfied that some sort of congealed memory resides by brute force in the materiality of monuments in some easy or obvious way. These debates were of course brought to the fore decades ago by French theorists, many of whom came from historical disciplines, such as Jacques Le Goff (1996), Philippe Ariès (1962, 1974, 1981), Pierre Nora (1989), and Georges Duby (1988), and later challenged by scholars like Paul Connerton (1989). Archaeology, whose business is the dual spheres of history and materiality, has arrived rather late on the scene yet is well placed to articulate the tensions between things, practices, intentions, and long-term outcomes.

ON CONCEALMENT AND TAXONOMY

Another theme taken up by several authors is the power of the unseen—the power of the imagination to shape and direct desire, fear, and a range of other visceral effects. As Mills describes, the power of secrecy and revelation is a dynamic that has wide valence in ancient societies. Moreover, that same dynamic is recognizable in our own if we think of our own fetishized viewing of or direct access to religious leaders, movie stars, royalty, and the like. It is the very lack of access, the forbidden zones, shielding, and limited viewing that heighten the intensity and perhaps even create sacred objects in religious or cultural terms or charismatic individuals. Other papers mention the very material effects of erasure, lack, scarring, and the power of negative spaces, which appear to offer a rich seam for archaeologists to pursue.

Of course just because something is not on public view, is buried or cached in a specific context, as Mills describes the dedicatory offerings deposited at Chaco, does not necessarily mean that the object is not *working*, not active or even agentic in specific cultures. Here I would recenter the work of Carolyn Nakamura on Neo-Assyrian apotropaic figurines buried within domestic contexts at sites such as Assur, Nineveh, Kish, Ur, and Babylon. Documentary evidence in her context similarly revealed the detailed instructions for an apotropaic or prophylactic ritual involving the making of figurines of mythological deities, demons, and monsters from consecrated wood and clay to be buried under house floors (Nakamura 2005). According to Nakamura, the priestly ritual entailed a choreographed series of specific and protracted gestures involving various objects, acts, substances, locations, incantations, and dedicatory rituals leading up to their final installation underground. Figurines were fashioned from conse-crated clay or wood cut from a sacred tree with golden and silver axes, and then taken to the riverbank and left there until sunrise. These secretive fig-urine deposits were explained by the Neo-Assyrians themselves as magical deposits that protected the individual and his house; the figures, as guar-dians, as protectors, "watched," "prayed," and "bore souls" away (Nakamura 2005). Here we could say that the "thing is the provocation of the nonliv-ing, the half-living, or that which has no life, to the living, to the potential of and for life" (Grosz 2005:131). From the Mayan context Lucero provides an account of objects made expressly for deposition that were never ani-mated and as such did not require ritual destruction, whereas items used in life had to be ritually killed before being buried because of their per-sonified forces. While the interpretive influences foregrounded in these papers are compelling and suggestive for other times and places, none can be applied universally, and all materials need to be examined contextually.

Pollard instructs us to think about deposition "as embodying a contin-uum of practices, some routinized and largely unconsidered, others overt performances. At one level the deposition of materials was a habitual action undertaken during the course of daily life, at other times a carefully contrived practice remarkable and memorable because of the objects involved (famed, tainted, or potent) and the spatial and temporal context of its enactment." The multiple gestures of concealment in the aforemen-tioned Neo-Assyrian figurine ritual suggest a play on the power of secrecy, namely, that the evocative physical details of the figures are sometimes completely obscured by a thick layer of white plaster, and that the figurines were first encased in boxes and then buried. Practices such as these may also connect to Mills's descriptions of a range of objects, natural and cul-tural, that were collected and cached, many of which had certain aesthetic properties and may have been prized by the Chacoans. Nielsen identifies a similar suite of evocative, perhaps even enlivened substances. Each of these cases challenges our notion of natural and cultural items, spirits and per-sons, people and things, the bodily boundaries of the individual, and so on. According to Grosz (2005:140), "Making, acting, functioning in the world, making oneself as one makes things—all these processes rely on and pro-duce things as the correlate of intellect, and leave behind the multiple, ramifying interconnections of the real out of which they were drawn and of which they are simplifications and schematizations." Those intercon-nections are also productive or generative domains where things direct and impact upon us as embodied persons, not simply as representations of the real. Nielsen effectively demonstrates this in his interpretation of monumentalized ancestors as a way of blurring the boundary between the ancestors of ephemeral thought and the material power of architectural mnemonics. On the basis of their weighty material presence, he suggests that *chullpa*-towers embodied ancestors that concomitantly played an important role in public gatherings, agricultural activity, and the like. Importantly, he takes this discussion right through to the present and confronts the erasure of indigenous memory in the Andes after the assaults of empire.

Joshua Pollard (2001) has previously described various depositional practices as fulfilling the role of a buried geography. Here he also discusses the aesthetics of practice; the careful deposition of animal bones; the arrangement of sherds, bones, lithic artifacts; and so on. This leads Pollard to trouble the subject-object duality and to disperse the notion of bounded, discrete people and things. Yet Pollard is correct in offering a measured response to object agency, writing that objects have "lives of their own outside of human constitution." Or following a Latourian development, Joyce and Pauketat ask us to consider the possibility of *actants* in overlapping networks of practice and meaning, of dispersed and entangled understandings of agency set within relational fields. And as Walker and others make clear, archaeologists equipped with this new suite of interpretative tools are required to rethink our old and comfortable taxonomies. His "dogs are people too" stance was a very welcome contribution—another example of where subject/object, human/inhuman, person/thing bifurcations do not always serve us. Breaking down anthropocentric privilege presents an important challenge, as Walker describes, to fully comprehend other belief systems and lifeways, and he does this skillfully by interweaving oral history and tradition into a sensuous and cross-categorical, cross-species mix.

Bruno Latour has been an outspoken critic of what we might call rational taxonomies. He wants to blur the categorical distinctions between objects and societies, cosmologies and sociologies. Past societies recognized this convergence, but the onslaught of terrifying revolutions has to some degree severed the link, that mixture of rational constraints and the needs of their societies. Latour's own neologism, *factishes*, reminds us that the dichotomy of facts and social constructions is nearly useless. He argues that "if religion, arts or styles are necessary to 'reflect,' 'reify,' 'materialize,' 'embody' society—to use some of the social theorists' favorite verbs—then are objects not, in the end, its co-producers? Is society not built literally —not metaphorically—of gods, machines, sciences, arts and styles?" (Latour 1991:54). Joyce (this volume) asks such questions in relation to the purposeful deposition of bowls in pits at Puerto Escondido. But just as humans initiate a first act, the material itself inspires future action and sets in motion a set of possible futures. That entanglement of people and things, humans and nonhumans, but also objects and imagery, associations, and aspirations, is another powerful way to rethink some classic themes in our discipline: ritualization, history and memory, practice, and personhood. Anthropologist Webb Keane (2003a, 2003b) sensibly warns of the false dichotomy between symbolic and materialist readings of the world. This is akin to the discursive taxonomies we instantiate, of ideas and things, where things are too often read as expressions or communications of ideas: things have been treated as basically epiphenomenal.

Along similar lines, feminist philosopher Elizabeth Grosz (2005:132) argues that "the thing has a history: it is not simply a passive inertia against which we measure our own activity. It has a 'life' of its own, characteristics of its own, which we must incorporate into our activities in order to be effective, rather than simply understanding, regulating, and neutralizing it from the outside. We need to accommodate things more than they accommodate us." Taking her vantage point from nature rather than culture, she posits, "Life is the growing accommodation of matter, the adaptation of the needs of life to the exigencies of matter....We find the thing in the world as our resource for making things, and in the process we leave our trace on things, we fabricate things out of what we find. The thing is the resource, in other words, for both subjects and technology" (Grosz 2005:132).

RITUALITY AND MATERIALITY

The irreducible connectedness of materiality with ritual practice is another thread that runs through this set of papers, as the previous sections make clear. Walker has raised some salient concerns about previous archaeologies of ritual and practice: they have been anthropocentric, to our detriment, foreclosing possibilities for other participants whether from quotidian or spiritual worlds. He can challenge this with some robust materials using oral tradition, ethnographies, and the material record, but cautions that putting the very matter of beliefs (spirits, souls, animate beings) back into the social world is disruptive to our tightly scripted and attenuated notions of agency. The spiritual power of objects in his Zuni example demonstrate that living things and objects were considered constitutive of the spatiotemporal patterns that reside at the center of social institutions, subsistence, and the workings of nature.

Linking to some of these themes, Stahl's paper prompts us to challenge the inherent conservatism we impute to ritual: instead she would like to recenter innovation and improvisation. This situation, she imputes, results from a fundamental bifurcation where the domain of ritual is hitched to questions of meaning and symbolism and is considered distinct from social arenas attuned to function and utility. She directs attention to the logics of practice and modes of circulation, rather than looking at static deposits as affirmations of presumed continuity. Ritual does not always reside exclusively in the depositional contexts of burials, monuments, and elaborate structures, but may be materialized in the seemingly quotidian, as archaeologists studying technologies such as ceramic and metallurgical production in African societies have acknowledged. Taking a biographical approach to classes of artifacts and using the rich ethnohistoric and anthropological sources at her disposal, Stahl considers depositional practices associated with shrines as a way to explore strategies of ritualization at Kuulo Kataa, specifically object pathways from shrines. Movements of things can thus create, sediment, or even disrupt ever more entangled social relations.

Pauketat gives us an altogether dramatic example of ritual and social disjuncture to some degree initiated with the founding of Cahokia. In the depositional genealogies that he outlines, enabled by a rigorous excavation methodology, we can see the significance of processing or cleaning fills, and the addition of ritually charged red pigments in the building of sacred structures. Construction practice here parallels large-festival activities with high densities of resonant objects: tobacco, crystals, human bone, and so on. There is an empirical richness to this work, which draws upon indigenous accounts of ritual and materiality gleaned from creation stories, historical writing, and cultural frames of reference. This renewed attention to the aesthetics of deposition has already been alluded to in the chapters by Pollard, Mills, and others. Color is obviously one symbolic constituent, as are materials such as plaster, ash, and burned earth, cautioning us to be more attentive to what some have traditionally considered fill, refuse, soil, and so on. Artificial soils, as he points out, were produced off-site, composed of socially significant and often sensual materials including sweetgrass, coniferous wood, and maize grass. Deposits themselves represent a kind of memory work, and those deposits, we must recall, also consist of human bodies, some sacrificial.

The mimetic possibilities of monuments mirror that which we cannot always apprehend—elements such as the sky—yet are similarly linked to the most tangible, such as earth. Pauketat underlines a specific Native American philosophy of materiality, something Danny Miller and Chris Tilley (1996) have suggested to be one of the strengths of an archaeological approach. Studies of materiality cannot simply focus upon the characteristics of objects but must engage in the dialectic of people and things. We might see this as a copresence or comingling. Webb Keane (2003a, 2003b) refers to this as *bundling*, the binding qualities that materiality allows, and in this way the concept harks back to Hegel, but also to anthropologists like Mauss, Munn, and Latour.

What strikes me here is that the authors' attention to materiality is articulated in a relational way, taking seriously the insights gathered from a more nuanced analysis of taxonomy and subject/object blurring. For example, I particularly like the way Mills outlines how both people and houses are adorned with jewelry in Chacoan society and how this interlaced with the projected identity of the dwelling. Lucero points out in her paper that Maya rites of animation and deanimation were performed for both houses and objects, "thus releasing their soul before renewal. Rites involve breaking objects, partially destroying houses, and burning incense."

This approach aligns with Gillespie's rethinking of Complex A at La Venta, embedded within a dynamic landscape, an enlivened place made possible through the actions of building and rebuilding. In this biographic account, people and things gather time and are mutually transforming through those processes. Specifically, the court and its platforms were "built and modified by the deposition of specially prepared earth; discrete episodes of digging through those deposits to cache stone and other materials; engineering for surface-water control; sweeping; refurbishment; and ceremonial offerings (including burned offerings), among other activities." Gillespie considers this suite of material and immaterial enactments within the constitution of emerging subjectivities in this spatiotemporal matrix, yet always framed by the resonances of cosmology, social identity, and embodied experience. From her perspective, the materiality of architecture, and its making, are inextricably linked to the making of persons at La Venta.

CONCLUDING THOUGHTS

Taken together, this is a remarkable set of essays. With the practice of structured deposition as a key starting point, the authors traverse a range of timely topics that resists disentangling. One cannot think of a buried object world without considering memory, forgetting, magic, secrecy, and so on. Could one consider embodiment without the modalities of performance, agency, or materiality, since all are indelibly meshed? Moreover, could we provide an account of subject making that is divorced from the forging and circulation of objects and the subsequent challenge to our own taxonomies and worldviews? The archaeologists in this volume have begun to truly embed things in creating accounts of embodied things or those that effectively blend with subjects, deities, entities, places, technologies, and so on. This new research is exciting for us as archaeologists and offers a compelling contribution to the broader framings of these issues for those in related disciplines.

References

Abercrombie, Thomas A.

1998   Pathways of Memory and Power: Ethnography and History among an Andean People. University of Wisconsin Press, Madison.

Ackerman, Kyle J., David J. Killick, Eugenia W. Herbert, and Colleen Kriger

1999   A Study of Iron Smelting at Lopanzo, Equateur Province, Zaïre. Journal of Archaeological Science 26:1135–1143.

Adams, E. Charles (editor)

2001   Homol'ovi III: A Pueblo Hamlet in the Middle Little Colorado River Valley. Arizona State Museum Archaeological Series 193. University of Arizona, Tucson.

Adler, Michael A., and Richard H. Wilshusen

1990   Large-scale Integrative Facilities in Tribal Societies: Cross-cultural and Southwestern U.S. Examples. World Archaeology 22:133–146.

Ahler, Steven R.

1999   Projectile Point Caches. In The Mound 72 Area: Dedicated and Sacred Space in Early Cahokia, by Melvin L. Fowler, Jerome Rose, Barbara Vander Leest, and Steven A. Ahler, pp. 101–115. Reports of Investigations No. 54. Illinois State Museum, Springfield.

Akins, Nancy J.

2003   The Burials of Pueblo Bonito. In Pueblo Bonito: Center of the Chacoan World, edited by Jill E. Neitzel, pp. 94–106. Smithsonian Institution Press, Washington, DC.

Alcock, Susan E.

2002   Archaeologies of the Greek Past: Landscape, Monuments and Memories. Cambridge University Press, Cambridge.

Aldunate, Carlos

1993   Arqueología en el Pukara de Turi. Actas del XII Congreso Nacional de Arqueología Chilena 61–77. Antofagasta.

Aldunate, Carlos, and Victoria Castro
1981   Las chullpa de Toconce y su relación con el poblamiento altiplánico en el Loa Superior, Período Tardío. Ediciones Kultrun, Santiago.

Alt, Susan M.
2002   Identities, Traditions, and Diversity in Cahokia's Uplands. Midcontinental Journal of Archaeology 27:217–236.

2006   Cultural Pluralism and Complexity: An Analysis of a Cahokian Ritual Outpost. Ph.D. dissertation, Department of Anthropology, University of Illinois, Urbana-Champaign.

Ambler, Richard
1994   The Shonto Junction Doghouse: A Weaver's Field House in the Klethla Valley. Kiva 59:455–473.

Ameyaw, Kwabena
1965   Tradition of Banda. In Traditions from Brong-Ahafo, Nos. 1–4, pp. 1–15. Institute of African Studies, University of Ghana, Legon.

Andersen, Joseph K.
1978   Arizona D:11:1161. In Excavation on Black Mesa, 1977: A Preliminary Report, edited by Anthony L. Klesert, pp. 117–121. Research Report No. 1. Center for Archaeological Investigations, Southern Illinois University, Carbondale.

Apentiik, Rowland
1997   Bulsa Technologies and Systems of Thought. Master's thesis, Department of Archaeology, University of Calgary.

Appadurai, Arjun
1986   Introduction: Commodities and the Politics of Value. In The Social Life of Things: Commodities in Cultural Perspective, edited by Arjun Appadurai, pp. 3–63. Cambridge University Press, New York.

Appadurai, Arjun (editor)
1986   The Social Life of Things: Commodities in Cultural Perspective. Cambridge University Press, Cambridge.

Argenti, Nicholas
2006   Remembering the Future: Slavery, Youth and Masking in the Cameroon Grassfields. Social Anthropology 14(1):49–69.

Argenti, Nicholas, and Ute Röschenthaler
2006   Introduction: Between Cameroon and Cuba: Youth, Slave Trades and Translocal Memoryscapes. Social Anthropology 14(1):33–47.

Arhin, Kwame
1970   Aspects of the Ashanti Northern Trade in the Nineteenth Century. Africa 40:363–373.

1979   West African Traders in Ghana in the Nineteenth and Twentieth Centuries. Longman, London.

Ariès, Philippe
1962   Centuries of Childhood. Knopf, New York.

1974   Western Attitudes to Death: From the Middle Ages to the Present. Johns Hopkins University Press, Baltimore.

1981   The Hour of Our Death. Penguin, London.

Aschero, Carlos

2000   El poblamiento del territorio. *In* Nueva Historia Argentina, Vol. 1, pp. 17–59. Sudamericana, Buenos Aires.

Ashmore, Wendy

2004   Social Archaeologies of Landscape. *In* A Companion to Social Archaeology, edited by Lynn M. Meskell and Robert W. Preucel, pp. 255–271. Blackwell Press, Oxford.

Ashmore, Wendy, and A. Bernard Knapp (editors)

1999   Archaeologies of Landscape: Contemporary Perspectives. Blackwell, Oxford.

Bailey, Garrick A.

1995   The Osage and the Invisible World: From the Works of Francis La Flesche. University of Oklahoma Press, Norman.

Bamford, Helen

1985   Briar Hill: Excavation 1974–1978. Northampton Development Corporation, Northampton.

Barrett, John C.

1999   The Mythical Landscapes of the British Iron Age. *In* Archaeologies of Landscape: Contemporary Perspectives, edited by Wendy Ashmore and A. Bernard Knapp, pp. 253–265. Blackwell, Oxford.

2001   Agency, the Duality of Structure, and the Problem of the Archaeological Record. *In* Archaeological Theory Today, edited by Ian Hodder, pp. 141–164. Polity, Malden, Massachusetts.

Baum, Robert M.

1999   Shrines of the Slave Trade: Diola Religion and Society in Precolonial Senegambia. Oxford University Press, Oxford.

Beaglehole, Ernest

1937   Notes on Hopi Economic Life. Yale University Publications in Anthropology No. 15. Yale University Press, New Haven.

Becker, Marshall

1992   Burials as Caches; Caches as Burials: A New Interpretation of the Meaning of Ritual Deposits among the Classic Period Lowland Maya. *In* New Theories on the Ancient Maya, edited by Robert J. Sharer, pp. 185–196. University Museum, University of Pennsylvania, Philadelphia.

Bell, Catherine M.

1992   Ritual Theory, Ritual Practice. Oxford University Press, Oxford.

1996   Modernism and Postmodernism in the Study of Religion. Religious Studies Review 22(3):179–190.

1997   Ritual: Perspectives and Dimensions. Oxford University Press, Oxford.

Bender, Barbara
1993   Introduction: Landscape—Meaning and Action. *In* Landscape: Politics and Perspectives, edited by Barbara Bender, pp. 1–17. Berg, Oxford.

Bender, Barbara (editor)
1993   Landscape: Politics and Perspectives. Berg, Oxford.

Berger, Rainer, John A. Graham, and Robert F. Heizer
1967   A Reconsideration of the Age of the La Venta Site. *In* Studies in Olmec Archaeology. Contributions of the University of California Archaeological Research Facility 3, pp. 1–24. Berkeley.

Bertonio, Ludovico
1984[1612] Vocabulario de la lengua aymara. CERES, Cochabamba.

Binford, M., A. Kolata, M. Brenner, J. Janusek, M. Seddon, M. Abbott, and J. Curtis
1997   Climate Variation and the Rise and Fall of an Andean Civilization. Quaternary Research 47:235–248.

Birmingham, Robert A., and Leslie E. Eisenberg
2000   Indian Mounds of Wisconsin. University of Wisconsin Press, Madison.

Birmingham, Robert A., and Amy Rosebrough
2003   On the Meaning of Effigy Mounds. *In* A Deep-Time Perspective: Studies in Symbols, Meaning, and the Archaeological Record, edited by John D. Richards and Melvin L. Fowler. Wisconsin Archeologist 84:21–36.

Blanton, Richard E., Gary M. Feinman, Stephan A. Kowalewski, and Peter N. Peregrine
1996   A Dual-Processual Theory for the Evolution of Mesoamerican Civilization. Current Anthropology 37:1–31.

Bleed, Peter
2001   Trees or Chains, Links or Branches: Conceptual Alternatives for Consideration of Stone Tool Production and Other Sequential Activities. Journal of Archaeological Method and Theory 8(1):101–127.

Boast, Robin
1997   A Small Company of Actors: A Critique of Style. Journal of Material Culture 2(2):173–198.

Bourdieu, Pierre
1977   Outline of a Theory of Practice. Translated by Richard Nice. Cambridge University Press, Cambridge.
1990   The Logic of Practice. Stanford University Press, Stanford.

Bourdieu, Pierre, and Loïc J. D. Wacquant
1992   An Invitation to Reflexive Sociology. Polity Press, Cambridge.

Bradley, Richard
1990   The Passage of Arms: An Archaeological Analysis of Prehistoric Hoards and Votive Deposits. Cambridge University Press, Cambridge.

1997   "To See Is to Have Seen": Craft Traditions in British Field Archaeology. *In* The Cultural Life of Images: Visual Representation in Archaeology, edited by Brian Leigh Molyneaux, pp. 62–72. Routledge, London.

1998   The Significance of Monuments: On the Shaping of Human Experience in Neolithic and Bronze Age Europe. Routledge, London.

2000   An Archaeology of Natural Places. Routledge, London.

2003   A Life Less Ordinary: The Ritualization of the Domestic Sphere in Later Prehistoric Europe. Cambridge Archaeological Journal 13(1):5–23.

2005   Ritual and Domestic Life in Prehistoric Europe. Routledge, London.

Brandt, Elizabeth A.

1980   On Secrecy and Control of Knowledge. *In* Secrecy: A Cross-Cultural Perspective, edited by Stanton K. Tefft, pp. 123–146. Human Sciences Press, New York.

Bravmann, René

1972   The Diffusion of Ashanti Political Art. *In* African Art and Leadership, edited by D. Fraser and H. M. Cole, pp. 153–171. University of Wisconsin Press, Madison.

1974   Islam and Tribal Art in West Africa. Cambridge University Press, Cambridge.

Bravmann, René, and R. Duncan Mathewson

1970   A Note on the History and Archaeology of "Old Bima." African Historical Studies 3:133–150.

Brown, Linda A.

2005   Planting the Bones: Hunting Ceremonialism at Contemporary and Nineteenth-Century Shrines in the Guatemalan Highlands. Latin American Antiquity 16(2):131–146.

Brown, M. E., and K. L. Brown

1993   Subsistence and Other Cultural Behaviors as Reflected by the Vertebrate Faunal Remains. *In* Across the Colorado Plateau: Anthropological Studies for the Transwestern Pipeline Expansion Project: Subsistence and Environment, Vol. 15, Part 3, edited by Joseph C. Winter, pp. 327–381. Office of Contract Archeology and Maxwell Museum of Anthropology, University of New Mexico, Albuquerque.

Brownlow, Alec

2000   A Wolf in the Garden: Ideology and Change in the Adirondack Landscape. *In* Animal Spaces, Beastly Places: New Geographies of Human-Animal Relations, edited by Chris Philo and Chris Wilber, pp. 141–158. Routledge, New York.

Brück, Joanna

1999   Ritual and Rationality: Some Problems of Interpretation in European Archaeology. European Journal of Archaeology 2(3):313–344.

2004   Material Metaphors: The Relational Construction of Identity in Early Bronze Age Burials in Ireland and Britain. Journal of Social Archaeology 4(3):307–333.

References

Brumfiel, Elizabeth M.

2000   On the Archaeology of Choice: Agency Studies as a Research Stratagem. *In* Agency in Archaeology, edited by Marcia-Anne Dobres and John E. Robb, pp. 249–255. Routledge, London.

Buchli, Victor

2004   Material Culture: Current Problems. *In* A Companion to Social Archaeology, edited by Lynn Meskell and Robert W. Preucel, pp. 179–194. Blackwell, Oxford.

Buchli, Victor (editor)

2002   The Material Culture Reader. Berg, New York.

Buikstra, Jane E., Douglas K. Charles, and Gordon F. M. Rakita

1998   Staging Ritual: Hopewell Ceremonialism at the Mound House Site, Greene County, Illinois. Kampsville Studies in Archeology and History 1. Center for American Archeology, Kampsville, Illinois.

Bullard, William R., Jr.

1962   The Cerro Colorado Site and Pithouse Architecture in the Southwestern United States prior to A.D. 900. Papers of the Peabody Museum of American Archaeology and Ethnology 44(2). Harvard University, Cambridge.

Bullock, Peter Y. (editor)

1998   Deciphering Anasazi Violence: With Regional Comparisons to Mesoamerican and Woodland Cultures. HRM Books, Santa Fe.

Bunzel, Ruth

1932   Introduction to Zuñi Ceremonialism. *In* The Forty-Seventh Annual Report of the Bureau of American Ethnology for the Years 1929–1930, pp. 467–474. Smithsonian Institution, Washington, DC.

Butler, Judith

1993   Bodies That Matter: On the Discursive Limits of "Sex." Routledge, London.

1997   The Psychic Life of Power: Theories in Subjection. Stanford University Press, Stanford.

Cameron, Catherine M.

2001   Pink Chert, Projectile Points, and the Chacoan Regional System. American Antiquity 66:79–101.

Cameron, Catherine M., and Steven A. Tomka (editors)

1993   Abandonment of Settlements and Regions: Ethnoarchaeological and Archaeological Approaches. Cambridge University Press, Cambridge.

Carlson, Roy L.

1963   Basket Maker III Sites near Durango, Colorado. University of Colorado Studies Series in Anthropology No. 8. University of Colorado, Boulder.

Caton, Alex

1997   Beads and Bodies: Embodying Change in Bead Practices in Banda, Ghana. M.A. thesis, Department of Anthropology, State University of New York at Binghamton.

Chapman, John

2000a   Fragmentation in Archaeology: People, Places and Broken Objects in the
        Prehistory of South Eastern Europe. Routledge, New York.

2000b   Tensions at Funerals: Social Practices and the Subversion of Community
        Structure in Later Hungarian Prehistory. *In* Agency in Archaeology, edited by
        Marcia-Anne Dobres and John E. Robb, pp. 169–195. Routledge, London.

Chase, Diane Z., and Arlen F. Chase

1998   Architectural Context of Caches, Burials, and Other Ritual Activities for the
        Classic Period Maya (as reflected at Caracol, Belize). *In* Function and Meaning
        in Classic Maya Architecture, edited by Stephen D. Houston, pp. 299–332.
        Dumbarton Oaks, Washington, DC.

Chesson, Meredith S.

2001   Social Memory, Identity, and Death: An Introduction. *In* Social Memory,
        Identity, and Death: Anthropological Perspectives on Mortuary Rituals, edited
        by Meredith S. Chesson, pp. 1–11. Archeological Papers of the American
        Anthropological Association No. 10. American Anthropological Association,
        Arlington, Virginia.

Chesson, Meredith S. (editor)

2001   Social Memory, Identity, and Death: Anthropological Perspectives on Mortuary
        Rituals. Archaeological Papers of the American Anthropological Association
        No. 10. American Anthropological Association, Arlington, Virginia.

Childs, S. Terry, and W. J. Dewey

1996   Forging Symbolic Meaning in Zaire and Zimbabwe. *In* The Culture and
        Technology of African Iron Production, edited by Peter R. Schmidt, pp.
        145–171. University of Florida Press, Gainesville.

Cieza de León, Pedro

1995 [1553] Crónica del Perú. 3 vols. Academia Nacional de la Historia, Lima.

Clark, John E.

1994   Los Olmecas en Mesoamerica. El Equilibrista and Turner Libros, Mexico and
        Madrid.

1997   The Arts of Government in Early Mesoamerica. Annual Review of
        Anthropology 26:211–234.

2004   The Birth of Mesoamerican Metaphysics: Sedentism, Engagement, and Moral
        Superiority. *In* Rethinking Materiality: The Engagement of Mind with the
        Material World, edited by Elizabeth DeMarrais, Chris Gosden, and Colin
        Renfrew, pp. 205–224. McDonald Institute, Cambridge.

Climo, Jacob J., and Maria G. Cattell

2002   Introduction: Meaning in Social Memory and History: Anthropological
        Perspectives. *In* Social Memory and History: Anthropological Perspectives,
        edited by Jacob J. Climo and Maria G. Cattell, pp. 1–36. AltaMira Press, Walnut
        Creek, California.

Cobo, Bernabé

1990 [1653] Inca Religion and Customs. University of Texas Press, Austin.

Coe, Michael D.

1960   Review of Excavations at La Venta, Tabasco, 1955, by Philip Drucker, Robert F. Heizer, and Robert J. Squier. American Journal of Archaeology 64:119–120.

1968   America's First Civilization: Discovering the Olmec. American Heritage Publishing, New York.

Coe, William R.

1959   Piedras Negras Archaeology: Artifacts, Caches, and Burials. University Museum, University of Pennsylvania, Philadelphia.

1965   Caches and Offertory Practices of the Maya Lowlands. *In* Handbook of Middle American Indians, Vol. 2, Archaeology of Southern Mesoamerica, Part 1, edited by Gordon R. Willey, pp. 462–468. University of Texas Press, Austin.

Coe, William R., and Robert Stuckenrath Jr.

1964   A Review of La Venta, Tabasco and Its Relevance to the Olmec Problem. Kroeber Anthropological Society Papers 31:1–43. Department of Anthropology, University of California, Berkeley.

Cohen, Abner

1974   Two-Dimensional Man: An Essay on the Anthropology of Power and Symbolism in Complex Society. University of California Press, Berkeley.

Cole, Brigitte F., and Phillip E. Koerper

2002   The Domestication of the Dog in General—and Dog Burial Research in the Southeastern United States. Journal of the Alabama Academy of Science 73(4):174–179.

Collins, James M.

1990   The Archaeology of the Cahokia Mounds ICT-II: Site Structure. Illinois Cultural Resources Study 10. Illinois Historic Preservation Agency, Springfield.

Comaroff, Jean, and John Comaroff (editors)

1993   Modernity and Its Malcontents: Ritual and Power in Postcolonial Africa. University of Chicago Press, Chicago.

Conlon, James M., and Jennifer J. Ehret

2002   Time and Space: The Preliminary Ceramic Analysis for Saturday Creek and Yalbac, Cayo District, Belize, Central America. *In* Results of the 2001 Valley of Peace Archaeology Project: Saturday Creek and Yalbac, edited by Lisa J. Lucero, pp. 8–20. Report submitted to the Department of Archaeology, Ministry of Tourism and Culture, Belize.

Connerton, Paul

1989   How Societies Remember. Cambridge University Press, Cambridge.

Creel, Darrell, and Roger Anyon

2003   New Interpretations of Mimbres Public Architecture and Space: Implications for Cultural Change. American Antiquity 68(1):67–92.

Crown, Patricia L., and W. H. Wills

2003   Modifying Pottery and Kivas at Chaco Canyon: Pentimento, Restoration, or Renewal? American Antiquity 68(3):511–532.

Cruz, Maria das Dores

2003   Shaping Quotidian Worlds: Ceramic Production in the Banda Area (West-Central Ghana): An Ethnoarchaeological Approach. Ph.D. dissertation, Department of Anthropology, State University of New York, Binghamton.

Cushing, Frank Hamilton

1883   Zuni Fetiches. Second Annual Report of the Bureau of Ethnology. Smithsonian Institution, Washington, DC.

1924   Origin Myth from Oraibi. Journal of American Folk-Lore 36:163–170.

1979   Zuñi: Selected Writings of Frank Hamilton. University of Nebraska Press, Lincoln.

Dalan, Rinita

1997   The Construction of Mississippian Cahokia. In Cahokia: Domination and Ideology in the Mississippian World, edited by Timothy R. Pauketat and Thomas E. Emerson, pp. 89–102. University of Nebraska Press, Lincoln.

David, Nicholas, and Carol Kramer

2001   Ethnoarchaeology in Action. Cambridge University Press, Cambridge.

Davis, Natalie Z., and Randolph Starn

1989   Introduction. Representations 26:1–6.

DeBoer, Warren R.

2005   Colors for a North American Past. World Archaeology 37(1):66–91.

de Certeau, Michel

1984   The Practice of Everyday Life. Translated by Steven Rendall. University of California Press, Berkeley.

DeCorse, Christopher R.

1992   Culture Contact, Continuity, and Change on the Gold Coast, AD 1400–1900. African Archaeological Review 10:163–196.

2001   An Archaeology of Elmina: Africans and Europeans on the Gold Coast, 1400–1900. Smithsonian Institution Press, Washington, DC.

de Maret, Pierre

1994   Archaeological and Other Prehistoric Evidence of Traditional African Religious Expression. In Religion in Africa. Experience and Expression, edited by Thomas D. Blakely, Walter E. A. van Beek, and Dennis L. Thomson, pp. 182–195. James Currey, London.

DeMarrais, Elizabeth, Chris Gosden, and Colin Renfrew (editors)

2004   Rethinking Materiality: The Engagement of Mind with the Material World. McDonald Institute Monographs. McDonald Institute for Archaeological Research, University of Cambridge, Cambridge.

Derrida, Jacques

1982   Signature, Event, Context. *In* The Margins of Philosophy, edited by Jacques Derrida, pp. 307–330. Harvester Press, Brighton.

Diehl, Richard A.

1981   Olmec Architecture: A Comparison of San Lorenzo and La Venta. *In* The Olmec and Their Neighbors: Essays in Memory of Matthew W. Stirling, edited by Elizabeth P. Benson, pp. 69–81. Dumbarton Oaks, Washington, DC.

2004   The Olmecs: America's First Civilization. Thames & Hudson, London.

Dietler, Michael

1998   Consumption, Agency and Cultural Entanglement: Theoretical Implications of a Mediterranean Colonial Encounter. *In* Studies in Culture Contact. Interaction, Culture Change, and Archaeology, edited by James G. Cusick, pp. 288–315. Occasional Paper No. 25. Center for Archaeological Investigations, Carbondale, Illinois.

Dirks, Nicholas B.

1996   Is Vice Versa? Historical Anthropologies and Anthropological Histories. *In* The Historic Turn in the Human Sciences, edited by Terrence J. McDonald, pp. 17–51. University of Michigan Press, Ann Arbor.

Dobres, Marcia-Anne

2000   Technology and Social Agency. Blackwell, Oxford.

Dohm, Karen M.

1988   Excavations in Area 7. *In* Dolores Archaeological Program: Anasazi Communities at Dolores: Grass Mesa Village, Book 2, pp. 847–871. US Bureau of Reclamation Engineering and Research Center, Boulder.

Dorsey, George A.

1997   The Pawnee Mythology. University of Nebraska Press, Lincoln.

Douglas, Mary, and Baron Isherwood

1996 [1979] The World of Goods: Towards an Anthropology of Consumption. Routledge, New York.

Drewett, Peter

1986   The Excavation of a Neolithic Oval Barrow at North Marden, West Sussex, 1982. Proceedings of the Prehistoric Society 52:31–51.

Drucker, Philip

1952   La Venta, Tabasco: A Study of Olmec Ceramics and Art. With a Chapter on Structural Investigations in 1943 by Waldo R. Wedel and Appendix on Technological Analyses by Anna O. Shepard. Smithsonian Institution Bureau of American Ethnology Bulletin 153. Government Printing Office, Washington, DC.

1981   On the Nature of Olmec Polity. *In* The Olmec and Their Neighbors: Essays in Memory of Matthew W. Stirling, edited by Elizabeth P. Benson, pp. 29–47. Dumbarton Oaks, Washington, DC.

Drucker, Philip, and Robert F. Heizer

1956   Gifts for the Jaguar God. National Geographic 110:366–375.

1965   Commentary on W. R. Coe and Robert Stuckenrath's Review of Excavations at La Venta, Tabasco, 1955. Kroeber Anthropological Society Papers 33:37–69. Department of Anthropology, University of California, Berkeley.

Drucker, Philip, Robert F. Heizer, and Robert J. Squier

1957   Radiocarbon Dates from La Venta, Tabasco. Science 126:72–73.

1959   Excavations at La Venta, Tabasco, 1955. Smithsonian Institution Bureau of American Ethnology Bulletin 170. Government Printing Office, Washington, DC.

Duby, Georges (editor)

1988   A History of Private Life: Revelations of the Medieval World. Vol. 2. Belknap Press of Harvard University, Cambridge.

Dumarest, Father Noel

1919   Notes on Cochiti, New Mexico. Memoir 6, No. 3. American Anthropological Association, Lancaster, Pennsylvania.

Durkheim, Emile

1995 [1912] The Elementary Forms of Religious Life. Translated by K. E. Fields. Free Press, New York.

Duviols, Pierre

1979   Un symbolisme de l'occupation, de l'amenagement et de l'exploitation de l'espace: Le monolithe "Huanca" et sa fonction dans les Andes préhispaniques. L'Homme 19(2):7–31.

Dwyer, Peter D.

1996   The Invention of Nature. In Redefining Nature: Ecology, Culture and Domestication, edited by Roy Ellen and Katsuyoshi Fukui, pp. 157–186. Berg, Oxford.

Echo-Hawk, Roger C.

2000   Ancient History in the New World: Integrating Oral Traditions and the Archaeological Record in Deep Time. American Antiquity 65:267–290.

Eddy, Frank W.

1966   Prehistory in the Navajo Reservoir District, Northern New Mexico. Papers in Anthropology No. 15. Museum of New Mexico, Albuquerque.

Edmonds, Mark R.

1999   Ancestral Geographies of the Neolithic: Landscapes, Monuments, and Memory. Routledge, London.

Emerson, Thomas E.

1997   Cahokia and the Archaeology of Power. University of Alabama Press, Tuscaloosa.

Emerson, Thomas E., Dale L. McElrath, and Andrew C. Fortier (editors)

2000 Late Woodland Societies: Tradition and Transformation across the Midcontinent. University of Nebraska Press, Lincoln.

Emslie, Steven D.

1978 Dog Burials from Mancos Canyon, Colorado. Kiva 43(3–4):167–182.

Evans, Edward Payson

1906 The Criminal Prosecution and Capital Punishment of Animals. Faber and Faber, London.

Evans, Susan Toby

2004 Ancient Mexico and Central America: Archaeology and Culture History. Thames & Hudson, New York and London.

Evans-Pritchard, E. E.

1937 Witchcraft, Oracles and Magic among the Azande. Clarendon Press, Oxford.

Fentress, James, and Charles Wickham

1992 Social Memory. Blackwell, Oxford.

Ferguson, T. J., and Chip Colwell-Chanthaphonh

2006 History Is in the Land: Multivocal Tribal Traditions in Arizona's San Pedro Valley. University of Arizona Press, Tucson.

Ferguson, T. J., and Robert W. Preucel

2005 Signs of the Ancestors: An Archaeology of Mesa Villages of the Pueblo Revolt. In Structure and Meaning in Human Settlement, edited by Toby Atkin and Joseph Rykwert, pp. 185–208. University of Pennsylvania Museum Press, Philadelphia.

Fewkes, Jesse Walter

1990 Tusayan Katcinas and Hopi Altars. Avanyu Publishing, Albuquerque.

Flannery, Kent V., and Joyce Marcus

2000 Formative Mexican Chiefdoms and the Myth of the "Mother Culture." Journal of Anthropological Archaeology 19:1–37.

Fletcher, Alice C., and Francis La Flesche

1992 The Omaha Tribe. Vols. 1–2. University of Nebraska Press, Lincoln.

Fortes, Meyer, and S. L. Fortes

1936 Food in the Domestic Economy of the Tallensi. Africa 9:237–276.

Forty, Adrian

1999 Introduction. In The Art of Forgetting, edited by Adrian Forty and Susanne Küchler, pp. 1–18. Berg, Oxford.

Forty, Adrian, and Susanne Küchler (editors)

1999 The Art of Forgetting. Berg, Oxford.

Foucault, Michel

1977 Language, Counter-Memory, Practice. Cornell University Press, Ithaca.

1979 Discipline and Punish: The Birth of the Prison. Vintage Books, New York.

Fowler, Chris

2004   The Archaeology of Personhood: An Anthropological Approach. Routledge, London.

Fowler, Melvin L.

1997   The Cahokia Atlas: A Historical Atlas of Cahokia Archaeology. Revised edition. Studies in Archaeology No. 2. Illinois Transportation Archaeological Research Program, University of Illinois, Urbana.

Fowler, Melvin L., Jerome Rose, Barbara Vander Leest, and Steven A. Ahler

1999   The Mound 72 Area: Dedicated and Sacred Space in Early Cahokia. Reports of Investigations No. 54. Illinois State Museum, Springfield.

Frank, Barbara E.

1998   Mande Potters and Leather Workers: Art and Heritage in West Africa. Smithsonian Institution Press, Washington, DC.

Frisbie, Theodore R.

1967   The Excavation and Interpretation of the Artificial Leg Basketmaker III–Pueblo I Sites near Corrales, New Mexico. Master's thesis, Department of Anthropology, University of New Mexico, Albuquerque.

Garber, James F.

1986   The Artifacts. In Archaeology at Cerros, Belize, Central America, Vol. 1, edited by Robin A. Robertson and David A. Freidel, pp. 117–126. Southern Methodist University Press, Dallas.

1989   Archaeology at Cerros, Belize, Central America, Volume II: The Artifacts. Southern Methodist University Press, Dallas.

Garber, James F., W. David Driver, Lauren A. Sullivan, and David M. Glassman

1998   Bloody Bowls and Broken Pots: The Life, Death, and Rebirth of a Maya House. In The Sowing and the Dawning: Termination, Dedication, and Transformation in the Archaeological and Ethnographic Record of Mesoamerica, edited by Shirley B. Mock, pp. 125–133. University of New Mexico Press, Albuquerque.

García Azcárate, Jorgelina

1996   Monolitos-Huancas: Un intento de explicación de las piedras de Tafí (Rep. Argentina). Chungará 28:159–174.

Gartner, William G.

2000   The Gottschall Strata. In The Gottschall Rockshelter: An Archaeological Mystery, edited by Robert Salzer and Grace Rajnovich, pp. 75–79. Prairie Smoke Press, Saint Paul, Minnesota.

Gell, Alfred

1992   The Technology of Enchantment and the Enchantment of Technology. In Anthropology, Art and Aesthetics, edited by Jeremy Coote and Anthony Shelton, pp. 40–63. Oxford University Press, Oxford.

1993   Wrapping in Images: Tattooing in Polynesia. Oxford University Press, Oxford.

1996   Vogel's Net Traps as Artworks and Artworks as Traps. Journal of Matérial Culture 1(1):15–38.

1998   Art and Agency: An Anthropological Theory. Clarendon Press, Oxford.

Geller, Pamela

2004   Transforming Bodies, Transforming Identities: A Consideration of Pre-
Columbian Maya Corporeal Beliefs and Practices. UMI, Ann Arbor.

Giddens, Anthony

1976   New Rules of Sociological Method. Hutchinson, London.

1979   Central Problems in Social Theory. Macmillan, London.

1984   The Constitution of Society: Outline of a Theory of Structuration. University
of California Press, Berkeley.

Gifford, James C., Robert J. Sharer, Joseph W. Ball, Arlen F. Chase,
Carol A. Gifford, Muriel Kirkpatrick, and George H. Myer

1976   Prehistoric Pottery Analysis and the Ceramics of Barton Ramie in the Belize
Valley. Peabody Museum of Archaeology and Ethnology Memoirs, Vol. 18.
Harvard University, Cambridge.

Gigerenzer, Gerd

2005   I Think, Therefore I Err (Errors in the Social Sciences). Social Research
72(1):195–218.

Gillespie, Susan D.

1999   Olmec Thrones as Ancestral Altars: The Two Sides of Power. *In* Material
Symbols: Culture and Economy in Prehistory, edited by John E. Robb, pp.
224–253. Center for Archaeological Investigations, Occasional Paper No. 26.
Southern Illinois University, Carbondale.

2000   Maya "Nested Houses": The Ritual Construction of Place. *In* Beyond Kinship:
Social and Material Production in House Societies, edited by Rosemary A.
Joyce and Susan D. Gillespie, pp. 135–160. University of Pennsylvania Press,
Philadelphia.

2001   Personhood, Agency, and Mortuary Ritual: A Case Study from the Ancient
Maya. Journal of Anthropological Archaeology 20:73–112.

2002   Body and Soul among the Maya: Keeping the Spirits in Place. *In* The Space
and Place of Death, edited by Helaine Silverman and David B. Small, pp.
67–78. American Anthropological Association Archeology Papers No. 11.
Arlington, Virginia.

Gisbert, Teresa

1994   El señorío de los Carangas y los chullpares del Río Lauca. Revista Andina
12(2):427–485.

Goldstein, Lynne G., and John D. Richards

1991   Ancient Aztalan: The Cultural and Ecological Context of a Late Prehistoric
Site in the Midwest. *In* Cahokia and the Hinterlands: Middle Mississippian
Cultures of the Midwest, edited by Thomas E. Emerson and R. Barry Lewis,
pp. 193–206. University of Illinois Press, Urbana.

González Lauck, Rebecca B.

1996   La Venta: An Olmec Capital. *In* Olmec Art of Ancient Mexico, edited by

Elizabeth P. Benson and Beatriz de la Fuente, pp. 73–81. National Gallery of Art, Washington, DC.

Goody, Esther

1970   Legitimate and Illegitimate Aggression in a West African State. *In* Witchcraft. Confessions and Accusations, edited by Mary Douglas, pp. 207–244. Tavistock Publications, London.

Goody, Jack

1957   Anomie in Ashanti? Africa 27(3):356–363.

1961   Religion and Ritual: The Definitional Problem. British Journal of Sociology 12(2):142–164.

1962   Death, Property and the Ancestors: A Study of Mortuary Customs of the Lodagaa of West Africa. Stanford University Press, Stanford.

1964   The Mande and the Akan Hinterland. *In* The Historian in Tropical Africa, edited by Jan Vansina, R. Mauny, and L. V. Thomas, pp. 192–218. Oxford University Press, London.

Gosden, Chris

1994   Social Being and Time. Blackwell, Oxford.

1999   Anthropology and Archaeology: A Changing Relationship. Routledge, London.

2001   Making Sense: Archaeology and Aesthetics. World Archaeology 33(2):163–167.

2004   Making and Display: Our Aesthetic Appreciation of Things and Objects. *In* Substance, Memory, Display: Archaeology and Art, edited by Colin Renfrew, Chris Gosden, and Elizabeth DeMarrais, pp. 35–45. McDonald Institute Monographs, Cambridge.

2005   What Do Objects Want? Journal of Archaeological Method and Theory 12:193–211.

Gosden, Chris, and Yvonne Marshall

1999   The Cultural Biography of Objects. World Archaeology 31(2):169–178.

Graham, John, and Mark Johnson

1979   The Great Mound of La Venta. *In* Studies in Ancient Mesoamerica IV, edited by John A. Graham. Contributions of the University of California Archaeological Research Facility 41, pp. 1–5. Berkeley.

Graves-Brown, Peter (editor)

2000   Matter, Materiality and Modern Culture. Routledge, London.

Grosz, Elizabeth

2005   Time Travels: Feminism, Nature, Power. Duke University Press, Durham.

Grove, David C.

1989   Olmec: What's in a Name? *In* Regional Perspectives on the Olmec, edited by Robert J. Sharer and David C. Grove, pp. 8–14. Cambridge University Press, Cambridge.

1997   Olmec Archaeology: A Half Century of Research and Its Accomplishments. Journal of World Prehistory 11:51–101.

Guamán Poma de Ayala, Felipe
1980 [1615] Nueva crónica y buen gobierno. Siglo XXI, Mexico.

Guderjan, Thomas H.
2004 Recreating the Cosmos: Early Classic Dedicatory Caches at Blue Creek. *In* Continuity and Change: Maya Religious Practices in Temporal Perspective, edited by Daniel Graña Behrens, Nikolai Grube, Christian M. Prager, Frauke Sachse, Stefanie Teufel, and Elisabeth Wagner, pp. 33–39. Acta Mesoamerica Vol. 14. Anton Saurwein, Markt Schwaben.

Guernsey, Samuel J., and Alfred V. Kidder
1921 Basket-maker Caves of Northeastern Arizona: Report on the Explorations, 1916–1917. Papers of the Peabody Museum of American Archaeology and Ethnology 12(1). Harvard University, Cambridge.

Haag, William G.
1966 Dogs from Tse-ta'a. *In* Excavations at Tse-ta'a, Canyon de Chelly National Monument, Arizona, edited by Charles R. Steen, pp. 131–135. Archaeological Research Series No. 9. National Park Service, Washington, DC.

Halbwachs, Maurice
1925 Les cadres sociaux de la mémoire. Les Travaux de L'Année Sociologique. F. Alcan, Paris.

1992 On Collective Memory. Edited, translated, and with an introduction by Lewis Coser. University of Chicago Press, Chicago.

Hall, Edward T.
1944 Early Stockaded Settlements in the Governador, New Mexico: A Marginal Anasazi Development from Basket Maker III to Pueblo I Times. Columbia University Studies in Archaeology and Ethnology, Vol. 2, Part 1. Columbia University, New York.

Hall, Robert L.
1997 An Archaeology of the Soul: North American Indian Belief and Ritual. University of Illinois Press, Urbana.

Hallam, Elizabeth, and Jenny Hockey
2001 Death, Memory and Material Culture. Berg, Oxford.

Halperin, Rhoda H.
1994 Cultural Economies: Past and Present. University of Texas Press, Austin.

Hammond, George P., and Agapito Rey
1928 Obregón's History of Sixteenth Century Explorations in Western America. Wetzel Publishing, Los Angeles.

Haraway, Donna
1991 Simians, Cyborgs, and Women: The Reinvention of Nature. Chapman and Hall, New York.

Harré, Rom, and E. H. Madden
1975 Causal Powers: A Theory of Natural Necessity. Rowman and Littlefield, Totowa, New Jersey.

Harris, Edward C.

1989 Principles of Archaeological Stratigraphy. 2nd ed. Academic Press, San Diego.

Hastorf, Christine A.

2003 Community with the Ancestors: Ceremonies and Social Memory in the Middle Formative at Chiripa, Bolivia. Journal of Anthropological Archaeology 22:305–332.

Haviland, William A.

1997 The Rise and Fall of Sexual Inequality: Death and Gender at Tikal, Guatemala. Ancient Mesoamerica 8:1–12.

Hawkes, Christopher

1954 Archeological Theory and Method: Some Suggestions from the Old World. American Anthropologist 56(2):155–168.

Hayes, Alden C.

1981 Contributions to Gran Quivira Archaeology: Gran Quivira National Monument. National Park Service Publications in Archaeology No. 17. Washington, DC.

Hayes, Alden C., and James A. Lancaster

1975 Badger House Community, Mesa Verde National Park. National Park Service, Washington, DC.

Healy, Frances

2004 Hambledon Hill and Its Implications. In Monuments and Material Culture, edited by Rosamund Cleal and Joshua Pollard, pp. 15–38. Hobnob Press, Salisbury.

Healy, Paul

1974 The Cuyamel Caves: Preclassic Sites in Northeast Honduras. American Antiquity 39:433–437.

Heckenberger, Michael J.

2005 The Ecology of Power: Culture, Place, and Personhood in the Southern Amazon, A.D. 1000–2000. Routledge, New York.

Heidegger, Martin

1977 Building Dwelling Thinking. In Basic Writings, edited by David Farrell Krell, pp. 323–339. Harper & Row, New York.

Heitman, Carolyn, and Stephen Plog

2005 Kinship and the Dynamics of the House: Rediscovering Dualism in the Pueblo Past. In A Catalyst for Ideas: Anthropological Archaeology and the Legacy of Douglas W. Schwartz, edited by Vernon L. Scarborough, pp. 69–100. School of American Research Press, Santa Fe.

Heizer, Robert F.

1959 Specific and Generic Characteristics of Olmec Culture. In Proceedings of the 33rd International Congress of Americanists, 1958, San Jose, Costa Rica, Vol. 2, pp. 178–182.

REFERENCES

1960   Agriculture and the Theocratic State in Lowland Southeastern Mexico.
        American Antiquity 26:215–222.
1961   Inferences on the Nature of Olmec Society Based upon Data from the La
        Venta Site. Kroeber Anthropological Society Papers 25:43–57. Department of
        Anthropology, University of California, Berkeley.
1962   The Possible Sociopolitical Structure of the La Venta Olmecs. In Proceedings
        of the 34th International Congress of Americanists, Vienna, pp. 310–317.
1964   Some Interim Remarks on the Coe-Stuckenrath Review. Kroeber
        Anthropological Society Papers 31:45–50. Department of Anthropology,
        University of California, Berkeley.

Heizer, Robert F., John A. Graham, and Lewis K. Napton
1968   The 1968 Investigations at La Venta. Contributions of the University of
        California Archaeological Research Facility 5, pp. 127–154. Berkeley.

Helms, Mary
1993   Craft and the Kingly Ideal: Art, Trade, and Power. University of Texas Press,
        Austin.

Hendon, Julia A.
2000   Having and Holding: Storage, Memory, Knowledge, and Social Relations.
        American Anthropologist 102(1):42–53.

Herbert, Eugenia W.
1993   Iron, Gender and Power: Rituals of Transformation in African Societies.
        Indiana University Press, Bloomington.

Hewett, Edgar L.
1936   The Chaco Canyon and Its Monuments. University of New Mexico Press,
        Albuquerque.

Hibben, Frank C.
1937   Mammal and Bird Remains. In Tseh So, a Small House Ruin, Chaco Canyon,
        New Mexico, edited by Donald D. Brand, Florence M. Hawley, and Frank C.
        Hibben, pp. 100–106. University of New Mexico Bulletin, Anthropological
        Series, Vol. 2, No. 2. Albuquerque.
1975   Kiva Art of the Anasazi at Pottery Mound. KC Publications, Las Vegas.

Hill, Erica
2000   The Contextual Analysis of Animal Interments and Ritual Practice in
        Southwestern North America. Kiva 65(4):361–398.

Hill, J. D.
1995   Ritual and Rubbish in the Iron Age of Wessex: A Study of the Formation of a
        Specific Archaeological Record. BAR Series 242. British Archaeological
        Reports, Oxford.

Hirsch, Eric, and Michael O'Hanlon (editors)
1995   The Anthropology of Landscape: Perspectives on Place and Space. Oxford
        University Press, Oxford.

Hobbes, Thomas

1991   Leviathan. Cambridge University Press, Cambridge.

Hobsbawm, Eric

1983   Introduction: Inventing Traditions. *In* The Invention of Tradition, edited by Eric Hobsbawm and Terence Ranger, pp. 1–14. Cambridge University Press, Cambridge.

Hobsbawm, Eric, and Terence Ranger (editors)

1983   The Invention of Tradition. Cambridge University Press, Cambridge.

Hodder, Ian

1982   Symbols in Action. Cambridge University Press, Cambridge.

1990   The Domestication of Europe: Structure and Contingency in Neolithic Societies. Blackwell, Oxford.

1992   Theory and Practice in Archaeology. Routledge, London.

Hodder, Ian, and Craig Cessford

2004   Daily Practice and Social Memory at Catalhuyok. American Antiquity 69:17–40.

Holley, George R., Rinitia A. Dalan, and Phillip A. Smith

1993   Investigations in the Cahokia Site Grand Plaza. American Antiquity 58:306–319.

Holtorf, Cornelius

2004   Incavation-Excavation-Exhibition. *In* Material Engagements: Studies in Honour of Colin Renfrew, edited by Neil Brodie and Catherine Hills, pp. 45–53. McDonald Institute Monographs, Cambridge.

Horton, Robin

1993 [1960] A Definition of Religion. *In* Patterns of Thought in Africa and the West: Essays on Magic, Religion and Science, pp. 19–49. Cambridge University, Cambridge.

Hoskins, Janet

1993   The Play of Time: Kodi Perspectives on Calendars, History, and Exchange. University of California Press, Berkeley.

1998   Biographical Objects: How Things Tell the Stories of People's Lives. Routledge, New York.

Hosler, Dorothy

1994   The Sounds and Colors of Power: The Metallurgical Technology of Ancient West Mexico. MIT Press, Cambridge.

Houston, Stephen, and David Stuart

1996   Of Gods, Glyphs and Kings: Divinity and Rulership among the Classic Maya. Antiquity 70:289–312.

Huffman, Thomas N.

1996   Snakes and Crocodiles: Power and Symbolism in Ancient Zimbabwe. University of Witwatersrand Press, Johannesburg.

Huyssen, Andreas

2003   Present Pasts: Urban Palimpsests and the Politics of Memory. Stanford University Press, Palo Alto.

REFERENCES

Hyslop, John
1977   Chulpas of the Lupaca Zone of the Peruvian High Plateau. Journal of Field
        Archaeology 4(2):149–170.

Ingold, Tim
1993   The Temporality of the Landscape. World Archaeology 25:152–174.
1995   Building, Dwelling, Living: How Animals and People Make Themselves at
        Home in the World. *In* Shifting Contexts: Transformations in Anthropological
        Knowledge, edited by Marilyn Strathern, pp. 57–80. Routledge, London.

Ingold, Tim (editor)
1988   What Is an Animal? Unwin Hyman, London.

Insoll, Timothy
2003   The Archaeology of Islam in Sub-Saharan Africa. Cambridge University Press,
        Cambridge.
2004   Archaeology, Ritual, Religion. Routledge, London.
2006   Shrine Franchising and the Neolithic in the British Isles: Some Observations
        Based upon the Tallensi, Northern Ghana. Cambridge Archaeological Journal
        16:223–238.

Isbell, W. H.
1997   Mummies and Mortuary Monuments: A Postprocessual Prehistory of Central
        Andean Social Organization. University of Texas Press, Austin.

Izko, Xavier
1992   La doble frontera: Identidad, política y ritual en el altiplano central. Hisbol,
        La Paz.

Jackson, Jason Baird
2003   Yuchi Ceremonial Life: Performance, Meaning, and Tradition in a
        Contemporary American Indian Community. University of Nebraska Press,
        Lincoln.

Jansen, Robert S.
2007   Resurrection and Appropriation: Reputational Trajectories, Memory Work,
        and the Political Use of Historical Figures. American Journal of Sociology
        112(4):953–1007.

Jeakle, Julie E.
2002   Social Integration and the Maya: The Multifunctionality of Mesoamerican Ball
        Courts. M.A. thesis, New Mexico State University, Las Cruces.

Jeakle, Julie E., Lisa J. Lucero, and Sarah Field
2002   SC-3: A Minor Center Temple Ball Court. *In* Results of the 2001 Valley of
        Peace Archaeology Project: Saturday Creek and Yalbac, edited by Lisa J.
        Lucero, pp. 47–64. Report submitted to the Department of Archaeology,
        Ministry of Tourism and Culture, Belize.

Jones, Andrew
2001   Drawn from Memory: The Archaeology of Aesthetics and the Aesthetics of

Archaeology in Earlier Bronze Age Britain and the Present. World Archaeology
33(2):334–356.

2002   Archaeological Theory and Scientific Practice. Cambridge University Press,
Cambridge.

2005   Lives in Fragments? Personhood and the European Neolithic. Journal of Social
Archaeology 5(2):193–224.

Jones, Andrew, and Gavin MacGregor (editors)

2002   Colouring the Past: The Significance of Colour in Archaeological Research.
Berg, Oxford.

Jones, Andrew, and Colin Richards

2003   Animals into Ancestors: Domestication, Food and Identity in Late Neolithic
Orkney. In Food, Culture and Identity in the Neolithic and Early Bronze Age, edited by Mike Parker Pearson, pp. 45–51. British Archaeological Reports, Oxford.

Jones, Owain

2000   (Un)ethical Geographies of Human–Non-Human Relations. In Animal Spaces,
Beastly Places: New Geographies of Human-Animal Relations. Routledge, New
York.

Jones, Owain, and Paul Cloke

2002   Tree Culture: The Place of Trees and Trees in Their Place. Berg, Oxford.

Joyce, Rosemary A.

1987   Ceremonial Roles and Status in Middle Formative Mesoamerica: The
Implications of Burials from La Venta, Tabasco, Mexico. Paper presented at the
Third Texas Symposium on Mesoamerican Archaeology: Olmec, Izapa, Maya.
Program in Latin American Studies, University of Texas, Austin.

1992   Ideology in Action: Classic Maya Ritual Practice. In Ancient Images, Ancient
Thought: The Archaeology of Ideology. Proceedings of the Twenty-third Annual
Conference of the Archaeological Association of the University of Calgary,
edited by A. Sean Goldsmith, Sandra Garvie, David Selin, and Jeannette Smith,
pp. 497–506. Department of Archaeology, University of Calgary.

1996   Social Dynamics of Exchange: Changing Patterns in the Honduran
Archaeological Record. In Chieftains, Power and Trade: Regional Interaction in
the Intermediate Area of the Americas, edited by Carl Henrik Langebaek and
Felipe Cardenas-Arroyo, pp. 31–46. Departamento de Antropología,
Universidad de los Andes, Bogota, Colombia.

1998   Performing the Body in Prehispanic Central America. RES: Anthropology and
Aesthetics 33:147–165.

1999   Social Dimensions of Pre-Classic Burials. In Social Patterns in Pre-Classic
Mesoamerica, edited by David C. Grove and Rosemary A. Joyce, pp. 15–47.
Dumbarton Oaks, Washington, DC.

2000a   Heirlooms and Houses: Materiality and Social Memory. In Beyond Kinship:
Social and Material Reproduction in House Societies, edited by Rosemary A.
Joyce and Susan D. Gillespie, pp. 189–212. University of Pennsylvania Press,
Philadelphia.

2000b   Gender and Power in Prehispanic Mesoamerica. University of Texas Press, Austin.

2001   Burying the Dead at Tlatilco: Social Memory and Social Identities. *In* Social Memory, Identity, and Death: Anthropological Perspectives on Mortuary Rituals, edited by Meredith S. Chesson, pp. 12–26. Archeological Papers of the American Anthropological Association Number 10. American Anthropological Association, Arlington, Virginia.

2003a   Making Something of Herself: Embodiment in Life and Death at Playa de los Muertos, Honduras. Cambridge Archaeological Journal 13:248–261.

2003b   Concrete Memories: Fragments of the Past in the Classic Maya Present (500–1000 AD). *In* Archaeologies of Memory, edited by Ruth M. Van Dyke and Susan E. Alcock, pp. 104–125. Blackwell, Oxford.

2004   Unintended Consequences? Monumentality as a Novel Experience in Formative Mesoamerica. Journal of Archaeological Method and Theory 11:5–29.

2005   Archaeology of the Body. Annual Review of Anthropology 34:139–158.

Joyce, Rosemary A., and Susan D. Gillespie (editors)
2000   Beyond Kinship: Social and Material Reproduction in House Societies. University of Pennsylvania Press, Philadelphia.

Joyce, Rosemary A., and John S. Henderson
2001   Beginnings of Village Life in Eastern Mesoamerica. Latin American Antiquity 12:5–24.

2002   La arqueología del Período Formativo en Honduras: Nuevos datos sobre el "Estilo Olmeca" en la Zona Maya. Mayab 15:5–18.

2003   Investigaciones recientes de la arqueología del Período Formativo en Honduras: Nuevos satos según el intercambio y cerámica pan-mesoamericana (o Estilo "Olmeca"). *In* XVI Simposio de Investigaciones Arqueológicas en Guatemala, 2002, edited by J. P. Laporte, B. Arroyo, H. Escobedo, and H. Mejía, pp. 819–832. Museo Nacional de Arqueología y Etnología and Asociación Tikal, Guatemala.

2004   Puerto Escondido: Exploraciones preliminares del Formativo Temprano. *In* Memoria del VII Seminario de Antropología de Honduras "Dr. George Hasemann," pp. 93–113. Instituto Hondureño de Antropología e Historia, Tegucigalpa.

Joyce, Rosemary A., and Julia A. Hendon
2000   Heterarchy, History, and Material Reality: "Communities" in Late Classic Honduras. *In* The Archaeology of Communities: A New World Perspective, edited by Marcel A. Canuto and Jason Yaeger, pp. 143–160. Routledge, London.

Joyce, Rosemary A., and Jeanne Lopiparo
2005   Doing Agency in Archaeology. Journal of Archaeological Method and Theory 12(4):365–374.

Judd, Neil M.
1954   The Material Culture of Pueblo Bonito. Smithsonian Miscellaneous

Collections No. 124. Smithsonian Institution, Washington, DC.

1959 Pueblo del Arroyo, Chaco Canyon, New Mexico. Smithsonian Miscellaneous Collections Vol. 138, No. 1. Smithsonian Institution, Washington, DC.

1964 The Architecture of Pueblo Bonito. Smithsonian Miscellaneous Collections Vol. 147, No. 1. Smithsonian Institution, Washington, DC.

Kammerer, Cornelia Ann, and Nicola Tannenbaum

2003 Introduction. *In* Founders' Cults in Southeast Asia: Ancestors, Polity, and Identity, edited by Nicola Tannenbaum and Cornelia Ann Kammerer, pp. 1–14. Yale University Southeast Asia Studies, New Haven, Connecticut.

Kaulicke, Peter

2001 Memoria y muerte en el Perú antiguo. Pontificia Universidad Católica del Perú, Lima.

Keane, Webb

2003a Self-Interpretation, Agency, and the Objects of Anthropology: Reflections on a Genealogy. Studies in Society and History 45:222–248.

2003b Semiotics and the Social Analysis of Material Things. Language and Communication 23:409–425.

2005 Signs Are Not the Garb of Meaning: On the Social Analysis of Material Things. *In* Materiality, edited by Daniel Miller, pp. 182–205. Duke University Press, Durham.

Keber, Eloise Quiñones

1991 Xolotl: Dogs, Death, and Deities in Aztec Myth. Latin American Indian Literatures Journal 7(2):229–239.

Kelly, John E.

1990 The Emergence of Mississippian Culture in the American Bottom Region. *In* The Mississippian Emergence, edited by Bruce D. Smith, pp. 113–152. Smithsonian Institution Press, Washington, DC.

Kertzer, David I.

1988 Ritual, Politics, and Power. Yale University Press, New Haven.

Klenck, Joel D.

1995 Bedouin Animal Sacrifice Practices: Case Study in Israel. *In* The Symbolic Role of Animals in Africa, edited by Kathleen Ryan and Pam J. Crabtree, pp. 57–72. MASCA Research Papers in Science and Archaeology, Vol. 12. MASCA, University of Pennsylvania Museum of Archaeology and Anthropology, Philadelphia.

Kluckhohn, Clyde, Paul Reiter, and Charles F. Bohannon

1939 Preliminary Report on the 1937 Excavations, Bc 50–51, Chaco Canyon New Mexico, with Some Distributional Analyses. Bulletin No. 3, Part 2. University of New Mexico, Albuquerque.

Knappett, Carl

2005 Thinking through Material Culture: An Interdisciplinary Perspective. University of Pennsylvania Press, Philadelphia.

Knight, Vernon James, Jr.

1989   Symbolism of Mississippian Mounds. *In* Powhatan's Mantle: Indians in the Colonial Southeast, edited by P. H. Wood, Gregory A. Waselkov, and M. T. Hatley, pp. 279–291. University of Nebraska Press, Lincoln.

Kopytoff, Igor

1986   The Cultural Biography of Things: Commoditization as Process. *In* The Social Life of Things: Commodities in Cultural Perspective, edited by Arjun Appadurai, pp. 64–91. Cambridge University Press, Cambridge.

Kovacik, Joseph J.

1998   Collective Memory and Pueblo Space. Norwegian Archaeological Review 31(2):141–152.

Krause, Elizabeth L.

2005   Encounters with the "Peasant": Memory Work, Masculinity, and Low Fertility in Italy. American Ethnologist 32(4):593–617.

Kruchten, Jeffery D.

2000   Early Cahokian Fluidity on the Fringe: Pfeffer Mounds and the Richland Complex. Paper presented at the 57th Southeastern Archaeological Conference, November 8–11, Macon, Georgia.

Kuba, Richard, and Carola Lentz

2002   Arrows and Earth Shrines: Towards a History of Dagara Expansion in Southern Burkina Faso. Journal of African History 43:377–406.

Küchler, Susanne

1987   Malangan: Art and Memory in a Melanesian Society. Man 22:238–255.

1988   Malangan: Objects, Sacrifice and the Production of Memory. American Ethnologist 15:625–637.

1992   Making Skins: Malangan and the Idiom of Kinship in Northern New Ireland. *In* Anthropology, Art and Aesthetics, edited by J. Coote and A. Shelton, pp. 94–112. Clarendon Press, Oxford.

1993   Landscape as Memory: The Mapping of Process and Its Representation in a Melanesian Society. *In* Landscape: Politics and Perspectives, edited by Barbara Bender, pp. 85–106. Berg, Oxford.

1997   Sacrificial Economy and Its Objects: Rethinking Colonial Collecting in Oceania. Journal of Material Culture 2:39–60.

1999   The Place of Memory. *In* The Art of Forgetting, edited by Adrian Forty and Susanne Küchler, pp. 53–73. Berg, Oxford.

2002   Malanggan: Art, Memory and Sacrifice. Berg, Oxford.

2005   Materiality and Cognition: The Changing Face of Things. *In* Materiality, edited by Daniel Miller, pp. 206–231. Duke University Press, Durham.

Küchler, Susanne, and Walter Melion (editors)

1991   Images of Memory: On Remembering and Representation. Smithsonian Institution Press, Washington, DC.

Kuwanwisiwma, Leigh
2004   Yupköyvi: The Hopi Story of Chaco Canyon. *In* In Search of Chaco: New
        Approaches to an Archaeological Enigma, edited by David Grant Noble, pp.
        41–47. School of American Research Press, Santa Fe.

Kwint, Marius
1999   Introduction: The Physical Past. *In* Material Memories: Design and Evocation,
        edited by Marius Kwint, Christopher Breward, and Jeremy Aynsley, pp. 1–16.
        Berg, Oxford.

LaMotta, Vincent L., and Michael B. Schiffer
1999   Formation Processes of House Floor Assemblages. *In* The Archaeology of
        Household Activities, edited by Penelope M. Allison, pp. 19–29. Routledge,
        London.

Larsson, Lars
2000   The Passage of Axes: Fire Transformation of Flint Objects in the Neolithic of
        Southern Sweden. Antiquity 74:602–610.

Latour, Bruno
1993   We Have Never Been Modern. Translated by Catherine Porter. Harvard
        University Press, Cambridge.
1994   Pragmatogonies: A Mythical Account of How Humans and Nonhumans Swap
        Properties. American Behavioral Scientist 37(4):791–801.
1999   Pandora's Hope: Essays on the Reality of Science Studies. Harvard University
        Press, Cambridge.
2005   Reassembling the Social: An Introduction to Actor-Network-Theory. Oxford
        University Press, Oxford.

Law, John, and John Hassard (editors)
1999   Actor Network Theory and After. Blackwell, Oxford.

Leach, Edmund R.
1966   Ritualization in Man in Relation to Conceptual and Social Development.
        Philosophical Transactions of the Royal Society of London 251:403–408.

Lechtmann, Heather
1984   Andean Value Systems and the Development of Prehistoric Metallurgy.
        Technology and Culture 25(1):1–36.

Lee, Daniel B.
2000   Old Order Mennonites: Rituals, Beliefs, and Community. Burnham Publishers,
        Chicago.

Le Goff, Jacques
1996   History and Memory. Columbia University Press, New York.

Lekson, Stephen H.
1986   Great Pueblo Architecture of Chaco Canyon. University of New Mexico Press,
        Albuquerque.

2007   Great House Form. *In* The Architecture of Chaco Canyon, New Mexico, edited by Stephen H. Lekson, pp. 7–44. University of Utah Press, Salt Lake City.

Lekson, Stephen H. (editor)

1983   The Architecture and Dendrochronology of Chetro Ketl, Chaco Canyon, New Mexico. Reports of the Chaco Center No. 6. Division of Cultural Research, National Park Service, Albuquerque.

Lentz, Carola

2000   Of Hunters, Goats and Earth-Shrines: Settlement Histories and the Politics of Oral Tradition in Northern Ghana. History in Africa 27:193–214.

Leroi-Gourhan, André

1964   Le geste et la parole. Albin Michelle, Paris.

Lewis-Williams, J. David, and D. G. Pearce

2004   San Spirituality: Roots, Expression, and Social Consequences. AltaMira Press, Walnut Creek, California.

Lightfoot, Ricky R., Alice M. Emerson, and Eric Blinman

1988   Excavations in Area 5, Grass Mesa Village (Site 5mt23). *In* Dolores Archaeological Program: Anasazi Communities at Dolores: Grass Mesa Village, pp. 561–766. US Bureau of Reclamation Engineering and Research Center, Boulder.

Lillios, Katina T.

1999   Objects of Memory: The Ethnography and Archaeology of Heirlooms. Journal of Archaeological Method and Theory 6:235–262.

2003   Creating Memory in Prehistory: The Engraved Slate Plaques of Southwest Iberia. *In* Archaeologies of Memory, edited by Ruth M. Van Dyke and Susan E. Alcock, pp. 129–150. Blackwell, London.

Linseele, Veerle

2002   Cultural Identity and the Consumption of Dogs in Western Africa. *In* Behaviour behind Bones: The Zooarchaeology of Ritual, Religion, Status and Identity, edited by Sharyn Jones O'Day, Wim Van Neer, and Anton Ervynck, pp. 318–326. Proceedings of the 9th ICAZ (International Council for Archaeozoology) Conference, Durham. Oxbow Books, Oxford.

Lister, Robert H.

1964   Contributions to Mesa Verde Archaeology I: Site 499, Mesa Verde National Park, Colorado. University of Colorado Studies Series in Anthropology No. 8. University of Colorado, Boulder.

Litzinger, Ralph A.

1998   Memory Work: Reconstituting the Ethnic in Post-Mao China. Cultural Anthropology 13(2):224–255.

Longyear, John M., III

1969   The Problem of Olmec Influences in the Pottery of Western Honduras. Proceedings, 38th International Congress of Americanists 1:491–498.

Lopinot, Neal H.
1991   Archaeobotanical Remains. *In* The Archaeology of the Cahokia Mounds ICT-II: Biological Remains, Part 1. Illinois Historic Preservation Agency, Springfield.

Lowe, Gareth W.
1978   Eastern Mesoamerica. *In* Chronologies in New World Archaeology, edited by R. E. Taylor and Clement W. Meighan, pp. 331–393. Academic Press, New York.

1989   The Heartland Olmec: Evolution of Material Culture. *In* Regional Perspectives on the Olmec, edited by Robert J. Sharer and David C. Grove, pp. 33–67. Cambridge University Press, Cambridge.

Lozano Machuca, Juan
1992 [1581] Carta del factor de Potosí...al virrey del Perú, en donde se describe la provincia de los Lípez. Potosí, 8 de Noviembre de 1581. Estudios Atacameños 11:30–34.

Lucas, F. A.
1897   A Dog of the Ancient Pueblos. Science 5(18):544–545.

Lucero, Lisa J.
2003   The Politics of Ritual: The Emergence of Classic Maya Rulers. Current Anthropology 44:523–558.

2006   Water and Ritual: The Rise and Fall of Classic Maya Rulers. University of Texas Press, Austin.

Lucero, Lisa J. (editor)
1997   1997 Field Season of the Valley of Peace Archaeological (VOPA) Project. Report submitted to the Department of Archaeology, Ministry of Tourism and the Environment, Belize.

2002   Results of the 2001 Valley of Peace Archaeology Project: Saturday Creek and Yalbac. Report submitted to the Department of Archaeology, Ministry of Tourism and Culture, Belize.

Lucero, Lisa J., and David L. Brown
2002   SC-18: A Wealthy Maya Farming Residence. *In* Results of the 2001 Valley of Peace Archaeology Project: Saturday Creek and Yalbac, edited by Lisa J. Lucero, pp. 18–25. Report submitted to the Department of Archaeology, Ministry of Tourism and Culture, Belize.

Lucero, Lisa J., Scott L. Fedick, Andrew Kinkella, and Sean M. Graebner
2004   Ancient Maya Settlement in the Valley of Peace Area, Belize. *In* Archaeology of the Upper Belize River Valley: Half a Century of Maya Research, edited by James F. Garber, pp. 86–102. University Press of Florida, Gainesville.

Lucero, Lisa J., Sean M. Graebner, and Elizabeth Pugh
2002a   SC-78: The Eastern Platform Mound of an Elite Compound. *In* Results of the 2001 Valley of Peace Archaeology Project: Saturday Creek and Yalbac, edited by Lisa J. Lucero, pp. 33–46. Report submitted to the Department of Archaeology, Ministry of Tourism and Culture, Belize.

Lucero, Lisa J., Gaea McGahee, and Yvette Corral

2002b   SC-85: A Common Maya Farming Household. *In* Results of the 2001 Valley of
        Peace Archaeology Project: Saturday Creek and Yalbac, edited by Lisa J.
        Lucero, pp. 26–32. Report submitted to the Department of Archaeology,
        Ministry of Tourism and Culture, Belize.

Luckert, Karl W.

1984   Coyote in Navajo and Hopi Tales. *In* Navajo Coyote Tales: The Curly Tó
        Aheedlíinii Version. University of Nebraska, Lincoln.

Lyman, R. Lee

1994   Vertebrate Taphonomy. Cambridge University Press, Cambridge.

MacDonald, Kevin C.

1995   Why Chickens? The Centrality of the Domestic Fowl in West African Ritual and
        Magic. *In* The Symbolic Role of Animals in Africa, edited by Kathleen Ryan
        and Pam J. Crabtree, pp. 50–56. MASCA Research Papers in Science and
        Archaeology, Vol. 12. MASCA, University of Pennsylvania Museum of
        Archaeology and Anthropology, Philadelphia.

MacNeish, Richard S.

1960   Review of Excavations at La Venta, Tabasco, 1955. American Antiquity
        26:296–297.

Maier, Donna J. E.

1983   Priests and Power: The Case of the Dente Shrine in Nineteenth-Century
        Ghana. Indiana University Press, Bloomington.

Malotki, Ekkehart (editor)

2001   Hopi Animal Stories. University of Nebraska Press, Lincoln.

2002   Hopi Tales of Destruction. University of Nebraska Press, Lincoln.

Malotki, Ekkehart, and Ken Gary

2001   Hopi Stories of Witchcraft, Shamanism and Magic. University of Nebraska
        Press, Lincoln.

Malotki, Ekkehart, and Michael Lomatuway'ma

1984   Hopi Coyote Tales: Istutuwutsi. University of Nebraska Press, Lincoln.

1987   Maasaw: Profile of a Hopi God. University of Nebraska Press, Lincoln.

Mandler, Jean M., and Nancy S. Johnson

1977   Remembrance of Things Parsed: Story Structure and Recall. Cognitive
        Psychology 9:111–151.

Martin, Debra L.

1997   Violence against Women in a Southwest Series (A.D. 1000–1300). *In* Troubled
        Times: Violence and Warfare in the Past, edited by D. Martin and D. Frayer,
        pp. 45–75. Gordon and Breach, New York.

Marx, Karl

1970   Theses on Feuerbach. *In* The German Ideology, edited by Christopher J.
        Arthur, pp. 121–123. International Publishers, New York.

Mason, Ronald J.

2000   Archaeology and Native North American Oral Traditions. American Antiquity
        65:239–266.

Mather, Charles

2003   Shrines and the Domestication of Landscape. Journal of Anthropological
        Research 59:23–45.

Mathews, Jennifer P., and James F. Garber

2004   Models of Cosmic Order: Physical Expression of Sacred Spaces among the
        Ancient Maya. Ancient Mesoamerica 15:49–59.

Mathien, F. Joan

2001   The Organization of Turquoise Production and Consumption by the
        Prehistoric Chacoans. American Antiquity 66:103–118.

2003   Artifacts from Pueblo Bonito: One Hundred Years of Interpretation. *In* Pueblo
        Bonito: Center of the Chacoan World, edited by Jill E. Neitzel, pp. 127–142.
        Smithsonian Institution Press, Washington, DC.

Mauss, Marcel

1992   Techniques of the Body. *In* Incorporations, edited by J. Crary and S. Kwinter,
        pp. 454–477. Zone Books, New York.

McAnany, Patricia A.

1995   Living with the Ancestors: Kinship and Kingship in Ancient Maya Society.
        University of Texas Press, Austin.

1998   Ancestors and the Classic Maya Built Environment. *In* Function and Meaning
        in Classic Maya Architecture, edited by Stephen D. Houston, pp. 271–298.
        Dumbarton Oaks, Washington, DC.

McAnany, Patricia A., Rebecca Storey, and Angela K. Lockard

1999   Mortuary Ritual and Family Politics at Formative and Early Classic K'axob,
        Belize. Ancient Mesoamerica 10:129–146.

McCaskie, Thomas C.

1981   Anti-Witchcraft Cults in Asante: An Essay in the Social History of an African
        People. History in Africa 8:125–154.

1983   R. S. Rattray and the Construction of Asante History: An Appraisal. History in
        Africa 10:187–206.

McCleary, Timothy P.

1997   The Stars We Know: Crow Indian Astronomy and Lifeways. Waveland Press,
        Prospect Hills, Illinois.

McFadyen, Lesley

2003   A Revision of the Materiality of Architecture: The Significance of Neolithic
        Long Mounds and Chambered Monuments, with Particular Reference to the
        Cotswold-Severn Group. Ph.D. thesis, University of Wales.

McGee, W. J.

1897   The Siouan Indians: A Preliminary Sketch. *In* Fifteenth Annual Report of the
        Bureau of American Ethnology, pp. 153–204. Government Printing Office,
        Washington, DC.

McGregor, John C.

1943   Burial of an Early American Magician. Proceedings of the American Philosophical Society 86(2):270–298.

McNaughton, Patrick R.

1988   The Mande Blacksmiths: Knowledge, Power, and Art in West Africa. Indiana University Press, Bloomington.

Mendonsa, Eugene L.

1982   The Politics of Divination: A Processual View of Reactions to Illness and Deviance among the Sisala of Northern Ghana. University of California Press, Berkeley.

Mercer, Roger

1981   Excavations at Carn Brae, Illogan, Cornwall, 1970–73. Cornish Archaeology 20:1–204.

Merrifield, Ralph

1987   The Archaeology of Ritual and Magic. Batsford, London.

Meskell, Lynn

1999   Archaeologies of Social Life: Age, Sex, and Class in Ancient Egypt. Basil Blackwell Press, Oxford.

2001   The Egyptian Ways of Death. In Social Memory, Identity, and Death: Anthropological Perspectives on Mortuary Rituals, edited by Meredith S. Chesson, pp. 27–40. Archeological Papers of the American Anthropological Association No. 10. American Anthropological Association, Arlington, Virginia.

2002   Negative Heritage and Past Mastering in Archaeology. Anthropological Quarterly 75(3):557–574.

2003   Memory's Materiality: Ancestral Presence, Commemorative Practice and Disjunctive Locales. In Archaeologies of Memory, edited by Ruth M. Van Dyke and Susan E. Alcock, pp. 34–55. Blackwell Publishers, Oxford.

2004   Object Worlds in Ancient Egypt: Material Biographies Past and Present. Berg, London.

2005   Introduction: Object Orientations. In Archaeologies of Materiality, edited by Lynn Meskell, pp. 1–17. Blackwell, Oxford.

2006   Trauma Culture: Remembering and Forgetting in the New South Africa. In Memory, Trauma, and World Politics, edited by D. Bell, pp. 157–174. Palgrave Macmillan, New York.

Meskell, Lynn (editor)

2005   Archaeologies of Materiality. Blackwell, Oxford.

Mick-O'Hara, Linda S.

1994   Nutritional Stability and Changing Faunal Resource Use in La Plata Valley Prehistory. Ph.D. dissertation, Department of Anthropology, University of New Mexico, Albuquerque.

Miller, Daniel

1987   Material Culture and Mass Consumption. Blackwell, Oxford.

2005   Materiality: An Introduction. *In* Materiality, edited by Daniel Miller, pp. 1–50.
            Duke University Press, Durham.

Miller, Daniel (editor)
2005   Materiality. Duke University Press, Durham.

Miller, Daniel, and Christopher Tilley
1996   Editorial. Journal of Material Culture 1:5–14.

Mills, Barbara J.
2000   Gender, Craft Production, and Inequality in the American Southwest. *In*
            Women and Men in the Prehispanic Southwest: Labor, Power, and Prestige,
            edited by Patricia L. Crown, pp. 301–343. School of American Research Press,
            Santa Fe.

2004   The Establishment and Defeat of Hierarchy: Inalienable Possessions and the
            History of Collective Prestige Structures in the Puebloan Southwest. American
            Anthropologist 106(2):238–251.

Mock, Shirley B.
1998   Prelude. *In* The Sowing and the Dawning: Termination, Dedication, and
            Transformation in the Archaeological and Ethnographic Record of
            Mesoamerica, edited by Shirley B. Mock, pp. 3–18. University of New Mexico
            Press, Albuquerque.

Moerman, Daniel E.
1986   Medicinal Plants of Native America. Technical Reports No. 19. University of
            Michigan, Museum of Anthropology, Ann Arbor.

Montgomery, Barbara
1993   Ceramic Analysis as a Tool for Discovering Processes of Pueblo Abandonment.
            In Abandonment of Sites and Regions, edited by Catherine M. Cameron and
            Steven A. Tompka, pp. 157–164. Cambridge University Press, Cambridge.

Moore, Henrietta L.
1982   The Interpretation of Spatial Patterning in Settlement Residues. *In* Symbolic
            and Structural Archaeology, edited by Ian Hodder, pp. 74–79. Cambridge
            University Press, Cambridge.

1986   Space, Text and Gender. Cambridge University Press, Cambridge.

Moore, Jerry D.
1996   Architecture and Power in the Ancient Andes. Cambridge University Press,
            Cambridge.

Moore, Sally Falk
1993   Changing Perspectives on a Changing Africa: The Work of Anthropology. *In*
            Africa and the Disciplines: The Contributions of Research in Africa to the
            Social Sciences and Humanities, edited by Robert H. Bates, V. Y. Mudimbe, and
            Jean O'Barr, pp. 3–57. University of Chicago Press, Chicago.

Morris, Earl H.
1921   The House of the Great Kiva at the Aztec Ruin. Anthropological Papers of the
            American Museum of Natural History 26(2). New York.

Morris, Elizabeth A.

1980   Basketmaker Caves in the Prayer Rock District, Northeastern Arizona. Anthropological Papers No. 35. University of Arizona, Tucson.

Morris, James N.

1988   Excavations in Area 8. *In* Dolores Archaeological Program: Anasazi Communities at Dolores: Grass Mesa Village, Book 2 of 2, pp. 873–932. US Bureau of Reclamation Engineering and Research Center, Boulder.

Moyes, Holley

2001   The Cave as a Cosmogram: The Use of GIS in an Intrasite Spatial Analysis of the Main Chamber of Actun Tunichil Muknal, a Maya Ceremonial Cave in Western Belize. M.A. thesis, Florida Atlantic University, Boca Raton.

Myers, Fred R.

2005   Some Properties of Art and Culture: Ontologies of the Image and Economies of Exchange. *In* Materiality, edited by Daniel Miller, pp. 88–117. Duke University Press, Durham.

Myers, Fred R. (editor)

2001   The Empire of Things: Regimes of Value and Material Culture. SAR Press, Santa Fe.

Nakamura, Carolyn

2005   Mastering Matters: Magical Sense and Apotropaic Figurine Worlds of Neo-Assyria. *In* Archaeologies of Materiality, edited by Lynn M. Meskell, pp. 18–45. Blackwell, Oxford.

Needham, Stuart, and Tony Spence

1997   Refuse and the Formation of Middens. Antiquity 71(271):77–90.

Neitzel, Jill E.

2003a   Artifact Distributions at Pueblo Bonito. *In* Pueblo Bonito: Center of the Chacoan World, edited by Jill E. Neitzel, pp. 107–126. Smithsonian Institution Press, Washington, DC.

2003b   The Organization, Function, and Population of Pueblo Bonito. *In* Pueblo Bonito: Center of the Chacoan World, edited by Jill E. Neitzel, pp. 143–149. Smithsonian Institution Press, Washington, DC.

Nielsen, Axel E.

1995   Architectural Performance and the Reproduction of Social Power. *In* Expanding Archaeology, edited by J. M. Skibo, W. H. Walker, and A. E. Nielsen, pp. 47–66. University of Utah Press, Salt Lake City.

2001   Evolución social en Quebrada de Humahuaca (AD 700–1536). *In* Historia argentina prehispánica, edited by E. Berberián and A. Nielsen, Vol. 1, pp. 171–264. Editorial Brujas, Córdoba.

2002   Asentamientos, conflicto y cambio social en el Altiplano de Lípez (Potosí, Bolivia). Revista Española de Antropología Americana (Madrid) 32:179–205.

2006   Plazas para los antepasados: Descentralización y poder corporativo en las formaciones políticas preincaicas de los Andes circumpuneños. Estudios Atacameños 31:63–89.

Nielsen, Axel E., and William H. Walker

1999　Conquista ritual y dominación política en el Tawantinsuyu: El caso de Los Amarillos (Jujuy, Argentina). *In* Sed non satiata: Teoría social en la arqueología latinoamericana contemporánea, edited by A. Zarankin and F. A. Acuto, pp. 153–169. Ediciones del Tridente, Buenos Aires.

Nora, Pierre

1989　Between Memory and History: Les Lieux de Mémoire. Representations 26:7–24.

Novecosky, Brad J., and Peter R. W. Popkin

2005　Canidae Volume Mineral Density Values: An Application to Sites in Western Canada. Journal of Archaeological Science 32:1677–1690.

Ogundiran, Akinwumi

2002　Of Small Things Remembered: Beads, Cowries, and Cultural Translations of the Atlantic Experience in Yorubaland. International Journal of African Historical Studies 35(2–3):427–457.

Olick, Jeffrey K., and Joyce Robbins

1998　Social Memory Studies from "Collective Memory" to the Historical Sociology of Mnemonic Practices. Annual Review of Sociology 24:105–140.

Olsen, Bjørnar

2003　Material Culture after Text: Re-membering Things. Norwegian Archaeological Review 36:87–104.

Olsen, Stanley J.

1972　The Small Indian Dogs of Black Mesa, Arizona. Plateau 45(2):47–54.

1976　The Dogs of Awatovi. American Antiquity 41:102–106.

Olszewski, D. L., R. M. Kohl, M. C. Trachte, and S. J. Gumerman

1984　Arizona D:7:2103. *In* Excavations on Black Mesa, 1982: A Descriptive Report, edited by Deborah L. Nichols and Francis E. Smiley, pp. 140–155. Research Paper No. 39. Center for Archaeological Investigations, Southern Illinois University, Carbondale.

Onar, Vedat, Altan Armutak, Oktay Belli, and Erkan Konyar

2002　Skeletal Remains of Dogs Unearthed from the Von-Yoncatepe Necropolises. International Journal of Osteoarchaeology 12:317–334.

Oswald, Alastair, Carolyn Dyer, and Martyn Barber

2001　The Creation of Monuments: Neolithic Causewayed Enclosures in the British Isles. English Heritage, London.

Owoc, Mary Ann

2005　From the Ground Up: Agency, Practice, and Community in the Southwestern British Bronze Age. Journal of Archaeological Method and Theory 12(4):257–281.

Palsetia, Jesse S.
2001   Mad Dogs and Parsis: The Bombay Dog Riots of 1832. Journal of the Royal
        Anthropological Society, Series 3, 11:13–30.

Parish, Jane
1999   The Dynamics of Witchcraft and Indigenous Shrines among the Akan. Africa
        69(3):426–447.
2000   From the Body to the Wallet: Conceptualizing Akan Witchcraft at Home and
        Abroad. Journal of the Royal Anthropological Institute 6(3):487–500.

Parker, John
2004   Witchcraft, Anti-Witchcraft and Trans-Regional Ritual Innovation in Early
        Colonial Ghana: Sakrabundi and Aberewa, 1889–1910. Journal of African
        History 45:393–420.

Parmentier, R. J.
1985   Times of the Signs: Modalities of History and Levels of Social Structure in
        Belau. *In* Semiotic Mediation: Sociocultural and Psychological Perspectives,
        edited by E. Mertz and R. J. Parmentier, pp. 132–151. Academic Press, New
        York.
1987   The Sacred Remains: Myth, History, and Polity in Belau. University of Chicago
        Press, Chicago.

Parsons, Elsie Clews (editor)
1924   The Origin Myth of Zuni. Journal of American Folk-Lore 36:135–166.
1929   The Social Organization of the Tewa of New Mexico. Memoir 36 of the
        American Anthropological Association.
1940   Taos Tales. Memoir 34 of the American Folk-Lore Society.
1994 [1926] Tewa Tales. University of Arizona Press, Tucson.
1996 [1939] Pueblo Indian Religion. 2 vols. University of Nebraska Press, Lincoln.

Pärssinen, Martti
1993   Torres funerarias decoradas en Caquiaviri. Pumapunku 5/6:9–31. La Paz.

Pauketat, Timothy R.
1993   Temples for Cahokia Lords: Preston Holder's 1955–1956 Excavations of
        Kunnemann Mound. Memoir No. 26. Museum of Anthropology, University of
        Michigan, Ann Arbor.
1998   The Archaeology of Downtown Cahokia: The Tract 15A and Dunham Tract
        Excavations. Studies in Archaeology 1. Illinois Transportation Archaeological
        Research Program, University of Illinois, Urbana.
2000   The Tragedy of the Commoners. *In* Agency in Archaeology, edited by Marcia-
        Anne Dobres and John Robb, pp. 113–129. Routledge, London.
2001   Practice and History in Archaeology: An Emerging Paradigm. Anthropological
        Theory 1:73–98.
2003a   Farmers and the Making of a Mississippian Polity. American Antiquity
        68:39–66.

2003b   Materiality and the Immaterial in Historical-Processual Archaeology. *In* Essential Tensions in Archaeological Method and Theory, edited by T. L. VanPool and C. S. VanPool, pp. 41–53. University of Utah Press, Salt Lake City.

2004   Ancient Cahokia and the Mississippians. Cambridge University Press, Cambridge.

2005   The Forgotten History of the Mississippians. *In* North American Archaeology, edited by Timothy R. Pauketat and Diana D. Loren, pp. 187–212. Blackwell Press, Oxford.

Pauketat, Timothy R. (editor)

2005   The Archaeology of the East St. Louis Mound Center: Southside Excavations. Illinois Transportation Archaeological Research Program, Research Reports 21. University of Illinois, Urbana.

Pauketat, Timothy R., and Susan M. Alt

2003   Mounds, Memory, and Contested Mississippian History. *In* Archaeologies of Memory, edited by Ruth Van Dyke and Susan Alcock, pp. 149–179. Blackwell Press, Oxford.

2004   The Making and Meaning of a Mississippian Axe Head Cache. Antiquity 78:779–797.

2005   Agency in a Postmold? Physicality and the Archaeology of Culture-Making. Journal of Archaeological Method and Theory 12:213–236.

Pauketat, Timothy R., Susan M. Alt, and Jeffrey D. Kruchten

2005   Final Report of the Cahokia Extension Waterline and Grand Plaza Test Unit Projects. Report submitted to the Illinois Historic Preservation Agency, Springfield.

Pauketat, Timothy R., and Thomas E. Emerson

1991   The Ideology of Authority and the Power of the Pot. American Anthropologist 93:919–941.

Pauketat, Timothy R., Lucretia S. Kelly, Gayle J. Fritz, Neal H. Lopinot, Scott Elias, and Eve Hargrave

2002   The Residues of Feasting and Public Ritual at Early Cahokia. American Antiquity 67:257–279.

Pauketat, Timothy R., and Mark A. Rees

1996   Early Cahokia Project 1994 Excavations at Mound 49, Cahokia (11-S-34-2). Report submitted to the Illinois Historic Preservation Agency, Springfield.

Pels, Peter

1998   The Spirit of Matter: On Fetish, Rarity, Fact, and Fancy. *In* Border Fetishisms: Material Objects in Unstable Spaces, edited by Patricia Spyer, pp. 91–121. Routledge, New York.

Pendergast, David M., and Clement W. Meighan

1959   Folk Traditions as Historical Fact: A Paiute Example. Journal of American Folklore 72(2840):128–133.

Pepper, George H.

1920   Pueblo Bonito. Anthropological Papers of the American Museum of Natural History No. 27. New York.

Pérez, José A.

2000   Los suplicantes: Una cartografía social. Temas de la Academia Nacional de Bellas Artes 21–36. Buenos Aires.

Piehl, Jennifer

2002   The Skeletal Remains from the 2001 Field Season at Saturday Creek. *In* Results of the 2001 Valley of Peace Archaeology Project: Saturday Creek and Yalbac, edited by Lisa J. Lucero, pp. 84–94. Report submitted to the Department of Archaeology, Ministry of Tourism and Culture, Belize.

Piña Chan, Román

1989   The Olmec: Mother Culture of Mesoamerica, edited by Laura Laurencich Minelli. Rizzoli, New York.

Pinney, Christopher

2005   Things Happen: Or, from Which Moment Does That Object Come. *In* Materiality, edited by Daniel Miller, pp. 256–272. Duke University Press, Durham.

Piot, Charles D.

1993   Secrecy, Ambiguity, and the Everyday in Kabre Culture. American Anthropologist 95(2):353–370.

Pizarro, Pedro

1921 [1571] Relations of the Discovery and Conquest of the Kingdoms of Peru. Cortes Society, New York.

Platt, Tristan

1987   Entre Ch´axwa y Muxsa: Para una historia del pensamiento político aymara. *In* Tres reflexiones sobre el pensamiento andino, pp. 61–132. Hisbol, La Paz.

Plog, Stephen

2003   Exploring the Ubiquitous through the Unusual: Color Symbolism in Pueblo Black-on-White Pottery. American Antiquity 68(4):665–695.

Plog, Stephen, and Carolyn Heitman

2006   Microcosm and Macrocosm: Pueblo World View during the Chaco Era. Paper presented at the 10th Biennial Southwest Symposium, Las Cruces, New Mexico.

Pollard, Joshua

1995   Inscribing Space: Formal Deposition at the Later Neolithic Monument of Woodhenge, Wiltshire. Proceedings of the Prehistoric Society 61:137–156.

2001   The Aesthetics of Depositional Practice. World Archaeology 33:315–333.

2004a   The Art of Decay and the Transformation of Substance. *In* Substance, Memory, Display: Archaeology and Art, edited by Colin Renfrew, Chris Gosden, and Elizabeth DeMarrais, pp. 47–62. McDonald Institute Monographs, Cambridge.

2004b A "Movement of Becoming": Realms of Existence in the Early Neolithic of Southern Britain. *In* Stories from the Landscape: Archaeologies of Inhabitation, edited by Adrian Chadwick, pp. 55–69. British Archaeological Reports, Oxford.

Pollard, Joshua, and Clive Ruggles
2001 Shifting Perceptions: Spatial Order, Cosmology, and Patterns of Deposition at Stonehenge. Cambridge Archaeological Journal 11(1):69–90.

Poppi, Cesare
1999 Secrecy as a Modality of Knowledge: Comparative Issues in West African and European Systems of Thought. A paper presented at Microcosms: Objects of Knowledge Alter/Orders Workshop, March 5–6. University of California Humanities Research Institute, Irvine.

Porter, Muriel N.
1953 Tlatilco and the Preclassic Cultures of the New World. Viking Fund Publications in Anthropology 19. New York.

Posnansky, Merrick
1972 Archaeology, Ritual and Religion. *In* The Historical Study of African Religion, edited by Terrence O. Ranger and I. N. Kimambo, pp. 29–44. University of California Press, Berkeley.

1979 Archaeological Aspects of the Brong-Ahafo Region. *In* A Profile of Brong Kyempim: Essays on the Archaeology, History, Language and Politics of the Brong Peoples of Ghana, edited by Kwame Arhin, pp. 22–35. Afram Publications, Accra, Ghana.

1987 Prelude to Akan Civilization. *In* The Golden Stool: Studies of the Asante Center and Periphery, edited by Enid Schildkrout, pp. 14–22. Anthropological Papers of the American Museum of Natural History, Vol. 65, Part 1. New York.

Powers, William K.
1977 Oglala Religion. University of Nebraska Press, Lincoln.

Preucel, Robert W.
2006 Archaeological Semiotics. Blackwell Publishing, Oxford.

Preucel, Robert W., and Alexander A. Bauer
2001 Archaeological Pragmatics. Norwegian Archaeological Review 34:85–96.

Preucel, Robert W., and Lynn Meskell
2004 Knowledges. *In* A Companion to Social Archaeology, edited by Lynn Meskell and Robert W. Preucel, pp. 3–22. Blackwell, Oxford.

Pryor, Francis
1998 Etton: Excavations at a Neolithic Causewayed Enclosure near Maxey, Cambridgeshire, 1982–7. English Heritage, London.

Radin, Paul
1948 Winnebago Hero Cycles: A Study in Aboriginal Literature. Waverly Press, Baltimore.

REFERENCES

1990   The Winnebago Tribe. University of Nebraska Press, Lincoln.

Rappaport, Roy A.
1999   Ritual and Religion in the Making of Humanity. Cambridge University Press,
         Cambridge.

Rattray, Robert Sutherland
1923   Ashanti. Clarendon Press, Oxford.

Ray, Keith, and Julian Thomas
2003   In the Kinship of Cows: The Social Centrality of Cattle in the Earlier Neolithic
         of Southern Britain. In Food, Culture and Identity in the Neolithic and Early
         Bronze Age, edited by Mike Parker Pearson, pp. 37–44. British Archaeological
         Reports, Oxford.

Renfrew, Colin
2001   Production and Consumption in a Sacred Economy: The Material Correlates
         of High Devotational Expression at Chaco Canyon. American Antiquity
         66:14–25.

Rice, Prudence M.
1999   Rethinking Classic Lowland Maya Pottery Censers. Ancient Mesoamerica
         10:25–50.

Richards, Colin, and Julian Thomas
1984   Ritual Activity and Structured Deposition in Later Neolithic Wessex. In
         Neolithic Studies: A Review of Current Research, edited by Richard Bradley
         and Julie Gardiner, pp. 189–218. British Archaeological Reports 133. Oxford.

Rivera, Mario
1995   The Preceramic Chinchorro Mummy Complex of Northern Chile: Context,
         Style, and Purpose. In Tombs for the Living: Andean Mortuary Practices,
         edited by T. Dillehay, pp. 43–77. Dumbarton Oaks, Washington, DC.

Roberts, Frank H. H., Jr.
1929   Shabik'eschee Village: A Late Basketmaker Site in the Canyon, New Mexico.
         Bulletin No. 92. Bureau of American Ethnology, Smithsonian Institution,
         Washington, DC.

1939   Archaeological Remains in the Whitewater District Eastern Arizona. Bulletin
         No. 121, Part 1. Bureau of American Ethnology, Smithsonian Institution,
         Washington, DC.

Robertson Smith, William
1956 [1894] The Religion of the Semites: The Fundamental Institutions. 2nd ed.
         Meridian Books, New York.

Röschenthaler, Ute M.
2006   Translocal Cultures: The Slave Trade and Cultural Transfer in the Cross River
         Region. Social Anthropology 14(1):71–91.

Rowe, John H.
1946   Inca Culture at the Time of the Spanish Conquest. In Handbook of South

American Indians, Vol. 2, edited by J. Steward, pp. 183–330. Smithsonian Institution, Washington, DC.

Rowlands, Michael
1993   The Role of Memory in the Transmission of Culture. World Archaeology 25(2):141–151.

Rowlands, Michael, and Kristian Kristiansen
1998   Introduction. *In* Social Transformations in Archaeology: Global and Local Perspectives, by Kristian Kristiansen and Michael Rowlands, pp. 1–26. Routledge, London.

Ruppel, Timothy, Jessica Neuwirth, Mark P. Leone, and Gladys-Marie Fry
2003   Hidden in View: African Spiritual Spaces in North American Landscapes. Antiquity 77(296):321–335.

Sahlins, Marshall
1985   Islands of History. University of Chicago Press, Chicago.

Saignes, Tierry
1993   Borrachera y memoria: La experiencia de lo sagrado en los Andes. Hisbol-IFEA, La Paz.

Salomon, Frank
1995   "The Beautiful Grandparents": Andean Ancestor Shrines and Mortuary Ritual as Seen through Colonial Records. *In* Tombs for the Living: Andean Mortuary Practices, edited by T. Dillehay, pp. 315–353. Dumbarton Oaks, Washington, DC.

Salzer, Robert J., and Grace Rajnovich
2000   The Gottschall Rockshelter: An Archaeological Mystery. Prairie Smoke Press, Saint Paul, Minnesota.

Sanchez, Gabriela, and Nick Chamberlain
2002   A Summary and Preliminary Analysis of Saturday Creek Burials. *In* Results of the 2001 Valley of Peace Archaeology Project: Saturday Creek and Yalbac, edited by Lisa J. Lucero, pp. 65–72. Report submitted to the Department of Archaeology, Ministry of Tourism and Culture, Belize.

Sanchez, Gabriela, and Jennifer Piehl
2002   Ancient Maya Household Ancestor Veneration at Saturday Creek, Belize. Paper presented at the 67th Annual Meetings of the Society for American Archaeology, March 20–24, Denver.

Sandstrom, Alan R.
2003   Sacred Mountains and Miniature Worlds: Altar Design among the Nahua of Northern Veracruz, Mexico. *In* Mesas and Cosmologies in Mesoamerica, edited by Douglas Sharon, pp. 51–70. San Diego Museum Papers 42. Museum of Man, San Diego.

Saunders, Nicholas J.
1999   Biographies of Brilliance: Pearls, Transformations or Matter and Being c. AD 1492. World Archaeology 31(2):243–257.

2001 A Dark Light: Reflections on Obsidian in Mesoamerica. World Archaeology 33(2):220–236.

Saville, Alan
1990 Hazleton North: The Excavation of a Neolithic Long Cairn of the Cotswold-Severn Group. English Heritage, London.

Savishinsky, Joel S.
1974 The Child Is Father to the Dog: Canines and Personality Processes in an Arctic Community. Human Development 17:460–466.

Schele, Linda, and David Freidel
1990 A Forest of Kings: The Untold Story of the Ancient Maya. William Morrow, New York.

Schele, Linda, and Mary Ellen Miller
1986 The Blood of Kings: Dynasty and Ritual in Maya Art. George Braziller, New York.

Schiffer, Michael B.
1972 Archaeological Context and Systemic Context. American Antiquity 37(2):156–165.
1975 Behavioral Chain Analysis: Activities, Organization, and the Use of Space. In Chapters in the Prehistory of Eastern Arizona, IV. Fieldiana: Anthropology 65:103–119. Field Museum of Natural History, Chicago.
1976 Behavioral Archaeology. Academic Press, New York.
1987 Formation Processes of the Archaeological Record. University of New Mexico Press, Albuquerque.
1991 The Portable Radio in American Life. University of Arizona Press, Tucson.
1994 Taking Charge: The Electric Automobile in America. With T. Butts and K. Grimm. Smithsonian Institution Press, Washington, DC.

Schiffer, Michael B., and Andrea R. Miller
1999 The Material Life of Human Beings. Routledge, New York.

Schiffer, Michael B., and James M. Skibo
1997 The Explanation of Artifact Variability. American Antiquity 62(1):27–50.

Schmidt, Peter R.
1997 Iron Technology in East Africa: Symbolism, Science and Archaeology. University of Indiana Press, Bloomington.

Sekaquaptewa, Emory, and Dorothy Washburn
2004 The Go Along Singing: Reconstructing the Hopi Past from Ritual Metaphors in Song and Image. American Antiquity 69:457ff.

Serpell, James
1995 The Domestic Dog: Its Evolution, Behavior, and Interactions with People. Cambridge University Press, Cambridge.
1996 In the Company of Animals: A Study of Human-Animal Relations. Cambridge University Press, Cambridge.

Shackel, Paul A.

2000   Archaeology and Created Memory: Public History in a National Park. Kluwer Academic/Plenum, New York.

Shanks, Michael, and Christopher Tilley

1987   Re-constructing Archaeology. Cambridge University Press, Cambridge.

Sharer, Robert J.

1989   The Olmec and the Southeast Periphery of Mesoamerica. *In* Regional Perspectives on the Olmec, edited by Robert J. Sharer and David C. Grove, pp. 247–271. Cambridge University Press, Cambridge.

1994   The Ancient Maya. 6th ed. Stanford University Press, Stanford.

Shaw, Rosalind

1997   The Production of Witchcraft/Witchcraft as Production: Memory, Modernity, and the Slave Trade in Sierra Leone. American Ethnologist 24(4):856–876.

2002   Memories of the Slave Trade: Ritual and the Historical Imagination in Sierra Leone. University of Chicago Press, Chicago.

Shennan, Stephen

2002   Genes, Memes and Human History: Darwinian Archaeology and Cultural Evolution. Thames and Hudson, London.

Sillar, Bill

1996   The Dead and the Drying. Journal of Material Culture 1:259–289.

Simmons, Leo W.

1942   Sun Chief: The Autobiography of a Hopi Indian: Don Talyesva. Yale University Press, New Haven.

Singer, Milton

1978   For a Semiotic Anthropology. *In* Sight, Sound and Sense, edited by Thomas A. Sebeok, pp. 202–231. Indiana University Press, Bloomington.

Smith, Isobel

1965   Windmill Hill and Avebury: Excavations by Alexander Keiller, 1925–1939. Clarendon Press, Oxford.

Smith, Watson

1952   Kiva Mural Decorations at Awatovi and Kawaika-a. Awatovi Expedition Report No. 5. Peabody Museum of American Archaeology and Ethnology, Paper 37. Harvard University, Cambridge.

1972   Prehistoric Kivas of Antelope Mesa, Northern Arizona. Awatovi Expedition Report No. 9. Peabody Museum of Archaeology and Ethnology, Harvard University, Cambridge.

Spyer, Patricia

1998   Introduction. *In* Border Fetishisms: Material Objects in Unstable Spaces, edited by Patricia Spyer, pp. 1–11. Routledge, New York.

Stahl, Ann Brower

1991   Ethnic Style and Ethnic Boundaries: A Diachronic Case Study from West Central Ghana. Ethnohistory 38(3):250–275.

REFERENCES

1999   The Archaeology of Global Encounters Viewed from Banda, Ghana. African
        Archaeological Review 16(1):5–81.

2001a   Historical Process and the Impact of the Atlantic Trade on Banda, Ghana,
        1800–1920. *In* West Africa during the Atlantic Slave Trade: Archaeological
        Perspectives, edited by Chris DeCorse, pp. 38–58. Leicester University Press,
        London.

2001b   Making History in Banda: Anthropological Visions of Africa's Past. Cambridge
        University Press, Cambridge.

2002   Colonial Entanglements and the Practices of Taste: An Alternative to
        Logocentric Approaches. American Anthropologist 104(3):827–845.

2004   Comparative Insights into the Ancient Political Economies of West Africa. *In*
        Archaeological Perspectives on Political Economies, edited by Gary M.
        Feinman and Linda M. Nicholas, pp. 253–270. University of Utah Press, Salt
        Lake City.

2007   Entangled Lives: The Archaeology of Daily Life in the Gold Coast Hinterlands,
        AD 1400–1900. *In* Archaeology of Atlantic Africa and the African Diaspora,
        edited by Toyin Falola and Akinwumi Ogundiran, pp. 49–76. Indiana
        University Press, Bloomington.

Stahl, Ann B., and Maria das Dores Cruz
1998   Men and Women in a Market Economy: Gender and Craft Production in West
        Central Ghana c 1700–1995. *In* Gender in African Prehistory, edited by Susan
        Kent, pp. 205–226. AltaMira Press, Walnut Creek, California.

Stahl, Ann B., and Peter W. Stahl
2004   Ivory Production and Consumption in Ghana in the Early Second Millennium
        AD. Antiquity 78:86–101.

Stephen, Alexander
1929   Hopi Tales. Journal of American Folklore 42:1–72.
1969 [1936] Hopi Journal of Alexander M. Stephen. 2 vols. Edited by Elsie Clews
        Parsons. AMS Press, New York.

Stirling, Matthew W.
1940   Great Stone Faces of the Mexican Jungle. National Geographic 78:309–334.
1943a   La Venta's Green Stone Tigers. National Geographic 84:321–332.
1943b   Stone Monuments of Southern Mexico. Smithsonian Institution Bureau of
        American Ethnology, Bulletin 138. Government Printing Office, Washington,
        DC.

Stirling, Matthew W., and Marion Stirling
1942   Finding Jewels of Jade in a Mexican Swamp. National Geographic 82:635–661.

Stoler, Ann Laura, and Karen Strassler
2000   Castings for the Colonial: Memory Work in "New Order" Java. Comparative
        Studies in Society and History 42(1):4–48.

Stoltman, James B.

2000   A Reconsideration of the Cultural Processes Linking Cahokia to Its Northern
        Hinterlands during the Period A.D. 1000–1200. *In* Mounds, Modoc, and
        Mesoamerica: Papers in Honor of Melvin L. Fowler, edited by S. R. Ahler,
        pp. 439–467. Illinois State Museum Scientific Papers, Vol. 28. Springfield.

Stoltman, James B., and George W. Christiansen

2000   The Late Woodland Stage in the Driftless Area of the Upper Mississippi Valley.
        In Late Woodland Societies: Tradition and Transformation across the
        Midcontinent, edited by T. E. Emerson, D. L. McElrath, and A. C. Fortier,
        pp. 497–524. University of Nebraska Press, Lincoln.

Strathern, Marilyn

1988   The Gender of the Gift: Problems with Women and Problems with Society in
        Melanesia. University of California Press, Berkeley.

1990   The Gender of the Gift. University of California Press, Berkeley.

2001   The Patent and the Malanggan. *In* Beyond Aesthetics: Art and the
        Technologies of Enchantment, edited by Christopher Pinney and Nicholas
        Thomas, pp. 259–286. Berg, Oxford.

Swanton, John R.

1942   Source Material on the History and Ethnology of the Caddo Indians. Bureau of
        American Ethnology, Bulletin 132. Smithsonian Institution, Washington, DC.

1985   The Indians of the Southeastern United States. Smithsonian Institution Press,
        Washington, DC.

2001   Source Material for the Social and Ceremonial Life of the Choctaw Indians.
        University of Alabama Press, Tuscaloosa.

Tait, David

1961   The Konkomba of Northern Ghana. Oxford University Press, London.

Tarlow, Sarah

1999   Bereavement and Commemoration: An Archaeology of Mortality. Oxford
        University Press, Oxford.

Tchernov, Eitan, and François F. Valla

1997   Two New Dogs, and Other Natufian Dogs, from the Southern Levant. Journal
        of Archaeological Science 24:65–95.

Theler, James L., and Robert F. Boszhardt

2000   The End of the Effigy Mound Culture: The Late Woodland to Oneota
        Transition in Southwestern Wisconsin. Midcontinental Journal of Archaeology
        25:289–312.

Thomas, Julian E.

1991   Rethinking the Neolithic. Cambridge University Press, Cambridge.

1996   Time, Culture and Identity: An Interpretive Archaeology. Routledge, London.

1997   The Materiality of the Mesolithic-Neolithic Transition in Britain. Analecta
        Praehistorica Leidensia 29:57–64.

1999a   Understanding the Neolithic. Routledge, London.

1999b   An Economy of Substances in Earlier Neolithic Britain. *In* Material Symbols: Culture and Economy in Prehistory, edited by John Robb, pp. 70–89. Center for Archaeological Investigations, Occasional Paper No. 26. Southern Illinois University Press, Carbondale.

2000   Reconfiguring the Social, Reconfiguring the Material. *In* Social Theory in Archaeology, edited by Michael B. Schiffer, pp. 143–155. University of Utah Press, Salt Lake City.

2001   Archaeologies of Place and Landscape. *In* Archaeological Theory Today, edited by Ian Hodder, pp. 165–186. Polity, Malden, Massachusetts.

Thomas, Nicholas

1991   Entangled Objects: Exchange, Material Culture, and Colonialism in the Pacific. Harvard University Press, Cambridge.

Tilley, Christopher

1993   Interpretative Archaeology. Berg, Oxford.

1994   A Phenomenology of Landscape. Berg, London.

Toll, H. Wolcott

1990   A Reassessment of Chaco Cylinder Jars. *In* Clues to the Past: Papers in Honor of William H. Sundt, edited by Meliha S. Duran and David T. Kirkpatrick, pp. 273–305. Papers of the Archaeological Society of New Mexico No. 16. Albuquerque.

2001   Making and Breaking Pots in the Chaco World. American Antiquity 66:56–78.

Townsend, Richard F. (editor)

2004   Hero, Hawk, and Open Hand: American Indian Art of the Ancient Midwest and South. Art Institute of Chicago and Yale University Press, New Haven.

Tozzer, Alfred M.

1941   Landa's Relación de Los Cosas de Yucatán. Papers of the Peabody Museum of American Archaeology and Ethnology, No. 28. Harvard University, Cambridge.

Trouillot, Michel-Rolph

1995   Silencing the Past: Power and the Production of History. Beacon Press, Boston.

Turnbull, David

2000   Masons, Tricksters and Cartographers. Harwood Academic Publishers, Amsterdam.

Turner, Christy G., II, and Jacqueline Turner

1999   Man Corn: Cannibalism and Violence in the Prehistoric Southwest. University of Utah Press, Salt Lake City.

Tylor, Edward B.

1871   Primitive Culture. John Murray, London.

Ulloa Mogollón, Juan de

1885 [1585] Relación de la provincia de los Collaguas para la descripción de las yndias que su magestad manda hacer. *In* Relaciones geográficas de indias perú, edited by Marcos Jiménez de la Espada, Vol. 2, pp. 38–50. Ministerio de Fomento, Madrid.

van Beek, Walter E. A.

1994   The Innocent Sorcerer: Coping with Evil in Two African Societies (Kapsiki and Dogon). *In* Religion in Africa: Experience and Expression, edited by Thomas D. Blakely, Walter E. A. van Beek, and Dennis L. Thomson, pp. 196–228. James Currey, London.

van der Merwe, Nikolaas J., and Donald H. Avery

1987   Science and Magic in African Technology: Traditional Iron Smelting in Malawi. Africa 57(2):143–172.

Van Dyke, Ruth M.

2003   Memory and the Construction of Chacoan Society. *In* Archaeologies of Memory, edited by Ruth M. Van Dyke and Susan E. Alcock, pp. 180–200. Blackwell Publishers, Oxford.

2004   Memory, Meaning, and Masonry: The Late Bonito Chacoan Landscape. American Antiquity 69(3):413–431.

Van Dyke, Ruth M., and Susan E. Alcock (editors)

2003   Archaeologies of Memory. Blackwell, Oxford.

Varien, Mark D.

1988   Excavations in Areas 1 and 2. *In* Dolores Archaeological Program: Anasazi Communities at Dolores: Grass Mesa Village, Book 1, pp. 75–316. US Bureau of Reclamation Engineering and Research Center, Boulder.

Vivian, R. Gordon, and Paul Reiter

1960   The Great Kivas of Chaco Canyon and Their Relationships. Monograph No. 22. School of American Research Press, Santa Fe.

Vivian, R. Gwinn, Dulce N. Dodgen, and Gayle H. Hartmann

1978   Wooden Ritual Artifacts from Chaco Canyon, New Mexico. Anthropological Papers of the University of Arizona, No. 32. University of Arizona Press, Tucson.

Vogt, Evon Z.

1970   The Zinacantecos of Mexico: A Modern Maya Way of Life. Holt, Rinehart and Winston, New York.

1993   Tortillas for the Gods: A Symbolic Analysis of Zinacanteco Rituals. University of Oklahoma Press, Norman.

1998   Zinacanteco Dedication and Termination Rituals. *In* The Sowing and the Dawning: Termination, Dedication, and Transformation in the Archaeological and Ethnographic Record of Mesoamerica, edited by Shirley B. Mock, pp. 21–30. University of New Mexico Press, Albuquerque.

von den Driesch, Angela

1976   A Guide to the Measurement of Animal Bones from Archaeological Sites. Peabody Museum Bulletin 1. Harvard University, Cambridge.

References

von Laue, Theodore H.

1976   Anthropology and Power: R. S. Rattray among the Ashanti. African Affairs 75:33–54.

Voth, H. R.

1901   The Oraibi Powamu Ceremony. Fieldiana, Anthropological Series 3(2):60–158.

Wagner, Roy

1991   The Fractal Person. *In* Big Men and Great Men: Personifications of Power in Melanesia, edited by Maurice Godelier and Marilyn Strathern, pp. 159–173. Cambridge University Press, Cambridge.

Walker, William H.

1995   Ceremonial Trash? *In* Expanding Archaeology, edited by James M. Skibo, William H. Walker, and Axel E. Nielsen, pp. 67–79. University of Utah Press, Salt Lake City.

1996   Ritual Deposits: Another Perspective. *In* River of Change: Prehistory of the Middle Little Colorado River Valley, Arizona, edited by E. Charles Adams, pp. 75–91. Arizona State Museum Archaeological Series 185. University of Arizona, Tucson.

1998   Where Are the Witches of Prehistory? Journal of Archaeological Method and Theory 5(3):245–308.

1999   Ritual, Life Histories, and the Afterlives of People and Things. Journal of the Southwest 41(3):383–405.

2002   Stratigraphy and Practical Reason. American Anthropologist 104:159–177.

2005   Witches, Practice, and the Context of Pueblo Cannibalism. *In* Multidisciplinary Approaches to Social Violence in the Prehispanic American Southwest, edited by Patricia Crown and Deborah Nichols. University of Arizona Press, Tucson.

Walker, William H., Vincent M. LaMotta, and E. Charles Adams

2000   Katsinas and Kiva Abandonments at Homol'ovi: A Deposit-Oriented Perspective on Religion in Southwest Prehistory. *In* The Archaeology of Regional Interaction, edited by Michelle Hegmon, pp. 341–360. University Press of Colorado, Boulder.

Walker, William H., and Lisa J. Lucero

2000   The Depositional History of Ritual and Power. *In* Agency in Archaeology, edited by Marcia-Anne Dobres and John Robb, pp. 130–147. Routledge, London.

Walker, William H., and Michael Brian Schiffer

2006   The Materiality of Social Power: The Artifact Acquisition Perspective. Journal of Archaeological Method and Theory 13(2):67–88.

Ward, B.

1956   Some Observations on Religious Cults in Ashanti. Africa 26:47–61.

Warren, Dennis M., and K. O. Brempong

1974   Techiman Traditional State. Part 1, Stool and Town Histories. Institute of African Studies, University of Ghana, Legon.

Waselkov, Gregory A., and Kathryn E. Holland Braund
1995   William Bartram on the Southeastern Indians. University of Nebraska Press, Lincoln.

Weiner, Annette
1992   Inalienable Possessions: The Paradox of Keeping-While-Giving. University of California Press, Berkeley.

Weltfish, Gene
1977   The Lost Universe: Pawnee Life and Culture. University of Nebraska Press, Lincoln.

Wertsch, James V.
2002   Voices of Collective Remembering. Cambridge University Press, New York.

White, Leslie A.
1935   The Pueblo of Santo Domingo, New Mexico. Memoir No. 43. American Anthropological Association, Menasha, Wisconsin.

Whittle, Alasdair
1991   Wayland's Smithy, Oxfordshire: Excavations at the Neolithic Tomb in 1962–3 by R. J. C. Atkinson and S. Piggott. Proceedings of the Prehistoric Society 57(2):61–102.

Whittle, Alasdair, and Joshua Pollard
1998   Windmill Hill Causewayed Enclosure: The Harmony of Symbols. *In* Understanding the Neolithic of North-Western Europe, edited by Mark Edmonds and Colin Richards, pp. 231–247. Cruithne Press, Glasgow.

Whittle, Alasdair, Joshua Pollard, and Caroline Grigson
1999   Harmony of Symbols: The Windmill Hill Causewayed Enclosure, Wiltshire. Oxbow Books, Oxford.

Wilkie, Laurie A.
1997   Secret and Sacred: Contextualizing the Artifacts of African-American Magic and Religion. Historical Archaeology 31(4):81–106.

Wilks, Ivor
1975   Asante in the Nineteenth Century: The Structure and Evolution of a Political Order. Cambridge University Press, Cambridge.

Willey, Gordon R.
1969   The Mesoamericanization of the Honduran-Salvadoran Periphery: A Symposium Commentary. Proceedings, 38th International Congress of Americanists 1:533–542.

Willey, Gordon R., William R. Bullard, John B. Glass, and James C. Gifford
1965   Prehistoric Maya Settlements in the Belize Valley. Papers of the Peabody Museum of Archaeology and Ethnology, Vol. 54. Harvard University, Cambridge.

Williams, Howard
2004   Potted Histories: Cremation, Ceramics and Social Memory in Early Roman Britain. Oxford Journal of Archaeology 23(4):417–427.

REFERENCES

Wilshusen, Richard H.

1986   The Relationship between Abandonment Mode and Ritual Use in Pueblo I Anasazi Protokivas. Journal of Field Archaeology 13:245–254.

1989   Unstuffing the Estufa: Ritual Floor Features in Anasazi Pitstructures and Pueblo Kivas. *In* The Architecture of Social Integration in Prehistoric Pueblos, edited by W. D. Lipe and Michelle Hegmon, pp. 89–112. Occasional Paper No. 1. Crow Canyon Archaeological Center, Cortez, Colorado.

Windes, Thomas C.

2003   This Old House: Construction and Abandonment at Pueblo Bonito. *In* Pueblo Bonito: Center of the Chacoan World, edited by Jill E. Neitzel, pp. 14–32. Smithsonian Institution Press, Washington, DC.

Wittry, Warren L.

1996   Discovering and Interpreting the Cahokian Woodhenges. Wisconsin Archeologist 77(2–3):26–35.

Wood, W. Raymond

1998   Archaeology on the Great Plains. University Press of Kansas, Lawrence.

Wylie, Alison

1985   The Reaction against Analogy. *In* Advances in Archaeological Method and Theory, Vol. 8, edited by Michael B. Schiffer, pp. 63–111. Academic Press, New York.

Yacobaccio, Hugo D.

2000   Inhumación de una cabeza aislada en la puna argentina. Estudios Sociales del NOA 4(2):59–72.

Yoffee, Norman

2001   The Chaco "Rituality" Revisited. *In* Chaco Society and Polity: Papers from the 1999 Conference, edited by Linda S. Cordell, W. James Judge, and June-el Piper, pp. 63–78. Special Publication No. 4. New Mexico Archaeological Council, Albuquerque.

Zuidema, Tom

1989   Reyes y guerreros: Ensayos de cultura andina. Fomciencias, Lima.

Zunie, Jerome, and Robert D. Leonard

1990   Faunal Remains. *In* Excavations at Three Prehistoric Sites along Pia Mesa Road, Zuni Indian Reservation, McKinley County, New Mexico, prepared by Mark Varien, pp. 166–172. Report No. 233, Research Series No. 4. Zuni Archaeology Program, Zuni Pueblo, New Mexico.

Index

School for Advanced Research Advanced Seminar Series

PUBLISHED BY SAR PRESS

AMERICAN ARRIVALS: ANTHROPOLOGY
ENGAGES THE NEW IMMIGRATION
Nancy Foner, ed.

VIOLENCE
Neil L. Whitehead, ed.

LAW & EMPIRE IN THE PACIFIC:
FIJI AND HAWAI'I
*Sally Engle Merry &
Donald Brenneis, eds.*

ANTHROPOLOGY IN THE MARGINS
OF THE STATE
Veena Das & Deborah Poole, eds.

PLURALIZING ETHNOGRAPHY: COMPARISON
AND REPRESENTATION IN MAYA CULTURES,
HISTORIES, AND IDENTITIES
John M. Watanabe & Edward F. Fischer, eds.

THE ARCHAEOLOGY OF COLONIAL
ENCOUNTERS: COMPARATIVE PERSPECTIVES
Gil J. Stein, ed.

COMMUNITY BUILDING IN THE TWENTY-
FIRST CENTURY
Stanley E. Hyland, ed.

GLOBALIZATION, WATER, & HEALTH:
RESOURCE MANAGEMENT IN TIMES OF
SCARCITY
Linda Whiteford & Scott Whiteford, eds.

A CATALYST FOR IDEAS: ANTHROPOLOGICAL
ARCHAEOLOGY AND THE LEGACY OF
DOUGLAS W. SCHWARTZ
Vernon L. Scarborough, ed.

COPÁN: THE HISTORY OF AN ANCIENT MAYA
KINGDOM
E. Wyllys Andrews & William L. Fash, eds.

AFRO-ATLANTIC DIALOGUES:
ANTHROPOLOGY IN THE DIASPORA
Kevin A. Yelvington, ed.

THE ARCHAEOLOGY OF CHACO CANYON: AN
ELEVENTH-CENTURY PUEBLO REGIONAL
CENTER
Stephen H. Lekson, ed.

THE SEDUCTIONS OF COMMUNITY:
EMANCIPATIONS, OPPRESSIONS, QUANDARIES
Gerald W. Creed, ed.

THE EVOLUTION OF HUMAN LIFE HISTORY
Kristen Hawkes & Richard R. Paine, eds.

IMPERIAL FORMATIONS
*Ann Laura Stoler, Carole McGranahan,
& Peter C. Perdue, eds.*

THE GENDER OF GLOBALIZATION: WOMEN
NAVIGATING CULTURAL AND ECONOMIC
MARGINALITIES
*Nandini Gunewardena &
Ann Kingsolver, eds.*

NEW LANDSCAPES OF INEQUALITY:
NEOLIBERALISM AND THE EROSION OF
DEMOCRACY IN AMERICA
*Jane L. Collins, Micaela di Leonardo,
& Brett Williams, eds.*

OPENING ARCHAEOLOGY: REPATRIATION'S
IMPACT ON CONTEMPORARY RESEARCH AND
PRACTICE
Thomas W. Killion, ed.

THE ANASAZI IN A CHANGING ENVIRONMENT
George J. Gumerman, ed.

REGIONAL PERSPECTIVES ON THE OLMEC
Robert J. Sharer & David C. Grove, eds.

THE CHEMISTRY OF PREHISTORIC HUMAN
BONE
T. Douglas Price, ed.

THE EMERGENCE OF MODERN HUMANS:
BIOCULTURAL ADAPTATIONS IN THE LATER
PLEISTOCENE
Erik Trinkaus, ed.

THE ANTHROPOLOGY OF WAR
Jonathan Haas, ed.

THE EVOLUTION OF POLITICAL SYSTEMS
Steadman Upham, ed.

CLASSIC MAYA POLITICAL HISTORY:
HIEROGLYPHIC AND ARCHAEOLOGICAL
EVIDENCE
T. Patrick Culbert, ed.

TURKO-PERSIA IN HISTORICAL PERSPECTIVE
Robert L. Canfield, ed.

CHIEFDOMS: POWER, ECONOMY, AND
IDEOLOGY
Timothy Earle, ed.

RECONSTRUCTING PREHISTORIC PUEBLO
SOCIETIES
William A. Longacre, ed.

Participants in the School for Advanced Research advanced seminar "The Archaeology of Ritual, Memory, and Materiality," Santa Fe, New Mexico, February 16–18, 2005. Left to right: Ann B. Stahl, Barbara J. Mills, Susan D. Gillespie, William H. Walker, Lisa J. Lucero, Axel Nielsen, Rosemary Joyce, Jason Pollard, Timothy Pauketat.